Collision Course

Collision Course

The Strange Convergence of Affirmative
Action and Immigration Policy in America

Hugh Davis Graham

OXFORD
UNIVERSITY PRESS

2002

OXFORD

UNIVERSITY PRESS

Oxford   New York
Athens   Auckland   Bangkok   Bogotá   Buenos Aires   Cape Town
Chennai   Dar es Salaam   Delhi   Florence   Hong Kong   Istanbul   Karachi
Kolkata   Kuala Lumpur   Madrid   Melbourne   Mexico City   Mumbai   Nairobi
Paris   São Paulo   Shanghai   Singapore   Taipei   Tokyo   Toronto   Warsaw

and associated companies in

Berlin   Ibadan

Published by Oxford University Press, Inc.
198 Madison Avenue, New York, New York 10016

Oxford is a registered trademark of Oxford University Press

Library of Congress Cataloging-in-Publication Data

Graham, Hugh Davis.
  Collision course : the strange convergence of affirmative action and immigration
policy in America / Hugh Davis Graham.
    p. cm.
  Includes bibliographical references and index.
  ISBN 0-19-514318-3
  1. United States—Emigration and immigration—Government policy. 2. Affirmative
action programs—United States. I. Title.

  JV6483 .G73 2002
  325.73—dc21   2001037476

1 3 5 7 9 8 6 4 2

Printed in the United States of America
on acid-free paper

For Holter and Janet

Contents

Preface and Acknowledgments

This book reconstructs the development of American national policy concerning civil rights and immigration issues over the entire twentieth century. My own expertise concentrates only on the second half of that century, and it emphasizes civil rights more than immigration policy. For the period prior to World War II, I rely chiefly on the secondary literature, and throughout the pages that follow I have limited citations to the main published sources. This includes, where possible, useful web sites on the Internet for many of the organizations in civil society seeking to influence policy outcomes. The bibliography is captured in the footnotes, not listed separately. This lightens the burden and clutter of research citation in the book. But it obscures the contributions to the book's analysis of years of archival research, most of it in the presidential libraries. Uncited in the pages that follow are tens of thousands of documents examined in the presidential libraries in the past twenty years.

My guides in this long, rewarding, and occasionally exhausting process of exploration were the unfailingly helpful archivists at the presidential libraries. For research on civil rights policy, this includes the full run of libraries covering the years 1961–1989—the Kennedy, Johnson, Nixon (a presidential papers project in the National Archives, not a presidential library), Ford, Carter, and Reagan libraries. Research in the Carter and Reagan libraries covered immigration as well as civil rights policy. For assistance in this research, I am especially grateful for the assistance of supervising archivists David Alsobrook and Martin I. Elzy at the Carter Library and Dennis Daellenbach at the Reagan Library.

Writing this book was delayed in the late 1990s by illness. The delay provided one advantage by permitting inclusion of the policy controversies surrounding the 2000 census and the substantive findings drawn from the census surveys. For patient support during this period, including generous financial assistance, I am indebted to a number of academic officers at Vanderbilt University. They include, in the College of Arts and Science, deans V. Jacque Voegeli, Madeleine M. Goodman, Ettore F. Infante, and John H. Venable. They also include deans Russell G. Hamilton and Peter

W. Reed in the Graduate School and History department chairmen Simon Collier and Marshall C. Eakin. For graduate research assistance I am pleased to thank Craig A. Kaplowitz at Vanderbilt and Christina Ziegler at the University of California, Santa Barbara. Throughout the research and writing the support at Vanderbilt of William S. Longwell and his staff in the Microcomputing Lab was generous, patient, and essential.

Hugh Davis Graham
Santa Barbara, California
July 2001

1

Introduction

In the early 1990s, against a backdrop of economic recession and rising job insecurity in the United States, controversy over affirmative action and immigration policy intensified. For the first time since the two issues emerged in the 1970s, they were connected in the public eye. Especially in California, where shrinking defense contracts and heavy immigration from Latin America and Asia increased economic anxiety, opponents of affirmative action preferences and high levels of immigration linked their arguments. Native-born Americans unfairly suffered rising unemployment, these critics claimed, because by hiring immigrants, employers bought cheap and docile labor while satisfying minority hiring requirements imposed by the government.[1]

In 1994, California voters passed Proposition 187, an initiative written to deny access by illegal immigrants to public schools, welfare assistance, and other public benefits. That same year, support for Proposition 187 helped California's Republican governor, Pete Wilson, win reelection. In 1995, the University of California regents, encouraged by Governor Wilson, an ex officio regent, prohibited affirmative action preferences in university admissions, employment, and contracts. In 1996, President Bill Clinton signed a bill stripping significant welfare and health benefits from unnaturalized immigrants, and California voters passed Proposition 209, the California Civil Rights Initiative (CCRI), banning affirmative action preferences by state and local governments. In 1998, voters in Washington state passed a similar initiative barring minority preferences by government agencies.

Also in 1998, California voters passed Proposition 227, which terminated the state's massive program of bilingual education and replaced it with English immersion as the standard instructional model. Backers of

1

Proposition 227 charged that bilingual education in California, over-whelmingly a Spanish-language program, isolated Hispanic students from the mainstream curriculum, replaced rigorous instruction in the basics with a curriculum keyed to boosting Latino self-esteem, worsened student test scores and dropout rates, and won jobs for thousands of Spanish-speaking teachers and aides who were otherwise unqualified for certifica-tion. The native-language instruction required in bilingual education progams, seen nationally by Latino political leaders as a key affirmative action remedy, was defended by teachers' unions and school administra-tors. Polls showed that Proposition 227 was supported by Republicans, whites, Asians, and older voters and was opposed by Latinos and blacks.[2]

News reports and press releases from groups opposing affirmative action in the 1990s featured stories of immigrants, legal as well as illegal, winning jobs through affirmative action preferences. It was indefensible, critics contended, to grant preferences on the basis of ancestry to recently arrived immigrants as a remedy to compensate for historic discrimination in the United States. News stories of immigrants winning affirmative action benefits periodically revealed bizarre examples. According to these reports, the Fanjul brothers in Miami, for example, multimillionaire busi-nessmen with major minority business set-aside contracts in Florida, fled Castro's revolution in 1960, yet retained their Cuban citizenship for tax-avoidance purposes. The Rodriguez brothers, immigrants from Portugal and owners of three large construction and paving companies in the Wash-ington, D.C., area, won 60 percent of the district's minority set-aside con-tracts between 1986 and 1990. A black businessman in Cincinnati, suing to prevent Governor George V. Voinovich from opening Ohio's minority con-tract set-aside program to Asian Indians, won a decertification order from the attorney general but lost in federal court. Federal Judge Tommy L. Thompson ruled that Asian Indians as "Orientals" were due the same priv-ileges as blacks under federal affirmative action regulations. At the Uni-versity of Michigan, the faculty senate discovered that large percentages of minority faculty recruited under the university's affirmative action pro-gram were foreign-born. University of Michigan faculty records showed that 18.8 percent of black faculty and 23.3 percent of Hispanic faculty were not U.S. natives. For Michigan faculty of Asian/Pacific Islander ancestry, 56 percent of them immigrants, affirmative action had become an engine of overseas recruitment.[3]

Supporters of affirmative action feared the newly conjoined opposition of antipreference groups and immigration restrictionists. According to Ricky Gaull Silverman, vice chairman of the Equal Employment Opportu-nity Commission (EEOC), immigrant participation in affirmative action "is the ultimate nightmare of affirmative action. It is its Achilles heel."[4] Lawrence II. Fuchs, former board member of the Mexican American Legal Defense and Education Fund (MALDEF), wrote in the *Washington Post* in 1995 that immigrant inclusion in affirmative action programs "is an historical accident for which there is no possible justification."[5] Defenders of affirmative action generally avoided the topic of immigrant participation. The Clinton administration's comprehensive review and defense of affirmative action programs, produced by a presidential task force in 1995, nowhere mentioned immigration or immigrant participation.[6] President Clinton's Dialogue on Race Commission, appointed in 1997 and chaired by historian John Hope Franklin, concentrated on black/white relations and criticized what Franklin called "imagined conflicts between African Americans and the Latino and Asian communities."[7]

Similarly, the major studies of immigration published during the 1990s avoided discussing affirmative action. *The New Americans*, a study of the effects of immigration on American life released in 1997 by the National Research Council, an arm of the National Academy of Sciences, addressed controversial social issues such as job displacement, residential segregation, racial identification, crime, illegal immigration, and interethnic tensions, but did not mention immigrant participation in affirmative action programs.[8] The U.S. Commission on Immigration Reform, in its fall 1997 final report, was equally silent on affirmative action. *Immigration in a Changing Economy*, a widely praised study of the California experience released in 1997 by RAND, discussed the benefits of affirmative action programs for African Americans but not for immigrants.[9]

Why, in the face of growing controversy during the 1990s over affirmative action for immigrants, have studies of immigration been silent on affirmative action and studies of affirmative action similarly silent on immigration? One reason is segregation of the evidence. Although mountains of statistical data have been published to document trends in both policy areas, almost no connection is made between them. Analysts wanting to chart immigrant use of affirmative action programs can find abundant documentation describing beneficiaries by race, gender, national origin, age, education, and many other attributes. But the documents generally do not include information on country of birth or citizenship status. The "rights revolution" that spun out of the 1960s protected individuals and members of racial and ethnic groups and rarely stipulated a citizenship requirement. The American constitutional tradition, generally strengthened by the federal courts since the 1960s, required equal protection for persons under government jurisdiction, not citizens of the United States per se. The Civil Rights Act of 1964 required confidentiality in records kept by the EEOC

and employers. The Immigration Reform and Control Act of 1986 prohibited employers from seeking national origin or citizenship status from job
applicants.

A second reason for the lack of connection between immigration and
affirmative action data is the desire of government officials and organizations representing minority groups to avoid the divisive issue. The civil
rights coalition, supporting both affirmative action and liberal immigration policies but anxious not to connect them, has benefited from the difficulty experienced by opponents in identifying immigrants in affirmative
action programs. Fearing that controversy over immigrants enjoying affirmative action preferences over native-born Americans would split the
coalition and endanger the programs, civil rights organizations have
avoided the topic. Elected officials who have supported the programs and
government agencies administering them have followed the same strategy.

The Liberal Coalition and the Politics
of Affirmative Action and Immigration

On both issues, the liberal coalition in Congress has been represented by
the Leadership Conference for Civil Rights, an umbrella lobby speaking for
more than 160 organizations, among them the American Federation of
Labor-Congress of Industrial Organizations (AFL-CIO), the National
Association for the Advancement of Colored People (NAACP), feminist
and Latino rights groups, and liberal religious organizations. Widely
respected for its lobbying acumen, the Leadership Conference effectively
supported the Johnson administration in passing the civil rights legislation
of the mid-1960s, including the immigration reform of 1965. In the Reagan
and Bush administrations, the Leadership Conference defended affirmative action programs and, especially in Reagan's second term, after the
economy strengthened and the Democrats recaptured the Senate, won
expanded affirmative action requirements in the large federal procurement
budgets for defense and transportation. Although the Leadership Conference's liberal constituencies generally also opposed immigration restriction efforts, the immigration expansion coalition was skewed toward
Latino groups, such as the National Council of La Raza and the Mexican
American Legal Defense and Education Fund (MALDEF), working closely
with the Hispanic Congressional Caucus. The expansionist coalition's lobbying was coordinated in the 1980s and 1990s by the National Immigration
Forum, an umbrella group funded substantially by the Ford Foundation
and modeled on the Leadership Conference.

Before 1960, the nation's leading African-American organizations (such as the NAACP) and labor organizations (such as the AFL-CIO) supported equal individual rights but opposed large-scale immigration as threatening to native American wage levels and job security. After 1970, however, these positions softened, partly because the growth of affirmative action programs with minority preferences broadened the coalition base for protected classes. Increasingly during the 1980s and 1990s, the civil rights and immigration expansionist coalitions meshed their coalition lobbying. The leading immigrant restrictionist organization, the Federation of American Immigration Reform (FAIR), was disappointed by weak support from black and labor organizations, even though FAIR's restrictionist argument emphasized the economic harm that mass immigration brought to low-wage workers.

Seeking to protect immigrants, illegal as well as legal, the liberal coalition successfully lobbied for language in immigration statutes (particularly the immigration amendments of 1986 and 1990) that prohibited employers from discriminating against potential hires on the basis of national origin or citizenship. The liberal coalition also backed provisions in the Immigration Reform and Control Act of 1986 (IRCA) providing amnesty for what would prove to be 3 million illegal immigrants who could document lengthy residence, and creating a weak system of employment eligibility identification that was easily evaded by illegal immigrants.[10]

Legislative leaders and political scientists have long valued the role of such interest-group lobbying in the process of bargaining and compromise that has built the complex American regulatory state. Journalists, however, refer to networks of knowledgeable insiders "inside the beltway" who shape regulatory regimes that bewilder American voters. The disconnection between these two worlds helps explain why public opinion on many major issues of public policy leans in one direction while policy heads in another. Examples include gun control, abortion rights, immigration restriction, and race-conscious remedies in civil rights (affirmative action). On these issues, citizen majorities in opinion polls persistently favored the first three and opposed the fourth, while legislative leaders, heavily lobbied by intensely committed organized interests, generally made policies in the opposite direction.

This is an old story in American political life, the story of interest groups winning benefits through insider deals not understood by the unorganized taxpayers. It is rational, self-interested political behavior, given our system of government, which thrives on bargains struck between organized interests seeking benefits, elected officials seeking campaign funds and votes, and government agencies seeking expanded programs and budgets. Journalists in the

1950s began calling these mutual back-scratching arrangements "iron trian-gles." They were originally forged in the century following the Civil War by economic interests (shippers, farmers, cattle and lumber combines, airlines) seeking government benefits (canals and dams, irrigation subsidies, public land grazing and timber rights, prime passenger routes) from congressional committees and the agencies they fund and oversee. Iron triangles were pro-duced by insider deal making between lobbyists and senior congressmen in closed markup sessions and conference committees. They were lawful but had the smell of pork, of tax dollars used to benefit special interests, usually at the expense of unorganized consumers. Understandably, groups benefit-ing from these arrangements have disliked the glare of publicity.[11]

In the 1960s, iron triangle bargaining spread to new constituencies and new government programs were created to serve them. Organizations rep-resenting racial and ethnic minorities, feminists, consumers, and environ-mentalists mobilized in social movements and demanded new laws and government programs to protect their interests.[12] In the breakthrough civil rights legislation of the 1960s, the governing principle was equal individ-ual rights. Discrimination on account of race, religion, and national origin was prohibited on a nationwide basis. By 1980, however, controversy arose over the spread of affirmative action programs requiring minority prefer-ences in employment, college admissions, and government contracts. Despite the success of a national conservative movement led by Republi-can Ronald Reagan, affirmative action programs continued to expand. By the 1990s, controversy over affirmative action preferences included immi-gration policy. Yet the contradictory political pattern seen since the late 1960s persisted. On the one hand, public opinion polls and voter initiatives showed substantial American majorities opposing minority preference policies and supporting restricted immigration. On the other hand, public policy on civil rights and immigration seemed remarkably immune from the rising discontents of public opinion.[13]

For example, on civil rights policy the Reagan administration called for deregulation and an end to government policies favoring one racial or eth-nic group over another. Yet during the Reagan-Bush years, Congress expanded minority contract set-asides in federal procurement, strength-ened affirmative-action regulation in higher education, and for the first time (in 1991), required a "disparate impact" standard of proportional minority representation in employment.[14] In immigration policy, the immigration expansionists emerged the legislative victor in both the Immi-gration Reform and Control Act of 1986 and the immigration amendments of 1990.[15] Despite the partisan reversals of the post-1968 pattern that pro-duced a Democratic president after 1992 and a Republican Congress after 1994, the elected branches in Washington continued largely the same affirmative action and immigration policies. The Republican Congress declined, despite extensive hearings in both chambers, to advance a bill curbing affirmative action preferences. In 1998, the Republican-controlled Congress quietly attached to an appropriation bill a minority contract set-aside requirement of 10 percent of the entire federal procurement budget. This congressional earmarking by racial and ethnic ancestry, totaling an unprecedented $117 billion, projected an expanding federal program of affirmative action into the twenty-first century. Yet it passed largely unnoticed in the American media.[16]

The Unintended Consequences of Reform

How can we account for this strange story of American policymaking, which produced such startling contradictions between the intended and unintended consequences of reform? Legislation passed in the 1960s to end a notorious and highly elaborated system of racial preference in the South did so with gratifying finality. But in the process of implementation in the 1970s, the civil rights reform movement extended nationwide another system of preferences based on ancestral, cultural, and bloodline distinctions among citizens. Parallel liberal reforms in immigration policy, passed to end national origin preferences but not appreciably to change the character or volume of immigration to America, led instead to massive immigration from Latin America and Asia.

The elected branches in the liberal breakthrough of 1964-65 passed three great civil rights laws: the Civil Rights Act of 1964, the Voting Rights Act of 1965, and the Immigration and Naturalization Act of 1965. All were based on the principle of nondiscrimination by race or national origin. In the years immediately following, the three laws were widely hailed for achieving their intended consequences. The Civil Rights Act broke the back of Jim Crow segregation in the South. The Voting Rights Act, by guaranteeing equal access to the voting booth, buried the racist demagoguery so long characteristic of white supremacy in the South, and built black voting strength (and, in the Southwest, Latino electoral power as well) that commanded courtship by politicians. The Immigration and Naturalization Act ended a long-standing policy, so repugnant to liberal values and so embarrassing in cold war competition, of immigration quotas by national origin preference. The spirit of the triumphant reforms of 1964-65 was captured by the image of a color-blind Constitution, where racial and ethnic origin was at long last ruled irrelevant to public policy.[17]

Then came the unintended consequences of reform. Government agencies and federal courts approved affirmative action policies, based ironically on the nondiscrimination laws of 1964-65, that imposed preferences, justified to compensate for past discrimination and designed to win proportional representation for minority groups in education, jobs, and government contracts. Similarly, in immigration policy, the reforms of 1965, intended to purge national origin quotas but not to expand immigration or to change its character, produced instead a flood of new arrivals that by the mid-1990s exceeded 30 million people, more than three-quarters of them arriving not from Europe but from Latin America and Asia. Despite the purging of racial and ethnic preferences by the 1964-65 laws, the ancestry of most immigrants in the 1990s entitled them to status as presumptive victims of historic discrimination in the United States. As members of protected classes, they enjoyed priority over most native-born Americans under affirmative action regulations.[18]

Congress in the 1960s never intended to create such a system. And it is doubtful that any Congress (or White House) today, in the 21st century, would build such a system anew and defend it before voters. So how did the intended consequences of the 1960s produce the unintended consequences of today? Something happened in the American political system that scrambled traditional political alignments and greatly weakened the connection between public opinion and the policymaking process.[19]

In the pages that follow I argue that a sea change in American political life occurred in the late 1960s that fundamentally changed the dynamics of political competition. The three-way election of 1968 ushered in a new American political order of divided government. It led not to a new majority party controlling both elected branches of government in Washington, as had commonly occurred in previous party realignments in American history. What emerged instead was a system of split partisan government in Washington, with one party dominating the presidency and the other controlling Congress (the single-term Carter administration was the exception proving the rule). One goal of this book is to explore how the new political order of divided partisan government affected the direction of civil rights and immigration policy. I argue that the unintended consequences of the 1960s reforms were shaped and accelerated by a fractious new system of divided authority that was sought by voters yet confused the electorate. It increased the capacity of organized interest groups to win expanded benefits from the regulatory state, and weakened the connection in policymaking between public preferences and government behavior. American voters were increasingly puzzled and dissatisfied by their national government. They were frustrated when majority opinion on major issues, such as abortion rights and gun control on the left, or color-blind rights enforcement and immigration restriction on the right, was ignored or short-circuited in government policy.

Telling the Story

The story of the origin and convergence of affirmative action and immigration policy is told in five narrative chapters, beginning with chapter 2. It describes the passage of the great civil rights laws of the 1960s. It includes an analysis of the chief target of civil rights reform, the biracial caste system of segregation in the South. Called the "Jim Crow" system from roots in antebellum minstrelsy, segregation was in part a product of conservative reformers before World War I in the southern states whose white supremacy regimes constituted an elaborate system of racial preference. The centerpiece of chapter 2 is the breakthrough legislation of 1964-65. The chapter also includes discussion of the original Kennedy-Johnson model of affirmative action, asking in what ways it was similar to and in what ways it differed from the nondiscrimination policies of 1964-65 and the race-conscious remedies of "hard" affirmative action developed in the 1970s.

Chapter 3 shifts to immigration policy. As in the chapter on civil rights, it reaches back to reconstruct the development of the system the reformers were attacking. The target in this case was the national origins quota system constructed by Congress in the 1920s. Immigration reform leaders in the Kennedy and Johnson administrations and in Congress were supported by the same liberal coalition backing civil rights reform. Both sets of reform rested on liberalism's core doctrines of nondiscrimination and equal individual rights. But there were important differences as well. Whereas civil rights reform was driven by a mass-based social movement and was characterized by intense controversy, polarized voting blocs, regional tension, and high media visibility, immigration reform was primarily an inside-the-beltway effort, engineered by policy elites largely in the absence of public demand or controversy.

Chapter 4 returns to civil rights policy and examines the puzzle of unintended consequences. Implementation in the 1970s of the nondiscrimination laws of the 1960s led to compensatory preferences for minorities (or "reverse discrimination," in the 1970s language of affirmative action critics). Beginning in 1969 with the Nixon administration, the nondiscrimination provisions were transformed into affirmative action programs benefiting an expanding array of protected class groups. African-Americans, the chief beneficiaries of both the intended reforms of 1964-65 and the minority preference programs of the 1970s, were joined as claimants by mobilizing constituencies representing feminists, Hispanics, the disabled, American Indians, and to a lesser extent the aged, Asians, and gays and lesbians. Paralleling this was an effective mobilization by environmentalists and advocates of consumer rights and worker safety. This was America's postwar "rights revolution." It was led, as in the 1950s and 1960s, by the black civil rights mobilization, but it generally enjoyed broad support from the liberal coalition. In the 1970s the left wing of the Democratic Party rallied to support race-conscious affirmative action policies that the liberal coalition had disavowed in the 1960s. This split the Democrats' New Deal coalition, alienating liberals faithful to equal individual rights and European ethnic workers resentful of minority preferences. As a consequence, the conservative Republican movement under the leadership of Ronald Reagan captured the presidency.[20]

Chapter 5 addresses unintended consequences in immigration policy. It describes the surprising growth in the 1970s and 1980s of immigration to America, both in numbers and in new patterns of national origin. Despite repeated pledges, and by all evidence despite sincere beliefs, by immigration reform leaders that the 1965 legislation would not significantly change the number or origin of immigrants, the 1965 law led to a tidal wave of immigration that coincided with economic distress during the 1970s. Polls showed rising public demand for Congress to restrict immigration and prohibit hiring undocumented workers. Congress passed a compromise immigration control law in 1986 with an employer sanctions program that failed and an amnesty provision for 3 million illegal immigrants that increased chain immigration. In the 1990s immigration exceeded 1 million annually and populist protests against immigrant job competition reshaped politics in high-immigration states, especially California.[21]

Chapter 6 describes the convergence of affirmative action and immigration policy. Convergence was unlikely and unanticipated, given the common 1960s grounding of both civil rights and immigration reforms in liberal nondiscrimination doctrine. But the preconditions for convergence were inadvertently set when early equal employment laws led government bureaucrats to design forms to identify who was a minority and where minorities were employed. From this emerged a color-coded minority identification scheme that made no distinction between native and immigrant workers. As a consequence, when immigration surged so dramatically from Latin America and Asia, immigrants increasingly competed with native workers, displacing black low-wage workers and unsettling the liberal coalition.

Collision Course

The title of this book, *Collision Course*, has a deterministic ring. It brings to mind an image of ships converging in the fog or of the *Titanic* heading for a disastrous rendezvous with an iceberg. But this book is not about a collision of catastrophic portent. And it is certainly not about inevitabilities.

The converging path of affirmative action and immigration policy in America, widely noticed in the economic recession of the early 1990s but little noticed before then, produced significant public agitation, especially in western states suffering from declining defense expenditures. The political and social collision of the 1990s, though eased by the end of the decade, sharpened questions about immigration and raised new questions about affirmative action that revealed deep fault lines in its policy logic.

The immigration debate of the 1990s, which followed restrictionist setbacks in the immigration laws of 1986 and 1990, sharpened both quantitative and qualitative questions. Why does American policy permit such a massive inflow of illegal entries? Why does policy for legal entry admit such huge numbers of poorly educated immigrants, ill suited for the knowledge-based economy of the future and requiring heavy social service expenditures? Why does U.S. policy allow immigration flows to be determined externally, and therefore arbitrarily, by kinship ties rather than internally by national needs? Why does the United States lack a modern, computer-based worker identification system, common to most other developed countries?

To these challenges by restrictionists, raised chiefly by FAIR, which led the drive behind the Simpson-Mazzoli bill in the 1980s, were added a green argument—that overpopulation and urban congestion were worsened by mass immigration, overburdening America's carrying capacity and accelerating destruction of the environment. Politically, however, these arguments proved less persuasive than the appeal of cheap labor and the Statue of Liberty tradition. As the economy rebounded in the 1990s, immigrants replenished an aging workforce, unemployment fell to thirty-year lows, the restrictionist drive weakened, and populist agitation over immigration subsided.

The intensified debate prompted by converging immigration and affirmative action issues had a more profound impact on the affirmative action controversy. News stories featuring Hispanic immigrants benefiting from minority contract set-aside programs, or featuring immigrants from Asia boosting minority employment statistics in university science and engineering faculties, raised questions about why these groups were privileged over native nonminority Americans. Why did immigrants qualify for affirmative action benefits at all? These questions led ineluctibly to others: Why were all Hispanics in the U.S. accorded protected-class status irrespective of income and education? Why were all affluent and privileged black Americans, a group that had grown substantially since the 1960s, given affirmative action benefits when impoverished white Americans were not? Why were Indonesian Americans, a recent and prosperous group with no history of oppression in the United States, given Small Business Administration grants and minority set-aside contracts under the federal government's 8(a) affirmative action program while Jews, with a long history of discrimination in America, were excluded? Why were women, who also had a long history of discrimination in America but who mirrored the general distribution of the population by socioeconomic class, accorded protected-class status as a group irrespective of wealth?

These were hard but important questions, searching the history and interrogating the logic of affirmative action, seeking a coherent rationale consistent with social justice. But the answers were difficult to find. When the census year 2000 turned the nation's calendars to a new century and a new millenium, a new generation of Americans, children of a mobile, racially and ethnically mixed society, challenged the very heart of the color-coded classification system upon which the entire system of affirmative action rested.

As the twenty-first century arrived, mass immigration, continuing unabated, and minority preference policies, weakened in the 1990s by federal court rulings and state referenda but still entrenched in the industrial economy and in government and academic institutions, were targets likely to be attacked again in the wake of the next economic downturn. We don't know whether or when this might occur. Our present task is to understand how the American political system, operating under significantly altered dynamics since the late 1960s, bent the parallel but largely unconnected trajectories of two liberal reforms of the 1960s toward a converging path that produced such unintended consequences.

Proponents of affirmative action, under attack during the Reagan presidency, drew strength from the immigration coalition and blunted most conservative reforms. Then the affirmative action coalition rallied in turn to help immigration expansionists neutralize the strong restrictionist reform drive of the 1980s. By the end of the 1990s, however, mass immigration from Latin America and Asia had undermined affirmative action's original, black-centered rationale. It did this by bringing to America more than 25 million immigrants whose national origins automatically qualified them as official minorities eligible for affirmative action benefits. This extraordinary development—affirmative action eligibility for millions of immigrants, illegal as well as legal—seemed constitutionally unavoidable in the reasoning of the federal courts. Yet politically and philosophically, it found almost no defenders in the ranks of American opinion leaders. By the early years of the new century, immigration expansion seemed secure but affirmative action was in retreat. How and why did these events occur, and with what consequences? Finding some answers to these questions is the goal of this book.

2

Civil Rights Reform in the 1960s

The story of civil rights reform in the 1960s should begin not with the reformers and their legislation but with their chief target, the Jim Crow system in the South. In their lifetimes they had watched segregation expand and harden its defenses against external attack. Foremost among their weapons was a liberal belief in equal individual rights and a vision of a color-blind Constitution. Since its founding in 1909 in an environment of national racial violence and southern apartheid, the NAACP had pressed relentlessly for a simple, radical remedy, lethal to Jim Crow, so that racial classifications would play no legitimate role in American public policy. Experience with segregation convinced liberals that racial designations by government, like the legal institution of slavery itself, were inherently pernicious and expansionist.[1]

The story of segregation's origins and development has been told in scores of books, some of them widely read, especially historian C. Vann Woodward's *The Strange Career of Jim Crow.*[2] For purposes of this study, however, two aspects of the story of segregation, as prelude to and target for the reforms of the 1960s, have not been well told or widely understood. One is the story of intended consequences, the story of segregation not only as white racist oppression, as a brutal assertion of racial hegemony of southern whites over blacks, but also as a story of conservative reform turned sour. It is a story of a new wave of race-conscious government policies, adopted between 1895 and 1915, whose intentions included not only the subordination of blacks but also the benign reformist goals of ending mob lynching, purging southern political life of corruption and violence, and educating the children of the freed men.

The second story is one of unintended consequences. Its inadvertent victims are southern whites themselves, trapped ironically in a political system designed to maintain white supremacy. It was a system loaded against the region's have-nots of both races. The South's racial caste system indisputably punished black southerners physically and traumatized them psychologically. But the creed of white supremacy also brutalized whites psychologically. Like an occupying army, southern whites were corrupted by the power and status derived from racial hegemony. North Carolina journalist Wilbur Cash, in his great cri de coeur of 1941, *The Mind of the South*, described a "proto-Dorian code" that bound poor whites in a brotherhood of solidarity with elite whites, a pact that reified whiteness and elevated the status of ignorant and impoverished whites over all blacks.[3] In 1942, a national poll showed only 2 percent of southern whites (compared with 40 percent of nonsouthern whites) agreeing with the statement that "white students and Negro students should go to the same schools." Only 21 percent of southern whites (compared with 47 percent of nonsouthern whites) agreed that "Negroes are as intelligent as white people."[4] By maintaining duplicate, poorly funded school systems in each state, the tax-poor South firmly anchored itself in the bottom tier of national rankings on school achievement for white as well as for black children.

Racial Segregation as a Conservative Reform

Conservative political leaders in the South in the 1890s, most of them Democrats and many of them later active in the southern Progressive movement, feared the violence, social turmoil, and populist insurgency that was rampant in the depressed region. There is no disputing that the construction of Jim Crow, separating the races in the turn-of-the-century South, was chiefly an act of racial subordination. But in the hands of the conservative political leaders who dominated state politics, segregation, though primarily a method of social control, was also a method of social amelioration. To stabilize a system of cheap and docile farm labor in the South, conservative landowners and their merchant-banker-lawyer allies needed to dampen racial violence and provide blacks with a minimum stakehold to anchor them to the system. To achieve this, they moved to protect black citizens from violence and to provide on a segregated basis social services that either were not previously available or were spotty and uncertain. Specifically the Jim Crow reformers, by disfranchising most African-Americans and large numbers of poor whites as well, sought to purge the South of widespread vote buying and electoral fraud and to shrink the electorate to a safe core of middle-class white voters interested in clean government, low taxes, and minimal social services. The reformers, as pro-business "New South" enthusiasts, and as both southern Progressives and segregationists, sought to end the contagion of lynching that depressed industrial investment in the South and mocked the region's civic claims to Christian virtue. Most positively, in common with Booker T. Washington, the reformers sought to guarantee a minimal standard of education to African-American citizens and to provide for the first time some systematic access to minimal social welfare services, such as hospitals and homes for the blind, deaf, and dumb.[5]

In *The Strange Career of Jim Crow*, Woodward emphasized the timing of Jim Crow's arrival, as documented by the spread of state and local segregation laws, initially by ordinances in the 1890s segregating passenger trains and steamboats. This first wave of Jim Crow laws in transportation—the type unsuccessfully challenged by Homer Plessy in the U.S. Supreme Court's landmark *Plessy v. Ferguson* decision of 1896, which upheld "separate but equal" schools—coincided with the explosion of racial lynching in the South. Lynching deaths doubled from 96 in 1890 to 184 in 1891, and averaged 154 a year until falling back below 100 in 1902. According to the statistics recorded by Tuskegee Institute, 1,689 lynchings were recorded in the South between 1891 and 1901. Of these, 452, or 27 percent, of the victims were white, a testimonial to the strength of the region's vigilante tradition irrespective of the race question. However, 73 percent of the victims were black. Typically, half of the black victims were accused of murder, a quarter were accused of rape, and a tenth were accused of theft. The alleged murder or rape of whites often produced a community auto-da-fé, accompanied by grotesque mutilation (often sexual) and burning of the victim's body. Especially in the rural and small-town South, racial lynchings provided a form of mass recreation, a spontaneous ritual of the church of White Supremacy.[6] Mississippi, the state with the highest proportion of African-Americans (almost 60 percent in 1900), was the most racially lethal as well. Between 1882 and 1930, 500 of Mississippi's 545 lynching victims were black. In 1910 a black man in Mississippi, Nelse Patton, was accused of cutting a white woman's throat, and he was lynched by a mob led by one of the state's United States senators, W. V. Sullivan. "I led the mob which lynched Nelse Patton and I'm proud of it," Sullivan boasted to newspaper reporters. "I directed every movement of the mob. I wanted him lynched. I saw his body dangling from a tree this morning and I'm glad of it. I aroused the mob and directed them to storm the jail. I had my revolver but did not use it. I gave it to a deputy sheriff and told him to shoot Patton and shoot to kill. I suppose the bullets from my gun were some of those that killed the Negro."[7] No charges were brought against any person for participating in the lynching.

Lynching, having accomplished its racist and vigilante purpose and, through its barbaric excesses, having generated internal opposition from business leaders, newspapers, and church women, declined steadily after 1901. In 1924, for the first time, there were no white lynching victims in the South and only sixteen black victims. But by then the point had been made: White terror had thoroughly intimidated and demoralized the black population.[8]

As lynching declined, segregation ordinances proliferated. Between 1900 and 1915, a wave of state and local laws segregated seating in municipal transportation (streetcars, waiting rooms, ticket windows), public accommodations (restaurants, hotels, theaters), and facilities (courtrooms, jails, libraries, parks, and swimming pools, including toilets and drinking fountains). Racial separation and its attendant (and expensive) duplication of facilities spread to schools, hospitals, and institutions of social welfare (orphanages, lunatic asylums, homes for the blind). Segregating the workplace was generally accomplished without ordinances. Segregating housing by law proved either impractical or unconstitutional. Historically, housing was more integrated in the South than in the North, slavery itself being incompatible with segregation. Efforts to impose segregation by ordinance were halted in 1917 when the U.S. Supreme Court, in a suit brought by the NAACP, invalidated a Louisville, Kentucky, ordinance designating residential blocks by race as violating the Fourteenth Amendment's equal protection clause.[9]

Because Woodward, in describing the "strange" career of Jim Crow, was sympathetic to the revolt of the white and black dirt farmers in the depressed 1890s, he emphasized the role of racial segregation as a weapon of class warfare. It was successfully exercised by conservative elites—the South's county courthouse oligarchy of merchants, bankers, planters, and lawyers and their political factotems—to split the populist insurgency by race baiting. To disrupt the dirt farmers' class solidarity, leaders of the propertied classes learned to shout, "Nigger!"[10] Woodward's class-based interpretation has held up fairly well. But his timing-centered analysis overemphasized both the fluidity of southern race relations before 1900 and the monolithic oppression of Jim Crow thereafter. Historian Howard Rabinowitz, taking issue with Woodward, argued that the crucial question was not *when* the shift to racial segregation occurred but what system it *replaced*. And according to Rabinowitz, what it replaced was racial exclusion, not integration.[11] Before segregation, blacks were largely excluded from hospitals, poorhouses, asylums, parks, hotels, restaurants, and theaters, and they found only limited access to schools and public transportation. A formal biracial caste system, however, like feudalism, conferred certain benefits on the lower social orders.

Thus paradoxically, segregation brought ostracism and humiliation, yet it also brought improved conditions in education, social welfare, and safety. New black institutions created stakeholders in the Jim Crow system. Black leaders learned to negotiate the parameters of Jim Crow to maximize their benefits. Having withdrawn en masse after the Civil War from white churches to build their own churches and staff them with African-American preachers, blacks demanded, and eventually won, black school teachers and support staff for their Jim Crow schools. Jim Crow thus contained a bargaining dynamic that produced compromises, a process that built stakeholders, such as black school teachers, while strengthening the conservative, racially segregated system. Similarly, black southerners benefited from the development of separate black hospitals and clinics, mental institutions, homes for the blind, and similar parallel institutions, even though the expanded services to black citizens unfailingly operated on barebones budgets.

The Biracial Trap of Segregation

The conservative reformist component of the white South's segregation movement produced some payoff for both races. It immediately reduced lynching and political corruption. Subsequently, it increased black access to education and social welfare services. The price of these benefits, however, kept ratcheting up as the logic of the white preference system polarized racial status. The decline of lynching, for example, left black southerners policed by all-white constabulary forces. Mass disfranchisement did indeed reduce the vote buying and political violence that prevailed in the last quarter of the nineteenth century. But losing the franchise stripped blacks of their political defenses, muting their voices before all-white governments and rendering them helpless before all-white police forces. The benefits of reduced political corruption from illiterate and purchasable voters were won at the cost of a radically shrunken electorate. Voter turnout in the South, which averaged a robust 66 percent of eligible voters of both races in the presidential elections of 1868 through 1892, plunged in the wake of disfranchisement to a state average of only 17.4 percent in 1924. Southern state electorates, thus purged of their lower orders (black and white alike) and hence allegedly of their ignorant and corrupting elements, pursued a path of government characterized by low taxes and scanty state services.

The steep price of Jim Crow for blacks, who were given little choice, was palpable, even in areas of intended benefit such as education. The "separate but equal" formula was a politically frail one even in the 1890s, when it was superimposed on existing first- and second-class railroad cars. As segregation spread, the separate-but-equal formula was everywhere honored in the breach. Black school terms were short and often excluded high schools. Black teachers were commonly paid a third less than white teachers, and black pupil-teacher ratios were twice that of whites. Black school buildings were typically dilapidated, and black school textbooks were white system castoffs. Florida and North Carolina made it illegal to give white pupils textbooks previously used by black students.

Segregated education in the poverty-ridden South was, by national standards, weak for white children and abysmal for black children. The average black adult in the South in 1940 had spent just five years in school, three and a half years less than the average southern white. Per pupil school expenditures in the southern states in 1940 averaged less than half of the national level. School systems in the Deep South spent more than three times more per pupil on whites than on blacks. In Mississippi, per pupil expenditures for whites were more than seven times that of blacks.

Similarly, the segregation reform's other benefits were modest in comparison with their long-term costs. The African-American stake in segregation's black job guarantees, although it sustained the region's tiny black middle class, was insufficient to sweeten the hatred that black southerners felt toward a system of degrading patronage everywhere dominated by white authority. The majority of southern blacks, confined to menial jobs as field hands and domestic servants, remained mired in poverty. By 1940, an estimated 80 percent of African-Americans in the southern and border states, where three-fourths of the nation's black citizens still resided, lived in poverty. While only one in seven southern white males had a skilled job of some kind in 1940, the figure for blacks was one in twenty-five.

By the 1950s, segregation was under attack in the national and international media, in the federal courts, and in Congress. A consensus among social scientists held that the white South, by adopting a formal biracial caste system, had built a destructive culture and, politically, had locked itself into a trap.[12] The South adopted a set of defensive political institutions—disfranchisement, legislative malapportionment, and the (Democratic) one-party system—that isolated the region from national life, crippled democratic processes, and blunted the forces of change, including economic revitalization and the development of a skilled and efficient workforce. The political scientist V. O. Key Jr.'s classic study of 1949, *Southern Politics in State and Nation*, described a region locked into a political system that punished the have-nots of both races.[13] Southern whites, long trapped by this system and lacking the political will to change it, were forced in the 1960s to abandon the system by mobilized southern blacks, allied with nonsouthern forces. It is a supreme irony that Martin Luther King, reviled by the southern white establishment in the 1950s and 1960s but celebrated elsewhere as the liberator of African-Americans in the South, numerically liberated far more whites than blacks from the crippling confines of the Jim Crow system.

Institutionalized Southern Defenses

The institutionalized system of white racial preference that the postwar liberals attacked was formidably defended in Congress. Over the years the South's one-party system had accumulated seniority for safe-seat Democrats, who as a consequence came to dominate congressional committee chairmanships after World War II. By 1960, southerners chaired twelve of the eighteen standing committees in the House and nine of the thirteen in the Senate. Key committees usually chaired by southern Democrats included the powerful House Rules Committee, the gatekeeper committee with authority to prevent bills from reaching the House floor, and the Senate Judiciary Committee, where civil rights bills could be similarly bottled up. In the Senate, rules of procedure required a supermajority vote (at least three-fifths of senators voting) to shut off debate and force a floor vote on legislation.[14]

As a consequence of these defenses, conservatives had always defeated liberal attacks on segregation or rendered them harmless. Senate filibusters led by southern Democrats, usually supported by conservative Republicans from the midwestern and Rocky Mountain states, had always been a successful last line of defense. Before 1964, no civil rights bill in the twentieth century had overcome a Senate filibuster. In 1957, legislative leaders Sam Rayburn in the House and Lyndon Johnson in the Senate, both Texas Democrats, avoided a filibuster because the civil rights bill passed that year was a symbolic bill about voting rights that powerful southern members of Congress believed unlikely to produce significant change (they were right) Lyndon Johnson, moreover, was nourishing presidential ambitions, and as Senate majority leader he supported voting rights compromises in the 1957 legislation that minimized its impact but helped shift his reputation from Texas segregationist to civil rights moderate.[15]

To overcome the South's defenses in Congress, reformers needed to build a coalition capable of winning a national mandate and capturing the elected branches of government in Washington. The liberal coalition that had passed Franklin Roosevelt's New Deal—an uneasy alliance of organized labor, southern white Democrats, northern blue-collar ethnics, African-Americans, academics and media intellectuals—was too divided by racial and cold war issues after World War II to overcome conservative defenses. This was changed, however, by the black civil rights movement in the South, led by courageous grassroots activists and inspired by the leadership of Martin Luther King.

The Civil Rights Movement

In retrospect, the triumph of "the Movement" in the 1960s seems inevitable. In reality, its path was halting, uncoordinated, and uncertain, especially before 1963. Its chief internal assets were a morally compelling cause, charismatic and courageous leadership that could overcome slipshod organization, and a rural black proletariat driven by a vision of justice and nurtured in the discipline of African-American churches. Its chief external assets were foolishly intransigent opponents in the white southern power structure, cold war competition with the Sino-Soviet bloc, a widespread belief by nonsouthern whites that racism was a southern problem, the federal courts, and television.

In the Montgomery, Alabama, protest of 1955, belligerent city officials fueled a bus boycott movement that had been quietly defused in other southern towns (Baton Rouge, Tallahassie, Rock Hill, South Carolina) by white politicians negotiating with moderate black leaders. Montgomery's veteran black leaders asked the new young preacher in town, King, to head the Montgomery Improvement Association not only because he offered a commanding voice and presence but also because the protest movement's leaders, many of them black schoolteachers and faculty at Alabama State College (formerly Alabama State College for Negroes) in Montgomery, were vulnerable to reprisal by white authorities. The Montgomery movement owed its victory in 1956 not only to courage and determination but also to the federal courts and television. But by the end of the decade, the movement was floundering. King's Southern Christian Leadership Conference (SCLC), formed in 1957 and successful in attracting northern foundation grants, was struggling against its own inept organizational skills, ineffective voter registration drives, and resentment from the NAACP for threatening its primacy.[16]

The revitalization of the movement in the early 1960s is the stuff of legend. The sit-ins of 1960 brought the vitality of the youth brigade, distilled in the liberal idealism and integrationist vision of the early Student Nonviolent Coordinating Committee (SNCC) and tailor-made for television news coverage. The sit-ins were more numerous and more successful in the rim South states (North Carolina, Tennessee, Virginia, Texas, Florida), although they spread to Deep South cities and often met violence there (Atlanta, Jackson). Sit-ins occurred most frequently, often with successful outcomes, in rim South cities possessing moderate political climates and black colleges as institutional bases (Greensboro, Nashville, Richmond, Houston, Tallahassie).[17]

The new, heavily televised activism accelerated in the early 1960s, as the limelight enjoyed by the SNCC attracted competing organizations and leaders. One was James Farmer of the Congress of Racial Equality (CORE), a Quaker-based pacifist and integrationist group active in northern cities in the 1940s. Farmer revitalized CORE in the early 1960s by repeating a tactic CORE had developed in the late 1940s of sponsoring interstate bus rides to integrate terminals in the southeastern seaboard states. CORE's "Freedom rides" in 1961 penetrated the Deep South and were violently attacked in Alabama. In 1962, however, King's demonstrations collapsed in failure in Albany, Georgia, where a shrewd and cool-headed police chief, Laurie Pritchett, jailed demonstrators en masse with polite efficiency. Deprived of confrontation, the press and television cameras left Albany, and the protest coalition of SCLC, SNCC, and the NAACP fell into bickering and recriminations. By the winter of 1963, Alabama governor George C. Wallace was setting the tone for career politicians in the South, and prospects for significant civil rights reform in Congress remained dim.

Then the political equation suddenly changed. A King-led strategic reassessment in the wake of the Albany fiasco produced a quiet and ironic consensus among movement leaders that nonviolent civil disobedience worked best not when peaceful demonstrators turned the other cheek in Christian love, as King had urged in his book *Stride toward Freedom*, but when the demonstrations provoked televised violence from die-hard white authorities. That new blueprint required a search for the most dependable racist police authorities, a strategy that brought the desegregation demonstrations to Police Commissioner T. Eugene "Bull" Connor in Birmingham in 1963 and to Sheriff James G. Clark in Selma, Alabama, in 1965.[18] The rest, as the scriptwriters say, is history.[19]

By the late spring of 1963, the televised police violence against the demonstrators in Birmingham, including police attacks using dogs, fire hoses, truncheons, and electric cattle prods on women and children, had stirred nationwide opposition to the South's caste system. This wave of revulsion against the ugly face of Jim Crow in turn prompted President John F. Kennedy to ask Congress to prohibit racial discrimination in public accommodations. "The Movement" had rallied the liberal coalition to a great moral crusade against Jim Crow oppression in the South, in the process mobilizing national church organizations in solidarity with many southern black church leaders. To the national electorate, the race problem was seen as the problem of racial segregation in the South and fixable by national legislation dismantling Jim Crow.[20]

The Triumph of Liberal Civil Rights Reform

The combination, in the early 1960s, of a robust economy, televised police violence against southern civil rights demonstrators, the martyrdom of President Kennedy in November 1963, the determined leadership of President Johnson, and Republican willingness to cooperate and compromise under the leadership of Senate Minority Leader Everett Dirksen of Illinois, produced a reform drive in Congress strong enough to overwhelm a southern filibuster and pass the Civil Rights Act in the summer of 1964. That same summer and fall, the ill-timed conservative crusade of Republican presidential nominee Barry Goldwater, who opposed the Civil Rights Act and threatened popular New Deal programs such as Social Security, gave Johnson a landslide victory that translated into a mandate backed by huge Democratic majorities in both houses of Congress.[21]

The election of 1964 created a window of opportunity for Johnson, whose party won majorities in the 89th Congress (1965-67) of 295 to 140 in the House and 68 to 32 in the Senate. During the campaign, Johnson had appointed high-level task forces to design an ambitious legislative agenda for his "Great Society" programs of 1965. At Johnson's prodding, the 89th Congress passed the Medicare and Medicaid bills, federal aid to schools and colleges, clean air and water laws, aid to urban mass transit, new cabinet departments of Housing and Urban Development (HUD) and Transportation, national endowments for the arts and humanities, and the voting rights law. The political sea change of 1964-65 transformed the role of the Leadership Conference for Civil Rights, the liberal, bipartisan organization formed to coordinate Washington lobbying for scores of civil rights, labor, civil liberties, and religious organizations, from traditional underdog in Congress to giant killer. Struggling uphill, since its founding in 1949, against the entrenched conservative defenses in Congress, the Leadership Conference led the coalition that shattered the southern defenses in 1964, and thereafter became a leading power within Washington's inside-the-beltway establishment.[22]

Thus Congress, following ineffective voting rights legislation in 1957 and 1960, responded to the liberal reform drive by passing four landmark antidiscrimination bills: the Civil Rights Act of 1964, the Voting Rights Act of 1965, the Immigration and Naturalization Act of 1965, and the Fair Housing Act of 1968. These laws were at once radical and traditional. The three domestic civil rights laws were radical because they extended centralized, permanent regulation from Washington to areas previously controlled by state and local authorities or the private marketplace: schools, colleges and universities, business firms, labor unions, owners of hotels and restaurants and places of amusement, voting registrars, realtors, and landlords. The immigration reform was radical because it abandoned a formula for permanent entry based on the national origins of immigrants, a formula enjoying broad congressional support in the years between the first and second world wars. The four reforms were traditional because they applied American liberalism's classic formula of nondiscrimination on account of race or ethnicity.[23]

The Liberal Accord of the 1960s

To destroy Jim Crow, the 1964 Civil Rights Act outlawed discrimination on account of race in employment and public accommodations, and one year later the Voting Rights Act banned racial discrimination in registration and voting. Together with the immigration reform and the fair housing legislation of 1968, these statutes reflected the liberal accord of 1964-68, a social compact forged from the fires of the black civil rights mobilization and hammered into law under the unlikely hand of Lyndon Johnson. The first two laws, in particular, forced changes in American society that were radical and rapid. The bedrock 1964 law destroyed the legal and economic foundation of Jim Crow segregation in the South, and the 1965 law empowered a formerly voiceless and defenseless majority of African-Americans who lived in the South to bargain politically with their ballots for protection and benefits.[24]

The great legislative breakthrough of the mid-1960s was a climax, long delayed by the hypocrisy of American racism, of the precepts of classical liberalism. It rested on six principles, and in at least five of them it enjoyed philosophical coherence and historical legitimacy. One foundation principle was *individualism*. Rights inhered in individuals, not in tribes or clans or races, or in corporatist groups such as royalty or aristocracy, capital, labor, the professions, churches, or ethnic organizations. A second principle was *universalism*. An inherently global value drawn from the Enlightenment, universalism in practice was qualified by the historic and legal reality of national boundaries. Within these boundaries, the fundamental rights of Americans, once discovered and proclaimed, were held to be the same for all citizens irrespective of wealth, social status, or location. And even outside the national boundaries, universalism implied a commonality of human rights, rooted in classic liberalism's natural rights doctrines and enlarged by the American origins of the United Nations Covenant, which added a global reach to liberalism's creed of equal individual rights.[25]

A third principle was *timelessness*. The equal rights of mankind were inherent in the human condition and were socially discovered through the unfolding of history, a process speeded by liberal protests and reform campaigns. Because the fundamental rights of Americans were natural and inherent rather than socially constructed, they were not socially variable (except perhaps in time of war). Once such immutable equal rights were proclaimed for Americans in the Constitution, the Bill of Rights, and subsequent amendments, they became permanent. They could be temporarily suspended by government in time of national emergency, but they could not be cancelled. Liberals conceded that some ancillary rights claims, derived from statutes and administrative regulations, were properly variable (age limits for driving or voting, residency requirements, spousal and parental obligations). But fundamental rights could not be temporary. Fourth, rights were best protected *negatively* in the Anglo-American liberal tradition, by government prohibitions against violations. The statutes of legislators and the decrees of judges banned discrimination. They commanded "Thou Shalt Not." They thereby avoided many dangers of ambiguity. Fifth, the essential guarantees of equal rights were *procedural*. They required equal treatment, not equal results. Equal opportunity meant freedom to demonstrate merit, not an entitlement to equal achievement.

A sixth principle of the liberal accord was modern, not classical. This was *centralization*. Like the New Deal, the liberal accord of the 1960s required enforcement from Washington because federalism, with its deference to local authority and tradition, had failed for too many generations to honor the first five principles. The Southern tradition of states rights had always defended white supremacy. As late as 1960, 60 percent of the nation's black citizens lived in the South under the humiliations of a racial caste system, and only 28.7 percent of the South's voting-age blacks were registered. Thus in its core policies the liberal accord provided for national enforcement of individual, universal, and timeless rights (as of 1964-68) through Washington-based negative procedures.

Achieving Consequences the Reformers Intended

The civil rights reforms of the 1960s quickly achieved their intended results. Consider the goals and achievements of the domestic civil rights reforms. The most radical provision in President Kennedy's civil rights bill of 1963, the ban on race discrimination in public accommodations, passed Congress in 1964 as Title II of the bill. The Johnson administration, fearing widespread defiance by southern whites over integrating restaurants and lodging, established a federal Community Relations Service in the bill to defuse explosive confrontations. Instead, except for some short-lived grandstanding, the race walls in hotels, restaurants, department stores, and theaters crumbled overnight throughout the South. Southern business and civic leaders, weary of the turmoil and commercial disruption of the early 1960s, quietly welcomed the change. Johnson's new Community Relations Service, almost unused, was soon disbanded.

The Civil Rights Act's other controversial provision, Title VII, created a national Equal Employment Opportunity Commission (EEOC) with a goal that was nonetheless regional: destroying race discrimination in the southern workforce. Because most states outside the southern and border regions had already established fair employment agencies like the EEOC—indeed, the EEOC was modeled on the fair employment commissions in northern states—Congress in 1964 required the EEOC to defer to established state agencies, freeing the new national commission to concentrate on the South, as Congress expected. Beginning in 1965, federal officials representing the EEOC, the Justice Department, the Pentagon, and the Labor Department mounted a combined attack on job bias by major southern employers, especially large defense contractors, such as Lockheed-Marietta in Georgia and Newport News Shipbuilding in Virginia. A key to their success was arm-twisting leverage provided by a little-noticed section of the Civil Rights Act, Title VI. It authorized Washington agencies to deny government contracts to businesses that treated their employees differently according to race. Title VI was designed to prevent the government from subsidizing the discrimination it was working to end.[26]

By 1970, these efforts had broken the back of segregation in the South. The rulings of the Justice Department and the requirements of federal agencies, when challenged in the federal courts, were almost always upheld. The economic consequences of these changes were striking. These were the years of greatest relative economic gain by African-Americans. Between 1959 and 1969, mean annual earnings by black men increased by 49 percent, while equivalent white earnings rose by 26 percent. In the decade following passage of the Civil Rights Act, the annual earnings of full-time black workers increased from 63 percent to 73 percent of that of white male workers, while among women workers the black-white earnings ratio rose from 68 percent to 90 percent. This surge in black income reflected primarily the dismantling of racial job barriers in the South.[27] By

1973, when the onset of race-conscious affirmative action programs coincided with a declining American economy and a shift away from manufacturing to service-based employment, the period of rapid gains for blacks was beginning to wane.[28]

On the political front, the Voting Rights Act similarly destroyed the basis of black powerlessness in the South. The law established a triggering formula for voter participation based on the percentage of voting-age minorities in each electoral district. If minority voter registrations were significantly below the threshold, federal officials were authorized to register voters themselves. Most electoral districts in the South quickly fell into line. Several Deep South jurisdictions defied the new requirements, and their voter registration processes were promptly "federalized." In the six southern states covered by the new voting law, the percentage of registered voting-age blacks jumped from 24.4 in 1964 to 60 in 1969.[29] By 1970, almost a million new black voters had been added to the South's voter rolls. Southern politicians, courting (and fearing) these new voters, abandoned the racist demagoguery that had marred southern politics for generations. In the 1970s a new breed of southern governor came to power across the region, men such as Jimmy Carter of Georgia, Reuben Askew of Florida, Richard Riley of South Carolina, and Bill Clinton of Arkansas. They welcomed the death of segregation and honored the civil rights movement for freeing southern whites as well as southern blacks from the bondage of the past. Even Governor Wallace of Alabama began to court black voters in the mid-1970s, seeking forgiveness for his earlier segregationist stands.

Is the Constitution Color-Blind?

The success of the civil rights laws in rapidly dismantling the South's racial caste system was due primarily to the clarity and force of Washington's new command to stop discriminating on account of race. This command summoned the famous imagery of Justice John Marshall Harlan of the U.S. Supreme Court, in his lonely dissent in Plessy v. Ferguson in 1896. "Our Constitution is color-blind," Harlan had proclaimed, "and neither knows nor tolerates classes among its citizens." In 1954 the New York Times greeted Chief Justice Earl Warren's ruling against school segregation in Brown v. Board of Education by observing that Harlan's visionary dissent in Plessy, which for a half-century had been "a voice crying in the wilderness," had at last been transformed by Brown into "the law of the land."[30]

Not surprisingly, blacks protesting against segregation had historically rallied to Justice Harlan's claim in Plessy that the Fourteenth Amendment's guarantee of equal protection of the law made the Constitution color-blind. That doctrine had been the keystone of black civil rights reformers since the formation of the NAACP in 1909. The chief political weapon of "the Movement" in the 1950s and 1960s was an appeal to the moral imperative of a color-blind Constitution. Thurgood Marshall, counsel for the NAACP in *Brown*, told the Warren Court that "the only thing the Court is dealing with is whether race can be used." "What we want from the Court," Marshall explained, is simply "the striking down of race."[31]

The *Times*'s celebration of *Brown* as confirming constitutional color blindness was widely shared in America. In the debates over the Kennedy-Johnson civil rights bill in 1963 and 1964, the bipartisan congressional leadership appealed to the classical liberal model of color-blind justice, leaning over backwards to deny charges by southern opponents that the law could lead to quotas or other forms of preference for minorities. Indeed, the legislative history of the Civil Rights Act shows what John David Skrentny, author of *The Ironies of Affirmative Action*, called "an almost obsessive concern" for maintaining fidelity to a color-blind concept of equal individual rights. Senator Hubert Humphrey of Minnesota, the majority (Democratic) whip behind the bill, explained simply: "Race, religion and national origin are not to be used as the basis for hiring and firing."[32]

Title VII required employers to treat citizens differing in race, sex, national origin, or religion equally, as abstract citizens differing only in merit. Section 703(j) of the Civil Rights Act states: "Nothing contained in this title shall be interpreted to require any employer . . . to grant preferential treatment to any individual or to any group because of the race, color, religion, sex, or national origin of such individual or group on account of an imbalance which may exist with respect to the total number or percentage of persons of any race, color, religion, sex, or national origin employed by an employer." The syntax was classic legalese, but the meaning was unambiguous. The Senate's floor managers for Title VII, Joseph S. Clark (D-Pa.) and Clifford P. Case (R-N.J.), told their colleagues, "The concept of discrimination . . . is clear and simple and has no hidden meanings. . . . To discriminate means to make a distinction, to make a difference in treatment or favor, which is based on any five of the forbidden criteria: race, color, religion, sex, or national origin." They continued:

> There is no requirement in Title VII that an employer maintain a balance in his work force. On the contrary, any deliberate attempt to maintain a racial balance, whatever such a balance may be, would involve a violation of Title VII because maintaining such a balance would require an employer to hire or refuse to hire on the basis of race. It must be emphasized that discrimination is prohibited to any individual.[33]

Humphrey, trying to lay to rest what he called the "bugaboo" of racial quotas raised by filibustering southerners in his own party and by some conservative Republicans as well, reaffirmed the bill's color-blind legislative intent: "That bugaboo has been brought up a dozen times; but it is nonexistent. In fact the very opposite is true. Title VII prohibits discrimination. In effect, it says that race, religion, and national origin are not to be used as the basis for hiring and firing." Humphrey even famously pledged on the Senate floor that if any wording could be found in Title VII "which provides that an employer will have to hire on the basis of percentage or quota related to color, . . . I will start eating the pages [of the bill] one after another."[34]

The Meaning of Kennedy-Johnson Affirmative Action

Conservative critics of affirmative action have pointed to the overwhelming consensus on requirements of color blindness shown in these debates to prove that affirmative action policy, in the controversial, race-conscious form it developed in the 1970s, violated the Civil Rights Act itself. These claims have particular force with respect to the EEOC, which in adopting race-conscious remedies in the late 1960s indisputably violated its own founding charter, Title VII, and got away with it. Yet the civil rights reforms of the 1960s included affirmative action of some sort from the start. President Kennedy's Executive Order 10925 of March 6, 1961, which was drafted by Kennedy's equal employment committee under the chairmanship of Vice President Lyndon Johnson, required government contractors to take "affirmative action" to ensure equal employment opportunity in their operations. What did that phrase mean? Why was it included?

Kennedy signed the executive order because he knew that Congress would not pass such a requirement as a statute. He had promised during the 1960 campaign, on the heels of the sit-in demonstrations that spread in February of that year, that he would act against racial unfairness in the South. As president, Kennedy held the executive's traditional authority to set the conditions for government contracts and to bar payments if contractors failed to meet the conditions stipulated. Typically, in the past, Washington's contractual conditions had been largely technical, for example, requiring that highway bridges and war machines must meet certain physical standards of performance. But Democrats in the 1930s had added a requirement (called Davis-Bacon, and hated by Republicans) that employees working on federally assisted projects must be paid "prevailing" (i.e., union) wages. So the idea of adding nontechnical requirements in government contracting, a form of "social regulation" to protect or benefit a deserving conotituency, was not entirely novel, especially to Democrats. The meaning of a command not to discriminate on account of race seemed clear, even if its implementation was difficult. But what did affirmative action mean? Kennedy's 1961 executive order offered no explanations. The term *affirmative action* was always ambiguous. It attracted little attention in Kennedy's executive order and was little noticed, much less understood, by Washington's policymaking community in the early 1960s. Veteran lawmakers with long memories might recall that the term had appeared in the Wagner Act of 1935. There Congress used it to define the authority of the newly created National Labor Relations Board (NLRB) to redress an unfair labor practice by ordering the offending party "to cease and desist from such unfair labor practice, and to take such affirmative action, including reinstatement of employees with or without back pay, as will effectuate the policies of this Act."[35] The NLRB, for example, could not only order the Ford Motor Company to stop firing workers who tried to organize labor unions but could also direct employers to rehire the fired union organizers and provide make-whole relief in the form of back pay (to make the complainant "whole," as if the termination and loss of wages had not occurred).[36]

Affirmative action in the Wagner Act sense implied an employer obligation, beyond avoiding unfair labor practices such as firing union organizers or breaking their knees (a favorite tactic of Henry Ford's union-busting hired goons in the 1920s), to accommodate the new norms of collective bargaining in industrial relations, to foster an environment in which organized labor was welcomed as a legitimate partner in the American industrial enterprise. But the nature and extent of such obligations remained vague. The Wagner Act's sole specific examples of affirmative action, job reinstatement and back pay, were identified in the statute establishing a new, permanent federal regulatory commission, the NLRB, as appropriate remedies to provide relief for a violation of law determined through the agency's quasi-judicial hearing process.

Kennedy's executive order of 1961, on the other hand, was not a congressional statute like the Wagner Act. It was an executive order rooted in the president's authority as chief executive to enforce government contracts. As administrative law, an executive order lacked the force of a legislative statute, except arguably under the president's authority as commander in chief in time of war or national emergency. President Franklin Roosevelt's Fair Employment Practices Committee (FEPC), established by executive order in 1941, was dismantled by a hostile Congress in 1946. Moreover, Kennedy's contract compliance order of 1961, unlike the Wagner

Act, did not provide remedies to punish violations. Instead, it directed that "the contractor will not discriminate against any employee or applicant for employment because of race, creed, color, or national origin" and that "the contractor will take affirmative action to ensure that applicants are employed, and that employees are treated during employment, without regard to their race, creed, color, or national origin."[37]

Kennedy's order, then, required affirmative action to ensure that government contractors followed color-blind employment practices. No examples of affirmative action were offered by the Kennedy administration, and few were asked. Contractors building government-funded submarines or airplanes or federally assisted highways or hospitals, or supplying government agencies with toilet paper or electricity, knew that the problem being attacked by the executive order was racial discrimination in the South, a problem that Congress was not ready to address in 1961. The best examples of affirmative action under Kennedy's executive order were to be found in the equal employment efforts of federal agencies themselves, where hiring offices interpreted affirmative action obligations during the Kennedy and Johnson administrations to mean extra recruiting efforts to boost the employment of underrepresented groups. According to this standard interpretation, not only should government employment officials not discriminate against minorities, but recruiting officers should advertise positions in minority newspapers and visit black college campuses. Some normative model of proportional representation seemed implicit in this notion. But so powerful was the animus against racial labeling and quotas that officials were careful to avoid such implications. And after 1964, the Civil Rights Act prohibited quotas or preferential treatment on account of race or ethnicity. The all-important imperative was to stop discriminating because of race.

Affirmative Action and the Long Hot Summers

The Civil Rights Act that President Johnson signed in 1964 took effect on July 1, 1965. Then on August 11, 1965, only five days after Johnson signed the Voting Rights Act, blacks angered by police arrests in the Watts neighborhood of Los Angeles began five days of rioting, looting, and arson. The Watts rioting left thirty-four persons dead, four thousand arrested, and $35 million in property damage. The following summer, there were forty-three racial disorders in northern and western cities. In 1966 King brought his nonviolent demonstration techniques, so successful when rooted in the disciplined rural and small-town culture of the southern black church, to

Chicago, where they quickly shattered in the brittle, fragmented culture of the urban ghetto. SNCC leader Stokeley Carmichael began a "Black Power" campaign in 1966 that rejected King's model of nonviolent protest and led SNCC toward a black nationalist stance that rejected the traditional goal of racial integration itself.

In the 1967 urban riots, there were 164 racial disorders, 8 involving National Guard intervention. In Newark, New Jersey, rioters systematically looted and burned white-owned businesses. In Detroit's mega-riot, 43 persons were killed, 7,000 were arrested, 1,300 buildings were burned, and 2,700 businesses were looted. In the spring of 1968, following the assassination in Memphis of Martin Luther King, dozens of cities were put to the torch. The most destructive riots in 1968 were in Baltimore and Washington, D.C. But the riots triggered by the King assassination marked an exception to a cooling-down trend that was evident by 1968. Thereafter, the rioting quickly faded. Rioting was expressive and cathartic, but it was also self-destructive, leaving a riot-scarred community further isolated, its stores closed, its services and security withered. Black inner-city neighborhoods almost never experienced a second riot.[38]

What lessons can we draw from the extraordinary race-triggered explosions of the long, hot summers? First, they demonstrate, by their rarity in the South, that the civil rights reforms of 1964-65, which were overwhelmingly directed at destroying the South's system of racial segregation, were successful. The riots of 1965-68 occurred almost entirely outside the South. Racial disturbances broke out in some southern cities, but none involved major destruction. Instead, these were solidarity demonstrations staged in largely African-American college communities, not spontaneous race riots marked by black looting and burning. The civil rights movement, after all, had won a massive payoff for black southerners. It brought Jim Crow crashing down and opened new opportunities for African-American advancement. Southern blacks thus had no incentive to riot. But outside the South, the Civil Rights Act and the Voting Rights Act had produced few tangible benefits for inner-city blacks, whose unemployment continued to double white rates and whose schooling and housing were racially isolated and deteriorating.

Second, coming on the heels of the impressive and effective nonviolent demonstrations in the South, the race riots alienated the American middle class. They ended the era of nonviolence and shattered the civil rights coalition. In the media, "We Shall Overcome" was supplanted as a movement slogan by "Burn, Baby, Burn," although most blacks still pursued peaceful integration strategies. By the end of 1968 the riots left 250 African-Americans dead, 8,000 wounded, and 50,000 arrested in more than 300 race riots and disturbances since 1965. An estimated half million blacks had participated in the burning and looting. Adding to the turmoil was growing protest against the Vietnam War. American voters in 1968, rejecting the party of Kennedy and Johnson, sent Republican Richard Nixon to the White House. Nixon and Alabama governor George Wallace, the protest candidate of the American Independent Party, together won 57 percent of the popular vote, a clear repudiation of the Johnson regime. The 1968 election was a major political watershed, marking a shift from an era of normal Democratic majorities since 1932 to a new era of divided partisan government, one in which voting majorities for the next quarter-century, reacting against race riots, black nationalism, rising crime rates and welfare rolls, and both the Vietnam War and antiwar radical protest, rejected Democratic candidates for the presidency (Jimmy Carter's single presidential term in 1977-81 was the exception that proved the rule).

Third, the riots spurred aggressive efforts by federal officials to dampen the violence by speeding delivery of benefits, especially jobs paying good wages, to urban minorities who found little payoff in the civil rights legislation of 1964-65. The Small Business Administration (SBA), seeking to aid proprietors of riot-damaged stores and to encourage minority ownership in urban rebuilding efforts, established in 1968 the section 8(a) program. Targeted to aid heavily damaged core areas through grants and subsidized business loans, the 8(a) program avoided the racial quota taboo by funneling aid to "socially disadvantaged" persons, not to minorities per se. But most participants in the 8(a) program were minority business entrepreneurs.

Labor Department officials, however, were less cautious than their counterparts in the Commerce Department's SBA. Charged by President Johnson in 1965 with coordinating contract compliance in federally assisted construction projects, the Labor Department began experimenting with expanding affirmative action requirements to goad federal contractors in the booming construction industry to hire more urban blacks. After failing to find a workable formula in St. Louis, San Francisco, and Cleveland in 1966 and 1967, they concentrated on Philadelphia. There contractors involved in federally supported construction projects costing $550 million were told of a new requirement: Their bids would not be found "in compliance" until negotiations over the number of minority workers on the job, shown in the builder's five-year manning table estimates, reached levels satisfactory to Labor Department officials. The officials making this judgment were fair employment monitors in the Labor Department's Office of Federal Contract Compliance (OFCC), a subagency formed in 1965 by labor secretary Willard Wirtz. The OFCC's job was to enforce equal employment opportunity (EEO) under the president's executive order program as strengthened by Title VI of the Civil Rights Act. In the five-county Philadelphia area in 1967, the OFCC interpreted fair employment to mean roughly proportional representation of minorities in the area workforce. Although technically the term *minorities* included Asians, American Indians, and national origin minorities vaguely described as "Spanish-speaking" or "Spanish-surnamed," for practical purposes *minorities* in government contract-compliance bureaucracies in the late 1960s meant blacks. For African-Americans in metropolitan Philadelphia, this translated into a target of approximately 30 percent of employees working on federally supported construction projects.

The Philadelphia Plan, announced in July 1967 in the wake of the Detroit riot, drew fierce attacks from both the unions and the builders. To the AFL-CIO, the Philadelphia Plan's racial hiring priorities violated labor's long-standing seniority principle, a centerpiece of every union contract. To the building contractors, the Philadelphia Plan violated union contracts and also violated federal bidding protocols. In 1968, the U.S. Chamber of Commerce and the National Association of Manufacturers joined the Associated Contractors of America in complaining to Congress and the Johnson administration. The ranking Republican on the House Public Works Committee, William Cramer of Florida, complained to the General Accounting Office (GAO), a watchdog agency charged with monitoring federal contracts. In reply, the GAO comptroller general, Elmer Staats, ruled that the Philadelphia Plan violated the federal government's blind, low-bid protocols, which were developed by Progressive reformers to combat widespread corruption by city machines. Moreover, Staats ruled, the minority preferences of the Philadelphia Plan violated the Civil Rights Act itself. Two weeks after the election of Richard Nixon in November 1968, the Labor Department quietly rescinded the Philadelphia Plan.

Nixon, reversing Goldwater, had pledged in his campaign to support the civil rights legislation of the 1960s and to consolidate its gains. He would vigorously enforce nondiscrimination but oppose racial quotas; he would support school desegregation in the South but oppose busing for racial balance. He called on Americans to "lower our voices," to concentrate not on passing more civil rights legislation but on making the laws already on the books work. Nixon had worked comfortably with the NAACP as a California senator, had chaired President Eisenhower's fair employment contract compliance committee, had differed little with Kennedy on civil rights issues in the 1960 presidential election, and had supported the civil rights legislation of 1964, 1965, and 1968. His election seemed to mark the closing of a long and tragic era in America, when a government-enforced system of white racial preference in the South was finally dismantled by the triumph of a color-blind Constitution and systematic enforcement of nondiscrimination in public policy. Similarly, American immigration policy, burdened early in the century with racial and national origin restrictions, was swept up in the liberal reform drive of the 1960s and purged of its ancestry-based preferences.

3

Immigration Reform in the 1960s

It was not surprising that immigration reform should reach the agenda of the civil rights coalition in the 1960s. American immigration policy since the 1920s had rested on a system of national origins quotas that favored immigration from northern and western Europe and that largely excluded Asians. The liberal reformers who dominated the heavily Democratic 89th Congress in 1965 deplored racial and ethnic quotas and banned them in the civil rights legislation of 1964 and 1965. The quota laws of the 1920s, however, had themselves been reform achievements, supported by a broad coalition that included middle-class "Progressives" (both Republicans and Democrats), organized labor, and the most prominent African-American leaders of the day. Immigration restrictionists from the left side of the political spectrum included leaders of organized labor, prominent spokesmen for black Americans, social justice Progressives, and conservationists. They argued that uncontrolled immigration, encouraged by industrial employers seeking docile low-wage workers, flooded the national labor pool, depressed wages, worsened working conditions and tenement housing, weakened organized labor, provided the basis for the corrupt city political machines, and threatened overpopulation.[1]

The immigration restriction coalition also included patrician conservatives such as Theodore Roosevelt and Massachusetts senator Henry Cabot Lodge, who sought to maintain the dominance in America of Anglo-Saxon stock. Madison Grant, a Park Avenue patrician, ardent student of the natural sciences and eugenics, and founder of the New York Zoological Society, in 1916 published *The Passing of the Great Race*, a popular text for "nativist" intellectuals.[2] Grant, though a racial determinist, showed little concern over relations between whites and blacks or Asians, but he brooded pessimistically over the "race suicide" produced by mixing Nordic stock

35

with bloodlines from southern and eastern Europe, especially Jews.[3] Other anti-immigration organizations were active, such as the Sons of the American Revolution, the American Protective Association, and the Immigration Restriction League, and emphasized Protestant America's older, anti-Catholic tradition.[4] Conservatives opposed importing European socialists, labor syndicalists, violent anarchists, and dependent classes. Out of this mixed coalition of the left and right came an immigration reform drive in the 1920s that was widely popular in Congress. Its immediate goal was to prevent the flood of immigrants from Europe, abruptly halted by the Great War, from resuming after the Armistice.

The "New Immigration" of 1880–1920

The centrality of mass immigration as a dominant fact of American life in the Progressive Era is hard to recapture a century later. In the economically distressed early 1990s, when populist resentment of the post-1960s mass immigration spread across the nation from California, the foreign-born constituted only 10 percent of the U.S. population. In prosperous 1965, when Congress abolished the national origins quota system, the foreign-born constituted only 5 percent of the U.S. population. America in the 1960s was an overwhelmingly native-born, English-speaking, culturally assimilated America (including the black/white divide) where ethnic pluralism chiefly took the form of religious diversity and ethnic cuisine. America's crisis of the 1960s centered on race, not ethnicity, and race meant native-born African-Americans, not immigrants.

In 1910, however, the foreign-born constituted 15 percent of the American population. This was also true in 1860. Immigrants in nineteenth-century America were a larger proportion of a smaller total population. Before the 1890s however, most immigrants were northern European in origin who were dispersed and rapidly assimilated throughout an America of farms, small towns, and modest-sized cities, the chief exception being Irish Catholics concentrated in northeastern seaports. Immigration from southern and eastern Europe began to quicken in the 1880s, however, and by 1910 almost 20 million new Americans had poured into the country's northern cities. Half the country remained largely unaffected—the South, the Great Plains, and the Rocky Mountain states. But in America's major industrial cities by 1910, typically three out of every four residents were immigrants or the children of immigrants. In the tenement slums, virtually all were immigrants. By 1910, immigrants and their children constituted more than 70 percent of the population of New York, Chicago,

Detroit, Cleveland, Boston, Milwaukee, and Buffalo. In other cities—San Francisco, Newark, Pittsburgh, Saint Louis, Philadelphia, Cincinnati—immigrants and their children were in the majority. A U.S. government survey of 1910 found that 58 percent of industrial workers were foreign-born. Between 1880 and 1920, 2.5 million immigrants came to Chicago alone, where they created ethnic neighborhoods of Poles, Russians, Italians, and Czechs.[5]

These were "New Immigrants" from new places. They were part of a great demographic tidal wave, the heart of which was a "Caucasian tsunami" that sent 50 million immigrants out of a Europe at first blessed by rising birth and falling death rates, then convulsed in the nineteenth century by industrial dislocation, farm mechanization, overpopulation, unemployment, and war. They fled to the "neo-Europes"—Australia and New Zealand, South Africa, Argentina and Brazil, Canada, and, most of all, to the United States, which received almost 60 percent of the total.

They were not the northern European Protestants who dominated the nation's Founding, or the Africans whose involuntary importation ceased early in the nineteenth century, or the Germans and Irish of pre-Civil War days. Instead, they were southern Italians, Hungarians, Greeks, Croats, and Slovakians. They were ethnic fragments of eastern Europe's crumbling empires, Austro-Hungarian and Russian and Ottoman Turk. They were Roman Catholics, Russian and Greek Orthodox, and Jews. America's Catholic population, 1.6 million in 1850, had jumped by 1900 to 12 million. American Catholicism, predominantly Irish in the nineteenth century, became increasingly Italian, Polish, and central European. By 1900 Catholics were the nation's largest single religious group, and their refusal to send their children to the American public schools alarmed patriotic and suspicious Protestants. In 1870 America's Jewish population of 250,000 was predominantly German, cosmopolitan, and rooted in Judaism's liberal or reform tradition. By 1920, 3.5 million Jews lived in America, most of them sharing the conservative or orthodox traditions of eastern Europe. Additionally, to the West Coast came 400,000 Chinese and 300,000 Japanese, 750,000 Mexicans, 450,000 from the West Indies, and 150,000 from Central and South America.[6]

Progressive Reformers and the Shame of the Cities

Who were the Progressives, and why were they such passionate reformers? Our history textbooks struggle with the Progressives because they poorly fit the standard model of America's reformers. Unlike the populists who preceded them in the 1890s or the New Dealers who followed them in the 1950s, reformers who attacked economic injustice through coalitions mobilized by dispossessed farmers, unemployed workers, union organizers, the impoverished elderly, and other suffering groups, the Progressives were typically middle-class Americans whose personal circumstances were reasonably secure. They were alarmed by the growth of industrial sweatshops, child labor, disease-ridden tenements, urban crime, corrupt city bosses, and labor violence driven by radical socialists and anarchists. It was difficult to identify a source of progressive concern that was not closely tied to the new mass immigration. These included the spread of slum tenements, infectious disease (typhoid, smallpox, scarlet fever, typhus), corrupt ethnic-based city machines, violent strains of anarchism and Bolshevism, and the devastation of families by alcohol and the saloon.[7]

The social justice wing of progressivism supported the settlement house movement, understood that immigrants were vulnerable victims of economic forces they could not control, and campaigned for maximum-hour legislation and laws limiting child labor. But most middle-class Progressives were animated by a different set of values. These included the canons of Protestant morality, a gospel of efficiency in business and government affairs, and faith in democracy, education, and professional and scientific expertise. Class tensions they found particularly worrisome, especially in the wake of the Bolshevik Revolution. Class tensions ran high throughout the Progressive Era, fueled by the downcycles of industrial capitalism, which increased unemployment and labor unrest; the conspicuous opulence of the wealthy, who paid no income taxes; and the arrival of hordes of impoverished immigrants from countries lacking democratic traditions and institutions.[8]

The captains of American industry, despised by the trust-busting Progressives, promoted mass immigration as a source of cheap labor and a curb against union growth. Such self-interested behavior was neither new nor contrary to government policy, and low-cost labor was a major engine of the extraordinary American industrial expansion following the Civil War. By 1913, the real per-capita Gross National Product in the United States was five times the average for European countries and 25 percent higher than that of Britain, the wealthiest country in Europe. But the boom-and-bust cycle of unregulated industrial capitalism produced sharp periodic recessions that brought soaring unemployment. Nonfarm unemployment rose above 10 percent in the recessions of 1900–1904 and 1907–11 and above 15 percent in 1914–15 and 1921–22. Native-born workers, resenting the immigrants' wage-lowering competition even in periods of high employment, agitated for restriction when unemployment rose. In 1921, when the Congress first imposed sharp limits on immigration, nonfarm unemployment stood at 19.5 percent.

What was to be done? Progressives attacked the problems of municipal corruption, urban decay, workplace safety, and monopoly directly through substantive reforms (child labor, workmen's safety and compensation, public health, juvenile justice, civil service, municipal government, antitrust) and procedural reforms (initiative, referendum, recall, direct primary, women's suffrage). But in the great northern cities, such piecemeal solutions seemed overwhelmed by a flood of immigration that between 1880 and 1920 had poured 25 million immigrants into America's squalid cities. The outbreak of war in Europe (and submarine warfare in the Atlantic) stopped transatlantic immigration between 1914 and 1919. In a war emergency mood, Congress in 1917 passed (over Wilson's veto) a literacy test excluding immigrants who were illiterate in English or their own language. "Tests of quality and purpose can not be objected to on principle," Wilson explained, "but tests of opportunity surely may be."[9] Wilson did not specifically object however, to an explicitly racist provision in the 1917 law. This was an "Asiatic barred zone" that defined by latitude and longitude a vast area of the Far East whose inhabitants were excluded from immigration to America. The provision, first passed on the floor of the Senate in 1916 without debate or a record vote, reflected a powerful consensus in Congress for a white immigration policy.[10]

The Armistice in 1919, however, threatened to renew the flood from a Europe economically shattered and awash in war refugees. Half a million immigrants entered U.S. ports in 1920. The immigration commissioner at the port of New York predicted that a million would enter in 1921, and reported that "more than ten millions are now waiting in various ports of war-stricken Europe to swarm to the U.S. as soon as they can obtain transportation."[11] Meanwhile, the economic recession of 1921 left 5 million unemployed in the United States. The American Federation of Labor (AFL), traditionally immigrant-based and non-nativist in its leadership, yet restrictionist on immigration since the 1890s, nonetheless called for a moratorium on all immigration.

The Immigration Reforms of the 1920s

Liberals of the 1960s, mobilized behind the civil rights movement against racial discrimination, objected to the national origins quota system created in the 1920s as a racist legacy of America's past that should be abolished, like the South's Jim Crow laws. American opinion leaders during the Progressive Era, most of them white Protestant men, widely accepted social Darwinist views of racial hierarchy that associated advanced civilization

with whiteness and backwardness with color. Scientific racism rationalized western imperialism and the tutelage of whites over what Rudyard
Kipling called "lesser breeds without the law." For these reasons, textbook
descriptions of American immigration reform in the 1920s typically root it
in the revolt of parochial, Protestant, small-town, middle America against
the urban-cosmopolitan America of the future. Such accounts emphasize
the adoption of prohibition in 1919, the "Red Scare" of the same year, the
revival of the Ku Klux Klan in small-town Protestant America, and the
Scopes "monkey trial" in Tennessee in 1925.

The context is legitimate, as far as it goes. Immigration restriction in the
1920s was driven by a reform coalition that had shifted to the right, strengthened by rural and small-town fears of cities flooded with such strange, "un-
Americanized" new immigrants. The national origins quota laws were
enacted by a Congress that significantly overrepresented rural interests. The
dominant reform impulse in America was still progressivism, even in the
1920s. But progressivism had always carried a strong "return" component, a
nostalgia for the moral certitudes of middle-class Protestant America that
legitimized "blue law" crusades against urban and often immigrant vices
such as saloons, gambling, Sabbath violation, and vulgar entertainment. Progressive enthusiasm for scientific professionalism often included a eugenics
concern about excessive breeding by the lower orders of mankind. Thus the
label of racism is generally apt, but also somewhat misleading, certainly in its
1960s context, when applied to immigration issues, especially for the 1920s.
In Progressive Era discourse, *race* was not taken to refer to the black/white/
yellow triad of the mid-twentieth century. Instead, race was used loosely to
refer not only to "Negroes" and "Orientals" but also to Italians, Jews, Germans, Slavs, Greeks, Turks—and Anglo-Saxons.

In the 1960s, racism was chiefly understood to mean discrimination by
whites against African-Americans. But in the immigration debate of the
Progressive Era, the nation's most prominent black leaders—most notably
the Republican conservative, Booker T. Washington, and the socialist intellectual, W.E.B. DuBois—supported the restrictionists. Washington, in his
famous Atlanta address at the Cotton States Exposition in 1895, pleaded
with industrial leaders to employ loyal, hardworking freedmen, rather
than import millions of European immigrants to take the industrial jobs
that otherwise might have freed native-born African-Americans from segregated misery in the rural South. Black immigration to the United States
had stopped with the repression of the slave trade early in the nineteenth
century. Immigration from Africa thus had no place on the policy agenda
of the 1920s, and no interest groups sought to place it there, including
Africans or African-Americans themselves.

Immigration by Asians, the other nonwhite "race" in the three-race formulation of Caucasuld, Mongoloid, and Negroid of classic European provenance, was an issue of diplomatic significance, given the sensitivity to racial insult of the proud, powerful, and strategically threatening Japanese. But Asian immigration had been halted almost completely before World War I. In the American West, Chinese laborers, who were brought in the mid-nineteenth century to mine gold and build the railroads, became the despised, alien "other" in the eyes of western workingmen, who feared competition with Chinese wages. Chinese laborers, grown to 10 percent of the California population by the 1870s, lived in segregated camps and Chinatowns, learned little English, and were stereotyped as unclean, illiterate, pigtailed coolies. China itself was an object of contempt, an ancient empire in full decay, fragmenting under the weight of despotic warlords, European incursions, corruption, and opium addiction. Thus China, like Africa, confirmed in American eyes the backwardness and undesirability of her immigrants. Western states taxed foreign mineworkers, segregated Asians in public schools, and hindered them in land ownership and business enterprise. Congress in 1882, responding to western populist demands, passed the Chinese Exclusion Act. Japanese and Korean immigrant laborers, arriving toward the end of the nineteenth century, stirred western protests that led to the negotiated Gentleman's Agreement of 1907–8, brokered by President Theodore Roosevelt, to halt immigration from Japan and Korea (a colony of Japan). In 1917 Congress created the Asiatic Barred Zone, a region of prohibited immigration for laborers (exceptions were provided for merchants, students, and spouses of American citizens) that included India.

The immigration reformers of the 1920s showed little dissent from this inherited pattern of Asian exclusion. Neither did the U.S. Supreme Court, which ruled in 1922, citing naturalization statutes dating back to 1790, that Asian aliens, unlike free white persons and aliens of African nativity, were "ineligible for citizenship."[12] In 1923 the Court upheld laws in western states seeking to discourage Japanese immigration by barring aliens ineligible for citizenship from owning or leasing agricultural lands. In that case, *Terrance v. Thompson*, the Court held that because the federal government by congressional statute recognized two classes of aliens—those who were eligible for citizenship (Caucasians and Africans) and those who were not (Asians)—states were not required to justify similar laws.[13]

In 1924, Congress, passed the Oriental Exclusion Act, which incorporated the Supreme Court opinion into law. Filipinos were not included in the Asian ban, owing to the status of the Philippine Islands as an American dependency. But the ban included the Japanese. In Japan, American flags were burned to protest an act of national humiliation (although the Japanese themselves banned immigration from China and Korea).

The great immigration debates of the 1920s, however, were about Europeans, not Asians or Africans. In the post-1960s context of racial controversy, race has centered chiefly on the black/white dyad, reflecting the African-American status as the descendants of slaves and the primary beneficiaries of race-conscious affirmative action programs, and secondarily on modern Latino or "brown" demands for protected class status and affirmative action benefits. But the racial debates of the 1920s concerned Caucasians (national origins quotas) and Asians (excluded), not blacks and browns. Immigrants of African and Hispanic ancestry continued to come to the United States in significant numbers from the Caribbean and Latin America because the Western Hemisphere was excluded from quota systems or caps. Even after the sharp restrictions of 1921 and 1924, immigration law in the late 1920s admitted an average of 287,000 immigrants a year, chiefly because of the Western Hemispheric exclusion.

"Race," then, was commonly used by the policymakers of the 1920s as a synonym for ethnicity. Neither term was used as a legislative category, however, because it would be unworkable in application. "National origins," on the other hand, was a practical surrogate for ethnicity. The problem of Europe's refugee explosion following the Great War, restrictionists agreed, was its size and its ethnocultural origin. No less an authority than political science professor Woodrow Wilson, later two-term president of the United States, wrote of the immigrants from southern and eastern Europe in his *History of the American People* (1902):

> Throughout the century men of the sturdy stocks of the north of Europe had made up the main strain of foreign blood which was every year added to the vital force of the country, or else men of the Latin-Gallic stocks of France and northern Italy; but now there came men of the lowest class from the south of Italy and men of the meaner sort out of Hungary and Poland, men out of the ranks where there was neither skill nor energy nor any initiative of quick intelligence . . . as if the countries of the South of Europe were disburdening themselves of the more sordid and hapless elements of their population."[14]

After he entered elective politics as a Democratic governor of New Jersey, Wilson backed away from those sentiments, dropping them in his textbook revisions and even opposing, as president, a bill in Congress that would screen immigrants for literacy in their native language. But most Progressive leaders agreed with the early Wilson. Like conservative leaders who otherwise opposed Progressive reforms to regulate child labor, working conditions, consumer safety, and monopolistic practices. Progressive leaders feared innundation by a post-Armistice flood of immigrants fleeing war-torn Europe. So they joined conservatives in devising a reform that would sharply restrict the immigration flow, providing in the short run a respite for planning through applied social science, a formula for replicating American society as they knew and loved it, and thus providing in the long run a period for assimilating the immigrants into the mainstream of American life.

A Breathing Space and a Formula for National Replication

The immigration reform coalition in the 1920s was worried that the nation's basic ethnocultural stock was being skewed, not by black or yellow races but by a mass of unassimilated immigrants from eastern and southern European cultures long alien to the western tradition of republican government, religious toleration, and technological progress. Being Progressives, they were optimistic that the New Immigrants in time could be Americanized by learning English and absorbing the values of American democracy. But this process of assimilation might take three generations. And the country desperately needed a breathing space. National immigration policy, they reasoned, should be based on a system of priorities that selected immigrants in accordance with American cultural and manpower needs, not in reaction to overseas wars, religious convulsions, or economic disasters.

Devising such a system would take time. Before the war, a congressional commission labored for three years (1907-10) to produce a forty-two-volume report on immigration. The commission, chaired by Senator William P. Dillingham, a Republican from Vermont, found the new immigrants from southern and eastern Europe on the whole less skilled, less literate, and poorer than earlier European groups. But the commission found somewhat less criminality among immigrants than among native-born Americans, and urged that immigration policy not concern itself primarily with "social defects," such as criminality and disease. Instead, immigration should be viewed primarily as an economic problem. Policy should aim to restrict the "oversupply of unskilled labor" in the country. In making these work force judgments, preference should be shown to those who "by reason of their personal qualities or habits" would be assimilated and make "desirable citizens."

How should they be selected? The Dillingham Commission recommended a literacy test in the immigrant's language and a ban on unskilled workers without families. Additionally, the commission recommended that Congress consider "the limitation of the number of each race arriving each year to a certain percentage of the average of that race arriving during a given period of years."[15] This suggestion, awkwardly phrased, would shape the heart of the national origins quota system in the 1920s. It hinged on a concept of European races that was nowhere defined, that reflected unexamined assumptions about bloodline and cultural hierarchy, and that, as a practical matter, could not be directly employed in an immigration classification scheme. Nation of origin would be used as a surrogate of the European "races."

In 1921, ten years after the release of the Dillingham Commission report, Congress took emergency action to stem the tide of postwar immigration by setting a cap of 355,000 visas a year and limiting each European country to a quota of 3 percent of its natives counted in the 1910 U.S. census (the 1920 census results were not yet tabulated). This stopgap measure achieved an immigration pause while Congress struggled to find a long-term solution. Ardent restrictionists, however, including nativists unhappy with heavy Catholic and Jewish immigration, complained that the 1921 law allocated almost half the total quota numbers to southern and eastern European nations. They countered with a proposal to shift the basis for quota allocation to the 1890 census, a shift that would favor immigrants from northern and western Europe because in 1890 there were fewer immigrants from southern and eastern Europe in America than in 1910. Republican congressman Albert Johnson of Washington state, chairman of the House Immigration Committee, sponsored such a bill in 1924.[16]

Republican senator David Reed of Pennsylvania, cosponsoring Johnson's bill, was nonetheless dissatisfied with a formula that shaped national policy by relying entirely on the past behavior of non-natives. The Dillingham formula, the 1921 emergency legislation, and Johnson's 1924 bill were all based on some calculation of the percentage of persons born in various countries who arrived in America. But this approach favored the foreign-born in America over the native-born. On the basis of the 1910 census, for example, about 12 percent of the American people derived from southern and eastern Europe. But in the 1921 law, based on the 1910 census, these regions were allocated 44 percent of the total quota immigration. Senator Reed believed that American immigration policy should be demographically based not on foreign-born persons but on the entire American people.

Hearings sponsored by the Senate Immigration Committee convinced Reed that what Americans wanted was an immigration policy that controlled immigration as a positive resource by regulating its flow at a modest level, not by halting it; that selected immigrants based on preferences

that served national needs (job skills, scientific attainment, family unification), and above all that continued to build America along the ethnocultural lines of the present. That is, immigration policy should be based on
"national origins," not foreign-born origins. It should mirror American
society and thereby replicate it, not shift its ethnocultural balance and spur
controversy. Immigration policy should thus be based on the whole American population, not on the numbers of natives of other countries, as in the
Dillingham Commission's recommendation, the 1921 emergency formula,
or the Johnson bill in the House.

   Accordingly, Reed proposed a bill that would set an aggregate annual cap
on immigration and base visa quotas for European nations on the national
origins of the entire American population, not on the numbers and origins
of foreign-born immigrants. It would ensure equal justice by counting the
ancestors of all Americans of European stock, not just the ancestors of European immigrants. Each year's immigration would thus mirror the United
States in its ethnocultural distribution. Assimilation, Reed argued, would
thereby be greatly eased. If "one were to imagine all the immigrants from
other countries in a given year congregated on board a single vessel," Reed
explained, "the ship's company, in the numerical relationships of the racial
stocks on board, would be in microcosm the United States of America."[17]

   The quota calculations would be based on the 1920 census, refined by
special studies needed to determine the national origin distribution of
more than 100 million American citizens. This was a task of unprecedented
magnitude and complexity. It would be undertaken by panels of demographers and social science specialists who were obliged to classify white
Americans according to a single or predominate national origin—a formidable task even in the absence of intermarriage. Once this was accomplished, all independent countries would get minimum quotas of 100, even
African and Asian countries, to provide a margin of consular flexibility.
Colonies could apply for visas under the quotas of governing nations. Visa
determinations would be made at the consular level overseas. This reform
was a crucial improvement over previous practice, which involved exit
visa determinations by foreign governments, and then sorting new arrivals
in America amid the chaos found at federal immigration facilities such as
Ellis Island. Immigration visas would thus be determined at point of origin by American consular officials, not by foreign governments or by
would-be immigrants themselves.

   What about the rest of the world outside Europe, specifically the nations
of the Western Hemisphere? The logic of comprehensive regulation, a
strong suit of Progressives, argued for hemispheric inclusion. The U.S. secretary of labor and some Texas congressmen urged controls on the heavy

use of Mexican nationals by growers in the Southwest. The Senate, however, was more responsive to lobbying by the growers, heavily reliant on the cheap, docile labor of Mexicans. This was partly because the Senate's constitutional formula of two senators per state overrepresented the interests of thinly populated agricultural states.

The Senate was also more responsive to lobbying by the State Department, a posture attributable to the Senate's special constitutional role in ratifying treaties. This gave the State Department leverage to argue for Western Hemispheric exemption from quota restrictions, an exemption that gave consular officials and State Department authorities great discretion in granting favors to smooth diplomatic intercourse in Latin America and Canada, freed from the bounds of quota limits. In Senate testimony, however, State Department officials based their request for American hemispheric exemption on special diplomatic traditions, including the Monroe Doctrine and the Pan American Union. Americans during the Progressive Era were accustomed to American gunboat diplomacy in the Caribbean and Latin America, where U.S. military forces had invaded Cuba, repeatedly intervened in Caribbean islands and Central American countries, acquired a slice of Panama to build and operate a canal, and invaded Mexico. Given the Monroe Doctrine tradition of a special sphere-of-influence status for Latin America and Canada, the Senate in 1924 not surprisingly found the State Department arguments persuasive. As a result, immigrants from Mexico, Central and South America, the Caribbean, and Canada would be exempt from quotas in the 1924 bill. Ironically, the national origins quota system curbed immigration from Europe but not from Latin America or the Caribbean.

There were other exceptions as well, exceptions that reflected the stipulated preferences of the new regulatory scheme. One class of preferences was for desirable occupational categories (professionals, skilled workers in short supply, ministers, college professors). Another was for reunifying the immediate family of immigrant male breadwinners, specifically, their wives and unmarried minor children. To encourage naturalization, the Reed bill extended the family unification preference only to immigrants who had become citizens.

A consensus formed around Senator Reed's version of the bill. This reflected not only the broad coalition supporting Reed's approach but also the weakening of the opposition. Since 1914, when the European war had stopped most immigration, industrial employers had learned that technical improvements in standardization and mass production had increased productivity per worker. Capital investments in machinery during the war were emancipating industry from its historic dependence on European manpower. Businessmen appreciated that the iron men did not strike or move to another city. Moreover, black workers recruited from the South offered both low-cost labor and leverage against unions.

The Reed bill passed both houses of Congress in 1924 with huge majorities—62-6 in the Senate and 323-71 in the House. Not surprisingly, the opposition was led by congressmen from New York and Chicago representing New Immigration constituencies, especially Jewish voters.[18] Although Congressman Johnson deferred in conference committee to Senator Reed's bill, which built its quotas from the 1920 census, Johnson and his supporters won use of their Nordic-favoring formula (2 percent of foreign-born residents counted in the 1890 census) during the interim period, while the special study panels grappled with determining the national origins of the white population, a process that was not completed until 1929. Immigration restriction by either formula was popular among Americans in the 1920s. It was also popular in the other neo-European nations for largely the same reasons. To prevent a worldwide flood of refugees from war-torn Europe, restrictionist reforms were implemented in the 1920s in Canada (preference for immigrants from Britain and France), Argentina and Brazil (preference for Portugal, Spain, and Italy), and Australia (preference for Caucasians).

The Strengths of the National Origins System

American history books since the 1960s have condemned the immigration laws of the 1920s as racist and xenophobic monuments to a benighted past. This view became standard among academics following World War II and the Holocaust, when American liberals stressed parallels between fascism and the scientific racist and eugenic beliefs shared by many Progressives. Unlike other controversial issues (slavery, imperialism, or communism), where historians were able to combine moral disapproval with intense study, the national origins quota system of the 1920s was morally rejected and little further studied. Most subsequent research has rested on John Higham's 1955 book, *Strangers in the Land*, a masterful intellectual and cultural analysis that emphasized the nativist impulses and their "Nordic victory" in the "tribal twenties."[19]

This posture helped fuel the immigration reforms of the 1960s, and has been little challenged since. Scant scholarly attention has been paid to the immigration reforms of the 1920s since the 1950s, and they merit a fresh reappraisal.[20] The American government spent almost the entire 1920s shaping a new system of immigration that produced far-reaching consequences. The record of the policymakers' motives, methods, and results is mixed, as is common in complex policy changes, and the assessment of their consequences almost a century later should reflect that variety.

A view that dwells on the national origin system's many weaknesses, especially its archaic racial underpinnings, obscures achievements that the immigration reformers of the 1920s might legitimately claim. First, the 1920s laws gave an ethnically tense country a needed breathing space, a pause that bought time for acculturation of pre-1920s immigrants to occur, time for the process of education and economic mobility to speed the acculturation of the second and third generation of the New Immigrants of 1880–1920. The American people, so ethnically fractured during World War I, may therefore have unified better in the face of the Great Depression and the war against fascism. The transition from a record of widespread interethnic hostility during World War I to one of greater tolerance and restraint during World War II—excepting the needless tragedy of Japanese-American internment—marks a remarkably successful process of ethnic acculturation in American life. Table 3.1 shows a sharply declining immigration rate following the reforms of the 1920s. Had the huge influx of 1880–1914 been allowed to continue after the 1920s, it is doubtful that this would have happened.

Second, the reforms of the 1920s were widely popular, both in Congress and in the nation at large. Press support for the new immigration policies, outside many ethnic and business journals, was almost universal. We have no opinion polls from the 1920s, but the extant evidence confirms a pow-

Table 3.1 U.S. Immigration by Decade, Rate per 1,000 Residents, and Percentage of European Origin, 1821–1960

Decade	Immigration	Rate	Percentage European
1821–30	143,439	1.2	68.9
1831–40	599,125	3.9	82.7
1841–50	1,713,251	8.4	93.2
1851–60	2,598,214	9.3	94.4
1861–70	2,314,824	6.4	89.2
1871–80	2,812,191	6.2	80.8
1881–90	5,246,613	9.1	90.3
1891–1900	3,687,546	5.3	96.4
1901–10	8,795,386	10.4	91.6
1911–20	5,735,811	5.7	75.3
1921–30	4,107,209	3.5	60.0
1931–40	528,431	.4	65.7
1941–50	1,035,039	.7	59.9
1951–60	2,515,479	1.6	52.7

Source: 1997 Statistical Yearbook of the Immigration and Naturalization Service, 24–25.

erful public consensus that the quantity of immigration should be sharply cut and that the new arrivals should ethnically replicate the America that received them. Future immigration, the nation decided, should mirror America. American society was changing so rapidly through industrial-ization, urbanization, and technological innovation, changes the public could scarcely avoid, that Americans applied the brakes where they could against the massive influx of foreign languages, cultures, and religions. Nathan Glazer, a leading sociologist of ethnicity in twentieth-century American life, said of the nation's decision to restrict immigration in the 1920s: "I think the racist thinking that accompanied the decision was rep-rehensible. The decision itself, however, one can understand. America had decided to stop the kaleidoscope and find out what it had become."[21]

Third, the Progressive reformers for the first time constructed a sys-tematic regulatory policy for immigration, one that tried to balance the public's felt needs for numerical control and cultural continuity with national priorities including manpower skills and family reunification. Famous for their faith in government regulation in the public interest through applied social science, Progressives had devised regulatory struc-tures to rationalize and control such broad areas of market transaction as interstate commerce, pure food and drugs, and the U.S. banking and mon-etary system. Immigration policy, somewhat similarly, had earlier featured a tradition of open-entry laissez-faire, punctuated by occasional govern-ment prohibitions, such as Chinese exclusion. This was the opposite of sys-tematic regulation in the public interest. Before 1920, Congress had patched on specific ad hoc quality controls, such as bans on lunatics, crim-inals, and diseased and illiterate immigrants, sorting them out only after arrival at ports of entry and deporting those rejected. After 1930, however, immigration would be governed not only by the national origins quota system but also by a scheme of visa preferences, applied by consular offi-cials in the countries of origin, that privileged skilled and professional immigrants and the close family relatives of breadwinners. Guided by these codified criteria, the State Department distributed a limited number of visas each year through U.S. embassies abroad, including 150,000 visas to European immigrants, and the Immigration Service admitted only immigrants who arrived with a valid visa.

Finally, two major constituencies harmed by the flood of immigrants were given much-needed relief. One was the large world of native-born nonfarm workers. Organized labor, battered by decades of business oppo-sition and court injunctions as well as wage-threatening immigration, mobilized a class-based social movement in the 1930s and following World War II enjoyed climbing real wages and robust union growth. Samuel

Gompers, himself an immigrant and founding president of the American Federation of Labor in 1886, had tirelessly preached that "so many immigrants coming into this country will break down the standard of living of our people. . . . There must be some restriction of immigration that will prevent disintegration of American economic standards."[22] Gompers died in 1924, still president of the AFL, witness to the changes that would bring sustained relief from mass immigration's relentless supply of labor.

The other major constituency that had suffered from the economic effects of mass immigration was black America, a constituency already overburdened with impediments of every kind. Booker T. Washington, in his Atlanta Cotton States Exposition address of 1895, pled with white society to "cast down your buckets where you are" by employing the former slaves rather than importing foreign workers. But black Americans remained stranded in the prostrate postbellum South as millions of European immigrants found jobs in America's northern industrial expansion. Blacks first took advantage of immigration restriction, during World War I, accelerating the Great Migration out of the South when the war rather than policy stopped the immigration flow. There was little patterned job migration during the Great Depression of the 1930s. But World War II, like the Great War, brought new opportunity. Fleeing racial oppression and destitution in the rural South, blacks increasingly found employment in northern industry and government, no longer competing with immigrant workers. For thirty years, there was a net outmigration from the South of 1.5 million blacks, lowering the percentage of African-Americans living in the South from 77 percent in 1940 to 53 percent in 1970. This movement in turn built black voting strength in the northern cities, which pulled both major political parties toward civil rights reform in the 1960s.

Weaknesses of the National Origins System

The chief weakness of the national origin immigration system was glaring. It was a racial and ethnic quota system grounded in nineteenth century doctrines of scientific racism. These genetic theories also undergirded the Jim Crow system, and the assault by the modern civil rights movement on racial segregation automatically brought the national origins system under fire. Liberal intellectuals of the New Deal generation, including Jewish leaders in coalition with African-American rights organizations, attacked the notion of group stereotyping and group rights that was implicit in quotas. Rights under the American Constitution, liberals said, inhered in individuals, not in groups. Assigning rights and privileges by group was a noxious legacy of the Old World, of feudal systems and ancient civilizations whore otatus was fixed at birth in steep hierarchies setting elites (royalty, aristocracy, priests) over subordinate masses (slaves, serfs, peasants). The primal sin of group prejudice lay in ignoring individual capacities by pre-judging them based on negative stereotypes. The war against fascism con-fronted liberals with the terrible logic of group prejudice embodied in law and manipulated by the state. The United Nations Charter, grounded in principles of liberal universalism, reaffirmed the philosophical and moral principles of the equality of all peoples.

A second weakness of the national origins quota system, little noticed in the 1960s or subsequently, is the profound conflict between a group sta-tus fixed by government pronouncement at a specific point in time and a reality of rapid demographic change in America through intermarriage and social mobility. The elaborate census studies of national origins of 1924–29 attempted an impossible task. Data from 1920 was used a decade later to set in stone for future decades classifications of Americans accord-ing to *one* unchanging country of "origin." In doing this, the national gov-ernment set the baleful precedent of classifying some citizens ("whites") but not others. Ironically, the immigration reforms of the 1920s accelerated a process of acculturation that fostered intermarriage and thereby daily undermined the original classifications themselves. The national origins classifications of the 1920s were doomed by the clock and by interethnic marriage patterns in ethnically diverse, socially mobile America. With each passing day, the snapshot assignments of 1929 grew more irrelevant, blind to the vagaries of depression, fascism, world war, or cold war.

Against charges that the national origins system was rooted in racial and ethnic prejudice, the system's defenders in the 1950s and 1960s had weak arguments. The baldest racial exclusions by then had been eased: After China, America's wartime ally against Japan, was given a small quota in 1943, no national or racial group was excluded per se, and the immigration revisions of 1952 (McCarran-Walter) formally ended such exclusions. After World War II, Congress permitted quotas unused by northern European countries to be mortgaged against the future, thus freeing unused quota visas to be shifted to relieve other pressure points. But the numbers remained small, and relief most commonly went to refugees fleeing the Soviet Iron Curtain, not to Asians or Africans. Defenders of America's national origins immigration system pointed out that it was similar to the systems of many other nations—Britain, Germany, Switzerland, Japan, Australia, Argentina—in privileging some national or ethnic groups over others. But such a system in the United States was in conflict with the claims of American Exceptionalism. The logic of the civil rights movement, that the American Constitution was color-blind, armed liberals with a powerful emotional weapon to use against the immigration quota system, once the liberals had achieved their primary goal, the destruction of racial segregation in the South.

The National Origins System in the Cold War

As a rallying cry for reform, no other complaint against the national origins system approached liberalism's crusade for equal individual rights against racial and ethnic prejudice and discrimination. But the cold war added its own urgent political imperatives. Both the South's Jim Crow laws and the nation's immigration policy provided propaganda advantages for Soviet and Chinese communist appeals to the colonies and emerging nations of the largely nonwhite Third World. Presidents Truman, Eisenhower, and Kennedy fought with Congress to admit refugees fleeing communism, irrespective of the quota system. Congress, resenting executive intrusion in shaping immigration policy, traditionally a legislative domain, reaffirmed the national origins system in the McCarran-Walter Act of 1952 (named after its chief sponsors, Senator Pat McCarran of Nevada and Rep. Francis Walter of Pennsylvania, both Democrats).[23]

In McCarran-Walter, Congress balanced tightened restrictions directed against subversives and illegal entry with liberalized measures that removed racial barriers to naturalization and hence to immigration. The law revised and codified the national origins quota system, largely in a technocratic fashion that avoided major policy shifts. President Truman and liberal leaders approved the law's removal of racial prohibitions on immigration. But they complained that the national origins quota system was retained and that the new token quotas extended to Asian and Pacific areas were based on applicants' racial ancestry, not national origin. Truman vetoed the bill, but liberal objections found little support in public opinion, and Congress easily overrode Truman's veto.

The McCarran-Walter law also toughened anticommunist restrictions. These provisions offended liberals by authorizing visa denial to applicants who had affiliations with allegedly subversive organizations in their native country, such as left-of-center political parties.[24] In the 1950s, civil liberties complaints such as these, especially as they applied to foreigners, persuaded few Americans. Nor did a third liberal argument, that the immigration restrictions of the 1920s, irrespective of their national origins bias, had gone too far in choking off international, cosmopolitan sources of pluralism. Since World War I the children and grandchildren of the New

Immigrants had seemed to assimilate so thoroughly into mainstream American life that by the 1950s, many social critics were savaging the bourgeois culture of suburban America as mindlessly homogenized. Middlebrow America, they said, was bland, conformist, materialist, and philistine. This complaint was voiced chiefly by sophisticated metropolitan elites in cities such as New York, and was muted because it risked offending mainstream America. It played little role in the immigration debates of the 1950s and 1960s, other than in a minor variant called the "new seed" concept, which called for adding, on a diversity rationale, immigrants not qualifying for family reunification or skills-based preferences.

Yet there was merit in the proposition that the combination of low immigration and accelerated acculturation since World War I had extracted a price in the coin of political and cultural comformity. By the 1950s the process of "Americanization," eagerly sought by the New Immigrants and their progeny, and by most evidence remarkably successful, had been warped at its edge into a narrow-minded assault against "un-Americanism."[25] The anticommunist rampages in Congress led by the Un-American Activities Committee in the House and by Wisconsin's Joseph McCarthy in the Senate intimidated liberal critics in the media, the entertainment industry, the universities, and even the State Department and the army.[26] American television and movies stereotyped not only blacks, Asians, and Latin Americans but also Russians and many European nationalities. Moreover, in the cold war competition for Third World allegiance, monolingual America had lost most of the multilinguistic capacity it had gained before 1920. Although liberal immigration reformers in the 1960s relied chiefly on their egalitarian political arguments, which tapped into the growing moral authority of the civil rights movement, there was weight to their cultural implication that a larger infusion of immigrants from across the globe would yield a richer, more cosmopolitan culture.

The immigration system constructed in the 1920s was not threatened by speculation over what might have happened under a more open system. It was threatened by growing evidence that it no longer worked. Like so many comprehensive systems established by government, the immigration "fix" of the 1920s eventually unraveled, eroded by the passage of time and circumstances, as if by a political law of entropy. The refugee crisis caused by the global devastation of World War II, the massive dislocations of postwar revolutions (China, Hungary, Cuba), and cold war demands on American foreign policy, together produced an incoherent patchwork of special government measures that worked mostly outside the immigration system. Political pressures in the cold war era moved both the executive branch and Congress to circumvent the annual quota system. The government offered large visa allotments to northern European nations that did not use them, especially Britain and Germany, and small allotments to Iron Curtain countries, which generally would not permit their use. In 1960, for example, these quotas included 6,524 visas for Poland, 2,874 for Czechoslovakia, 2,712 for Russia, and 859 for Hungary. Truman and Eisenhower, anxious to welcome refugees from communism and blocked by the quota limits, used executive parole authority between 1945 and 1960 to admit 700,000 political refugees.[27]

Congress, though reaffirming the quota system for two decades after World War II, responded to the same political and cold war pressures by expanding the use of special statutes that worked outside the annual immigration quotas. This included displaced persons admissions, private bills to admit groups represented by effective lobbies, and nonquota status granted to spouses and children of U.S. citizens (chiefly military personnel). Between 1952 and 1965, 44,200 Japanese women immigrated to the United States as wives of U.S. servicemen, although Japan's annual immigration quota was only 185. Congress also made special exceptions, such as the Bracero program of 1942–64, which admitted temporary agricultural workers. During the 1950s the Bracero Program imported on average 360,000 low-wage workers a year from Mexico alone. Like "temporary" guest worker programs throughout modern history, it produced a deepening channel of migration and expanding lodgments of permanent settlement in the host nation. Between 1945 and 1965, more than 40 percent of all immigrants came to America from the Western Hemisphere, which continued to be exempt from the quota limitations.[28]

As a result of these patchwork measures, by 1960 fully two-thirds of all immigrants, many of them refugees, entered the United States each year without a quota number. For example, China, with a yearly quota allotment of only 105, sent more than 70,000 immigrants to the United States between 1950 and 1965, an average of 4,480 annually. In 1965, the annual quota for Italy was 5,666, but 15,686 Italian immigrants were admitted. The quota for Greece that year was 308, but more than 3,000 Greek immigrants arrived. In the decade 1955–65, almost a million immigrants came to America with nonquota visas.

By 1960, then, when John F. Kennedy, the great-grandson of Irish immigrants and a champion of liberalized immigration, won the Democratic nomination for president, immigration reformers were armed with an inventory of potentially powerful weapons to use against the national origins quota system. Kennedy's election set the stage for successful immigration law reform in the 1960s much as it had for civil rights reform.[29]

The Politics of Immigration Reform in the Kennedy-Johnson Years

A series of political changes occurred in the early 1960s that cleared the ground for a comprehensive immigration reform bill. Kennedy's election ensured that immigration reform, though not a priority for the new administration, would find a place on the new president's agenda. It did this by staffing the presidency with a critical mass of political appointees, northern liberal Democrats who would nourish the immigration reform constituencies, seeking a window of opportunity. Such an occasion arose in May 1963, when Representative Francis Walter, a major opponent of reform, died of leukemia. Chairman of the House Immigration Committee since 1949, Walter had sponsored the McCarran-Walter Act of 1952 and was the most effective defender in Congress of the national origins system.[30] Kennedy, who in 1961 had directed his staff to develop an immigration reform bill but not send it to Congress as long as Walter chaired the House Immigration Committee, sent his bill to the Hill within a month of Walter's death. There it joined similar bills proposed by leading immigration reform legislators. The most important of these bills were those sponsored in the Senate by Michigan Democrat Philip Hart and in the House by Brooklyn Democrat Emanuel Celler, chairman of the Judiciary Committee, and Cleveland Democrat Michael Feighan, who replaced Walter as chairman of the Immigration Committee.[31]

Kennedy's assassination in November 1963 sidetracked immigration reform legislation for a year, as President Johnson concentrated on passing Kennedy's three top-priority bills (civil rights, tax cut, and antipoverty). In Johnson's election campaign against Republican senator Barry Goldwater in 1964, Goldwater opposed the civil rights bill, and thus civil rights issues played a major role. But immigration issues did not—aside from a brief flare-up when Goldwater's running mate, New York congressman William Miller, warned that increased immigration would threaten the jobs of native-born Americans.

Johnson's victory over Goldwater in 1964 devastated Republican ranks in Congress as well. The 89th Congress enjoyed huge Democratic majorities: 68-32 in the Senate and 295-140 in the House. Especially important, the 1964 elections, by greatly weakening the conservative coalition in Congress of Republicans and southern Democrats, removed the major roadblocks to liberal legislation in the House that had frustrated President Kennedy. The 89th Congress obliged Johnson by passing most of his Great Society legislation. The political environment in 1965 was bright for immigration reform. When the Voting Rights Act was passed in July 1965, the administration's main agenda for African-American rights was achieved, and this opened the door for rapid approval of immigration reform.[32]

These circumstances, especially the egalitarian thrust from the civil rights movement, virtually ensured that the 89th Congress would be pressed by the White House and the congressional leadership to abolish the national origins quota system in 1965. But what system of immigration would replace it? The existing system depended on numerical caps and country quotas. If these disappeared, the result might be a return to massive, uncontrolled immigration. Yet all evidence indicated that the American public seemed satisfied with the existing system and opposed increased immigration. Immigration reformers, to be successful, would have to build convincing arguments (1) that the national origins quota system was discriminatory and should be abolished, but (2) that doing so would not change the quantity or quality of immigration.[33]

To accomplish this, the immigration coalition concentrated on the first argument. Like the civil rights coalition (and greatly overlapping with it), the immigration coalition in the 1960s was led by an umbrella organization to coordinate the lobbying of constituent groups. This was the New York-based American Immigration and Citizenship Council (AICC), the immigration analog of the Washington-based Leadership Conference on Civil Rights. The AICC's most visible lobbying organizations were ethnic-based groups, such as the American Committee for Italian Migration, the American-Hellenic Education Program Association, the Sons of Italy, and the Japanese American Citizens League. Most of these groups were small and modestly funded, but they made up in activist zeal what they lacked in political throw-weight. Like the civil rights coalition, the immigration coalition under the AICC umbrella also included liberal religious organizations—the National Catholic Welfare Conference, Catholic Relief Services, National Council of Jewish Women, Lutheran Immigration Service, National Council of Churches of Christ—and liberal action groups, including the American Civil Liberties Union and the American Council of Volunteer Agencies. Some of the newer and larger labor unions associated with the Congress of Industrial Organizations (CIO) also joined the attack on the national origins quota system, including the steelworkers, auto workers, clothing workers, and unions with heavy ethnic representation from eastern and southern Europe.[34]

Most important for the content of immigration reform, the driving force at the core of this movement, reaching back to the 1920s, were Jewish organizations long active in opposing racial and ethnic quotas. These included the American Jewish Congress, the American Jewish Committee, the Anti-Defamation League of B'nai B'rith, and the American Federation of Jews

from Eastern Europe. Jewish members of Congress, particularly representatives from New York and Chicago, had maintained steady but largely
ineffective pressure against the national origins quotas since the 1920s. But
the war against Hitler and the postwar movement against colonialism
sharply changed the ideological and moral environment, putting defenders of racial, caste, and ethnic hierarchies on the defensive. Jewish political
leaders in New York, most prominently Governor Herbert Lehman, had
pioneered in the 1940s in passing state antidiscrimination legislation.
Importantly, these statutes and executive orders added "national origin"
to race, color, and religion as impermissible grounds for discrimination.

Following the shock of the Holocaust, Jewish leaders had been especially active in Washington in furthering immigration reform. To the public, the most visible evidence of the immigration reform drive was played
by Jewish legislative leaders, such as Representative Celler and Senator
Jacob Javits of New York. Less visible, but equally important, were the
efforts of key advisers on presidential and agency staffs. These included
senior policy advisers such as Julius Edelson and Harry Rosenfield in the
Truman administration, Maxwell Rabb in the Eisenhower White House,
and presidential aide Myer Feldman, assistant secretary of state Abba
Schwartz, and deputy attorney general Norbert Schlei in the Kennedy-
Johnson administration.

Shaping a New Immigration Preference System

American immigration policy from the beginning has embraced opposite
tendencies in a carrot-and-stick fashion, on the one hand discouraging
unwanted arrivals through exclusion and restriction, on the other hand
encouraging desirables by favoring certain occupations and encouraging
family cohesion. On the positive side of immigration preferences, Congress has exempted from its various exclusions certain desirable occupational categories, such as professionals including ministers and college
professors, and skilled workers in short supply. In doing so Congress commonly provided for executive branch expertise in certifying national
needs, as in the immigration statute of 1917, which stipulated certification
by the secretary of labor. At the same time Congress traditionally preferred
family immigration over single-male "sojourner" or "commuter" immigration by providing visa preferences for spouses and minor children of
immigrants. In these legislative deliberations, Congress by tradition fully
debated the merits and evidence bearing on various occupational preferences
but did not debate the relative effects and merits of family reunification

preferences. Also by tradition, Congress stressed the primacy of occupational preferences and the supplemental nature of family unification preferences. When the quota system was developed in the 1920s, for example, Congress privileged occupational preferences by giving them nonquota status, but assessed the family unification preferences against the national origins quotas for each country. In the comprehensive codification of the national origin system in the McCarran-Walter Act of 1952, Congress established a 50 percent first preference for desired occupational skills, a 30 percent second preference for parents of adult citizens, and a 20 percent third preference for spouses and children of lawfully admitted aliens.[35]

In the immigration reform debates of the 1960s, however, these priorities got reversed. Occupational preferences slipped downward in priority, driven by the determination of organized labor, a strong voice in the Kennedy and Johnson administrations and especially in the 89th Congress, to narrow the incentives for skilled worker importation. At the same time, family unification preferences ratcheted upward and expanded, driven by the ethnic lobbies and encouraged by Congress's tradition of not debating such provisions. The result of this reversal was a quiet, unplanned, unanticipated policy revolution.

Not surprisingly, the concentration in the early 1960s of lobbying by ethnic and religious groups with strong ties to eastern and southern Europe produced an emphasis on family reunification priorities in the immigration policy deliberations. Americans in the early 1960s, recent witnesses to the crushed Hungarian revolution of 1956, the Sputnik scare of 1957, the flight to the United States of Cuba's middle and professional classes in 1959–60, and the building of the Berlin Wall in 1961, were sympathetic to the plight of freedom-loving, God-fearing families trapped behind communist borders. Congressional committees listened attentively to testimony describing the plight of relatives of American citizens behind the Iron Curtain where the state attacked their Catholic, Jewish, or Orthodox Christian faith. In this cold war environment, supporting liberalized family reunification policies offered members of Congress, especially from metropolitan areas heavy with ethnic voters, great political payoff with virtually no negatives.[36]

Organized labor in the 1950s and 1960s, though historically restrictionist, was nonetheless an urban ethnic constituency with strong family ties to the immigrants of 1880–1920. Still resisting increased skilled worker immigration, union leaders in the immigration reform debates lobbied for rigorous Labor Department screening and certification of skilled worker visas to protect American jobs. As a consequence, union lobbying helped shift the balance in the Kennedy-Johnson negotiations away from national needs, which emphasized the economic contribution of immigrant skills, toward family reunification priorities, which emphasized private needs and kinship relations. The Johnson administration was quick to assure labor that the immigration bill would have no appreciable impact on employment. Labor Secretary Willard Wirtz told Congress that once the act became fully operative, the total number of immigrants entering the workforce every year "will be equal to about one tenth of 1 percent of the workforce."[37]

Reassured, union leaders generally joined the call for expanded family reunification preferences. Because American immigration law for years had exempted from the quota ceilings immediate family members of U.S. citizens (spouses and minor children), the consensus on family reunification meant growing political pressures on Congress and the president to include not only the parents and minor children but also the adult sons and daughters and even the brothers and sisters of U.S. citizens. Given the presumption in naturalization law that immigrants would seek citizenship and become American voters, Congress was urged to include in an expanded formula of family reunification the close family members of permanent resident aliens as well.

As a consequence, "family reunification" became a powerful slogan that was difficult to oppose and hence difficult to limit. Representative Michael Feighan, alarmed by his narrow reelection margin in 1964 in an urban Cleveland district heavy with recent eastern European immigrants, responded to intense pressures for expanded family reunifications by strengthening his bill's family preference provisions in 1965. A man of volatile temperament and a heavy drinker, Feighan was locked in a bitter contest with Celler to claim authorship of the new immigration law. As the political window of opportunity for immigration reform opened in 1963, these kinds of pressures produced a bidding war that expanded family reunification preferences. It seemed heartless to oppose such proposals. Given generally low levels of immigration since the 1920s, American policymakers had no experience with the "chain immigration" that expanded family reunification preferences would invite. Not surprisingly under these circumstances, all of the major immigration reform bills introduced in Congress between 1963 and 1965, those submitted by Kennedy and Johnson, and those sponsored by Senator Hart and Representatives Celler and Feighan, converged on a common compromise formula for visa preferences.[38]

As the new compromise formula emerged by the summer of 1965, it listed seven visa preferences proposed for the new immigration law, in order of priority:

1. Unmarried adult sons and daughters of U.S. citizens (maximum of 20 percent).
2. Spouse and unmarried sons and daughters of permanent resident aliens (20 percent).
3. Members of the professions and scientists and artists of exceptional ability (10 percent).
4. Married adult sons and daughters of U.S. citizens (10 percent).
5. Brothers and sisters of U.S. citizens (24 percent).
6. Skilled and unskilled workers in occupations for which labor is in short supply (10 percent).
7. Refugees (6 percent).

Family reunification, garnering five of the seven preferences and four of the first five, dominated the proposed new system. The preferences would not apply, however, to immigrants from the Western Hemisphere. Presidents Kennedy and Johnson in their initial reform proposals had placed relatively greater stress on national needs and individual immigration skills. But they offered no objection when Congress shifted the emphasis toward expanded family reunification.[39]

The Debate over Numerical Limits: Reforming Immigration While Maintaining the Status Quo

Would a new system without country quotas still have numerical limits? All parties to the debate knew that it would. The leaders of immigration reform, politically astute realists, knew that the price of abolishing the quota system would be a pledge not to increase total immigration by any significant margin. Moreover, passage would also require assurances that the new law would not significantly alter the demographic structure of the nation. American public opinion in the 1960s was forming a new national consensus that racial and ethnic discrimination should be purged from public policy. But in the public mind this applied to the constitutional rights of American citizens, not to foreigners. A Harris poll reported in the *Washington Post* on May 31, 1965, found that Americans by a 2 to 1 margin (56 percent to 24 percent) opposed "changing immigration laws to allow more people to enter this country." In a Gallup poll in July, respondents ranked the most important criteria for admitting immigrants to the United States as follows: occupational skills 71 percent, relatives in the United States 55 percent, country in which born 33 percent. When asked whether immigration should be kept at its present levels, 40 percent said yes, 32 percent said decrease, and only 7 percent said increase. The *Post* article reporting the Harris poll concluded that "Americans prefer people from Canada and northern and western Europe as immigrants and tend to oppose immigrants from Latin America, southern and eastern Europe, Russia, the Middle East, and Asia."[40] Even "Manny" Celler agreed that "there is no burning desire in the grassroots of this country to change our immigration policy."[41]

Under these circumstances, the Johnson administration and congressional sponsors of immigration reform assured the public that although the administration's bill (which was most similar to the Hart and Celler bills) would abolish the government's racial and ethnic preference system, the practical result would be to maintain the status quo. Future potential immigrants would need to have close family ties in the United States, due to prior immigration, to gain entry. The new family reunification policy would thus perpetuate traditional patterns of immigration, the reformers explained. The argument seemed persuasive: Heavy immigration from Asia, for example, would not seem possible under family reunification provisions because Asian immigration had slowed to a trickle by the beginning of the twentieth century. Congress heard testimony to this effect from Secretary of State Dean Rusk, Deputy Attorney General Norbert Schlei, and Attorney General and later Senator Robert Kennedy. Administration and congressional leaders told the public that, far from threatening to ethnically transform the nation, the immigration reform bill would, as a practical matter, produce a national origins system of immigration, but without the offensive quotas.[42]

Given Johnson's huge voting majorities in the 89th Congress, conservatives could not hope to salvage the national origins system, and few seemed interested in trying. Abolishing that system seemed an idea whose time had come. Opposing organizations were few and weak: the National Association of Evangelicals, the anticommunist Liberty Lobby. By 1965 even the American Legion and the American Coalition of Patriotic Societies were no longer actively opposing immigration reform. In the Senate, North Carolina Democrat Sam Erwin, a leading opponent of the civil rights reforms of 1964 and 1965, emerged as the immigration reform bill's chief critic.

In hearings held by the immigration subcommittee of the Judiciary Committee in the summer of 1965, Erwin asked Justice Department spokesmen why the Johnson administration opposed discrimination by country-of-origin quotas, yet would discriminate in the new immigration bill by continuing to exempt Western Hemisphere countries from the immigration ceilings and visa preferences that applied elsewhere in the world. Arguing that a coherent system of immigration preferences must apply its numerical ceilings to all countries of the world, Erwin also raised the issue of world population growth. He pointed out that at present rates of growth the Earth's population would increase from 3 billion to 6 billion in only forty years, and that the administration's proposal of 350,000 immigrants a year would expand into 80 million people in one hundred years.[43]

Erwin's arguments against the civil rights bills had been rejected by most Americans and by most members of Congress. But on the immigration issue, where the American public was inattentive, Erwin was more successful in convincing his colleagues. He argued that numerical limits were essential to prevent a flood of immigration to America and that the limits wouldn't work if half the globe, including Latin American nations experiencing a population explosion, remained exempt. None of the immigration reform leaders could offer persuasive reasons why the nations of the Western Hemisphere should remain exempt. Erwin's opposition forced the administration to compromise by accepting an annual numerical ceiling of 120,000 per year for the Western Hemisphere. For the Western Hemisphere countries, exempt from the reform bill's system of seven family reunification and skills preferences, immigrants would be admitted on a first-come, first-served basis consistent with standard immigration law. For the rest of the world, the numerical cap would be 170,000 per year, with immigrants admitted on the basis of the new system of seven preferences, and with no single country permitted more than 20,000 visas per year. Thus approximately 300,000 immigrants would be admitted annually under the numerical ceilings. Additionally, the administration estimated that 30,000 to 40,000 annually would be admitted outside the numerical limits—chiefly, as in the past, the spouses, minor children, and, after 1965, the parents of U.S. citizens. This added up, administration spokesmen pointed out, to annual immigration under 350,000. Numerically this was little more than the immigration America had been receiving in the early 1960s under the old system (roughly 300,000 a year) but no longer marred by the racial and ethnic quotas.

The compromise with Erwin in August 1965 brought the negotiations to a successful close for the Johnson administration. Unlike the high-profile, high-demand reforms in civil rights, immigration reform was a low-profile negotiation driven by inside-the-beltway elites. It was covered only routinely by the press and was scarcely noticed in the television newscasts. The liberal coalition, which had touted the Civil Rights Act as a path to epoch-ending changes, sold the Immigration Act as a reform whose principles were vital but whose effects would scarcely be noticed. Faced with this rationale and with a strong economy as well, the two core constituencies of the liberal coalition that had historically been restrictionist, labor unions and African-Americans, maintained liberal solidarity by supporting immigration reform. Labor leaders, by lobbying to control an influx of skilled labor while supporting the bill's family reunification provisions, helped lower the priority of work-related visas to the next-to-last (sixth) preference. African-American leaders, cheered by the success of the civil rights bills, shaken by the eruption of racial rioting, and reassured by administration promises that the new immigration law would produce little new immigration, supported the bill in the common cause of nondiscrimination and unity within the liberal coalition.

Business interests not surprisingly supported the bill as well, but were not a driving force behind it. Because the baby boom was pouring new workers into the economy, and the assault on racial discrimination promised to feed millions of underemployed blacks into the workforce as well, employers did not seem to be looking for workers overseas. Even the growers were quiet. Sponsors of the Bracero farm worker program that had imported hundreds of thousands of mostly Mexican contract workers since 1942—the program averaged 430,000 guestworkers a year from Mexico during its peak 1955–60 years—the growers had been attacked by organized labor, religious, and civil rights organizations for exploiting foreign workers and depressing labor standards.[44] The same liberal coalition that backed the civil rights and immigration reforms of 1964–65 had persuaded Congress to terminate the Bracero program in 1964. Agricultural interests were aware, however, that illegal entry by Mexican nationals had increased sharply with the growth of the Bracero program and that the immigration reform bill's cap of 20,000 visas a year from any single country would not apply to Western Hemisphere nations such as Mexico.[45]

The *Wall Street Journal*, commenting on the conservative nature of the immigration reform, noted on October 4, 1965, that the family preference priorities would ensure that "the new immigration system would not stray radically from the old one." The historically restrictionist *American Legion Magazine* agreed, reassured by the promises of continuity. As Senator Edward Kennedy had pledged in the Senate hearings on immigration, first, "Under the proposed bill, the present level of immigration remains substantially the same," and second, "the ethnic mix of this country will not be upset."[46] The Japanese American Citizens League also agreed, but resentfully. Noting that Asians formed less than 1 percent of the population of the United States, they complained that in actual operation under the new law, "immigration will still be controlled by the now discredited national origins system and the general pattern of immigration which exists today will continue for many years to come."[47]

On August 25, the House passed the Celler bill by a vote of 318 to 95. On September 20, the Senate passed its version (the Hart bill) by a vote of 76 to 18. In the final vote on the immigration bill in 1965, every Jewish member of Congress in both chambers voted for it, as did all Catholics in the Senate and all but 3 (of 92) in the House. Most of the opposition came from southern Democrats.[48] On September 30, the Hart-Celler bill was reported out of conference committee, with both houses soon concurring, and on October 3, Johnson signed the Immigration and Naturalization Act of 1965 at the foot of the Statue of Liberty in New York harbor. "This is not a revolutionary bill," President Johnson explained at the signing ceremony. "It does not affect the lives of millions." Johnson was unquestionably sincere. As was his vice president, Hubert Humphrey, when pledging to his Senate colleagues in 1964 that if the civil rights bill led to racial quotas or ratios, he would eat its pages one at a time. Both men captured the intended consequences of the reforms they defended. And both turned out to be profoundly wrong.

4

Origins and Development of Race-Conscious Affirmative Action

One of the great puzzles of modern American history is the speed with which race-conscious implementation policies in the 1970s followed the triumph of liberal nondiscrimination in the 1960s. As sociologist John David Skrentny pointed out in his 1996 book, *The Ironies of Affirmative Action*, so powerful was the American belief in the principle of color-blind law by the 1970s that advocacy of racial preference became one of the "third rails" of American politics: Touch it and you die.[1] *Race-conscious* affirmative action is a familiar term of journalistic convenience. It identifies unambiguously the controversial element of minority preferences in distributing benefits. But it also conflates racially targeted civil rights remedies with affirmative action preferences for groups, such as Hispanics and women, given protected class status irrespective of race. For this reason, editors of *The New Republic* substituted the term *hard* affirmative action. It includes nonracial as well as racial preferences, and it distinguishes such remedies, available only to officially designated protected classes, from the *soft* affirmative action of the Kennedy-Johnson administrations, which emphasized special outreach programs for recruiting minorities but did so within a traditional liberal framework of equal individual rights for all Americans. In these pages, the descriptors *race-conscious* and *hard* affirmative action will be used interchangeably.

The architects of race-conscious affirmative action, Skrentny observes, developed their remedy in the face of public opinion heavily arrayed against it. Unlike most public policy in America, hard affirmative action was originally adopted without the benefit of any organized lobbying by the major interest groups involved. Instead, government bureaucrats, not

65

benefiting interest groups, provided the main impetus. The race-conscious model of hard affirmative action was developed in trial-and-error fashion by a coalition of mostly white, second-tier civil servants in the social service agencies of the presidency (Labor, Housing and Urban Development, Health, Education, and Welfare). This was a network of Kennedy-Johnson liberals in Washington's mission agencies, working with a small cadre of young, often black policy entrepreneurs, coordinating with allies in the Justice Department and the EEOC, and linked to counterparts in regional and municipal government by the sprawling federal grant network. Once started in this way, hard affirmative action spread during the 1970s with surprisingly little attempt by conservatives to stop it.

To Skrentny's core irony, we may add three further ironies. First, the key to political survival for hard affirmative action was persistent support from the Republican Party, despite that party's strong shift toward the right following the 1960s. Second, the theories of compensatory justice supporting minority preference policies were devised only *after* the adoption of the policies themselves. Finally, affirmative action preferences which supporters rationalized as necessary to compensate African-Americans for historic discrimination, and which for twenty years were successfully defended in federal courts primarily on those grounds, soon benefited millions of immigrants newly arrived from Latin America and Asia.

This chapter tells the story of how race-conscious affirmative action, contrary to all expectations and against steep political odds, was born and nurtured in the national policymaking system. It begins quietly in the late 1960s, in parallel developments within two small new government agencies. One, the EEOC, which was attacked by mobilizing feminists for concentrating on black employment discrimination, had shifted its enforcement rhetoric by 1968 from classic liberalism's procedural focus on nondiscrimination to a results-oriented focus on "underutilization." This was a low-visibility, internal debate among relatively obscure government officials, one with consequences little noticed until the Supreme Court, in the *Griggs* decision of 1971, surprised observers by approving the EEOC's enforcement model of statistical proportionality for minorities in the workforce. The other new agency, the Labor Department's OFCC, floundered in obscurity during the riot-torn years of the Johnson administration. The Labor Department's awkwardly named new contract compliance subagency then surged surprisingly into prominence in 1969, the first year of the Nixon administration, in the battle over the Philadelphia Plan. Because this conflict featured a battle between the new Republican president and the Democratic-controlled Congress, it captured public attention and launched a controversy over racial quotas and "reverse discrimination" that simmered throughout the 1970s and beyond.[2]

The origins and development of hard affirmative action is best described by connecting a series of stories reaching across the Nixon, Ford, and Carter administrations. They include the rebirth under Nixon of the Philadelphia Plan; the growth of social regulation from Washington, surging out of the 1960s and driven by captured agencies; the search for a theory to legitimize a program of race-conscious affirmative action begun without a theory; the favorable rulings of the federal courts; the development of bilingual/bicultural education as affirmative action for Hispanics; and finally, the creation by Congress of minority contract set-aside programs in the Carter administration. The story thus concludes with action dominated by liberal Democrats in elective office. But in its beginning, oddly, it is a distinctively Republican story.

Richard Nixon and the Philadelphia Plan

During his first year in office, President Nixon resurrected the Philadelphia Plan, rushed it through the Labor Department's notice-and-comment process for issuing regulations, and cracked the whip of Republican loyalty in Congress when opponents moved to block it.[3] This first-year performance was both surprising and effective. It caught opponents off-guard. Nixon exploited both the president's advantages of control over his cabinet departments, including the newly developing regulatory offices in several mission agencies, and the public's inability to understand the complex, obscure, bureaucratic technicalities of the regulatory process. By 1970, the once moribund Philadelphia Plan, with its prescriptive norm of racial and ethnic proportionality in the American workplace, had been established as the federal government's pathbreaking model of affirmative action. It endowed the lowly Labor Department, by tradition a small, low-budget agency largely captured by organized labor, with a muscular new regulatory authority that would transform it into a major player in American economic regulation.

The affirmative action requirements designed by the Labor Department's OFCC provided a model for the federal government's new sub-agencies of civil rights regulation: the Office of Civil Rights (OCR) in the Department of Health, Education, and Welfare (HEW), the Civil Rights Division of the Justice Department, the EEOC, and a score of contract compliance offices scattered throughout the mission agencies. By the end of 1971, federal courts had upheld the minority preferences of the Philadelphia Plan against lawsuits claiming that they violated both the equal protection clause of the Fourteenth Amendment and Titles VI and VII of the Civil Rights Act itself.[4] The Nixon administration's new, race-conscious remedies spread quickly as required standards of employment in federal, state, and local governments and in private employment assisted by U.S. tax dollars—which is to say, in virtually all large businesses in the nation.

Why did President Nixon do this? Such a large expansion of federal regulatory power over state and local governments and private firms seemed to violate long-standing Republican precepts. The chief beneficiaries of hard affirmative action were, after all, African-Americans, a group solid in its loyalty to the Democratic Party. Nixon's motives for action were often mixed, shifting, and contradictory. But his main impulses can be teased out of the story of that first year's revival of the Philadelphia Plan.

The initiative was taken early in 1969 by Nixon's newly appointed labor secretary, George P. Shultz, an economist and former business dean at the University of Chicago. Shultz was familiar with the first Philadelphia Plan, the unsuccessful attempt under President Johnson's labor secretary, Willard Wirtz, to require proportional representation of minority workers in construction projects aided by federal dollars. As a labor economist, Shultz had long been critical of the exclusionary, father-son traditions of the skilled construction trades, where ethnic guilds had traditionally dominated the AFL craft unions (plumbers, electricians, sheet metal workers, stone masons). Shultz saw in Labor's moribund Philadelphia Plan a way to force the hiring halls of the skilled trades to include more minority workers. This would enlarge and diversify the nation's skilled workforce, lower construction costs, open high-wage jobs to minorities, and ease social unrest in the wake of urban rioting.[5]

In a story full of ironies, one irony of affirmative action is that the Labor Department, through the Revised Philadelphia Plan, took advantage of a shrinking pocket of discrimination in construction unions outside the South to impose a permanent regime of federal social regulation on all government contractors. For this purpose, the plan came in the nick of time, because the antidiscrimination laws and court orders of the 1960s had accelerated a process of desegregating unions that was well advanced by 1969. In the progressive unions of the CIO, African-Americans were reasonably well integrated among the 4.5 million members of the large industrial unions—auto, rubber, chemical, and steel workers (although black workers, generally newer to union membership, commonly found themselves in the 1960s at the bottom of labor's seniority system). In the older but declining AFL (9 million members in 1969), resistance to racial integration by local father-son unions in the skilled crafts was stronger, and progress by African-American workers was slower. The AFL's building trades unions, often ethnically based, had the worst record of racial integration in organized labor outside the South. Yet by 1969, black Americans, representing 11 percent of the U.S. labor force, exceeded 8 percent of membership in the nation's construction trade unions.

Even in Philadelphia, where the Labor Department sought and found lily-white targets among the building trade locals to legitimize the Philadelphia Plan, most of the five-county area's 75,000 workers in construction unions in 1967 were in racially integrated locals, as were most of the 28,000 workers in the twenty-two building trades locals. The Philadelphia Plan's architects could identify only six locals, with a total membership of less than 5,000, where racial exclusion was blatant. The plumbers, steamfitters, and electrical workers locals had token black membership, the structural steamfitters had only 6 blacks out of 800 members, and all 1,350 members of the sheet metal workers and 650 members of the elevator constructors were white. The civil servants sponsoring the Philadelphia Plan in the late 1960s were sincere in their attack on the racial exclusion found in the skilled building trades, and were genuine in their alarm over the explosive racial tensions in America's cities. But they were also, in hindsight, racing the clock. The tide of liberal antidiscrimination reform was sweeping away most barriers of racial exclusion in the American labor force, including the unions, and was doing so without recourse to the controversial practice of compensatory minority hiring preferences. The black disadvantage in seniority was a serious problem, but federal court orders and the passage of time were building black seniority. The Labor Department needed the bad-apple craft unions in Philadelphia to accomplish two compatible goals: speed minority access to good jobs in the riot-torn cities, and build a minor player among cabinet departments in Washington into a regulatory powerhouse. The resurrected Philadelphia Plan allowed them to achieve both.

Labor Secretary George Shultz's concern in 1969 over racial unfairness and the high economic costs of a restricted labor force was reinforced by pressure from another cabinet quarter. Nixon's secretary of Housing and Urban Development (HUD), former Michigan governor (and Republican presidential contender) George W. Romney, sent the White House a sobering report in the late spring of 1969. Romney warned that the soaring cost of housing construction, worsened by the scarcity of skilled workers, threatened a sharp spiral of inflation. At the same time, Nixon's senior counselor for domestic policy development, Columbia University economist Arthur Burns, warned the president that the rising cost of construction threatened to worsen inflationary pressures already intensified by Vietnam War expenditures and Great Society social programs.

Thus when Shultz resurrected the Philadelphia Plan, he easily persuaded Nixon of its several benefits. It would free employers from shackles forged by the craft unions, expand the national pool of skilled labor, ease wage pressures on employers, reduce urban violence, and strengthen national defense. There is little evidence that the nation's building contractors were dissatisfied with the status quo and backed Shultz's plan. To the contrary, contractors relied on the union hiring halls to procure their skilled labor force and quickly sued the Labor Department to stop Shultz's revived Philadelphia Plan.

In addition to offering the economic and social benefits of increasing the labor supply, attractive to the academic economist, Shultz, the Philadelphia Plan appealed to Nixon's political instincts. It did this in two ways. First, the threat of inflation endangered Nixon's prospects for reelection in 1972. For all of Richard Nixon's unpredictable political style and his penchant for the unexpected—for example, his presidential trip to Moscow and Beijing, proposing a guaranteed annual income for poor Americans, establishing the Environmental Protection Agency (EPA) to police American business, and imposing wage and price controls in 1972—his one reliable constant was a determination to win the next election. A fear of the political consequences of inflation explains in part Nixon's surprising sponsorship of race-conscious affirmative action at the beginning of his first administration and his imposition of wage and price controls at its end.

Second, the Philadelphia Plan coincided with Nixon's interest in fostering what he called "black capitalism." As Herbert Parmet observes in his biography of Nixon, throughout his career Nixon had favored a jobs strategy to invest black Americans with a stake in the system. Expanding black capitalism promised to strengthen the Republican Party.[6] Alarmed by the urban riots of the late 1960s, Nixon wanted to speed the acquisition by blacks of a middle-class stake in American society. Middle-class Americans didn't riot. They had something to lose, homes and families to protect. Valuing good schools and law and order, Nixon reasoned, middle-class blacks like suburban whites should rally to Republican virtues. During his first hundred days as president, Nixon's sole civil rights initiative was to issue an executive order on March 5, 1969, establishing an Office of Minority Business Enterprise (OMBE) in the Commerce Department. The OMBE was largely a paper enterprise with no budget or program authority. But it reflected Nixon's hopes for building a Republican-leaning black middle class and incorporating it in a new Republican majority, one built on the traditionally Republican suburbs and Rocky Mountain West, and enlarged by newly recruited white Protestant voters in the South and Catholic voters among blue-collar European ethnics and Latinos.

The courtship of southern and Catholic voters complicated the politics of the Philadelphia Plan within the Nixon administration, since these voters could be expected to resent policies favoring minorities in job competition. But by the fall of 1969, Nixon had additional incentives to support the Philadelphia Plan. In September and October, organized labor teamed up with civil rights organizations to attack Nixon's Supreme Court nomination of Clement F. Haynsworth Jr., chief judge of the 4th U.S. Circuit Court of Appeals. A scholarly jurist with an impressive list of publications, Haynsworth was a wealthy, conservative South Carolinian whose rulings had angered labor and civil rights forces. When the vigorous objections of the labor-civil rights alliance persuaded the Democratic-controlled Senate in November to reject Haynsworth, Nixon sought revenge. Thus the Philadelphia Plan, despised by organized labor as a threat to the seniority principle in union-management bargaining, was sweetened in the aftermath of the Haynsworth rejection as an instrument of retaliation against the AFL-CIO. By pushing the Philadelphia Plan, Nixon could drive a wedge between two traditional Democratic constituencies, organized labor and black civil rights groups. "Nixon thought that Secretary of Labor George Shultz had shown great style," John Ehrlichman, Nixon's chief domestic aide, wrote in his memoirs, "in constructing a political dilemma for the labor union leaders and civil rights groups" by "tying their tails together."[7]

Nixon's support for the Philadelphia Plan was bolstered by yet another factor. In addition to fear of inflation, concern for reelection in 1972, support for black capitalism, and splitting the Democrats' labor-civil rights coalition, Nixon moved to defend the prerogatives of the presidency against attack by Congress. Despite his early career in Congress, Nixon's years as Eisenhower's vice president had hardened him against congressional encroachment in executive branch affairs. In the fall of 1969, both organized labor and the contractors associations, customary opponents politically and in the collective bargaining process, lobbied their supporters in Congress to oppose the Philadelphia Plan. And once again, Comptroller General Elmer Staats, head of the GAO, ruled that the revised Philadelphia Plan, like its 1967 predecessor, violated federal bidding protocols and the Civil Rights Act as well. Staats, seeing the battle over the revived Philadelphia Plan as an opportunity to strengthen the authority of the GAO, persuaded Senator Robert Byrd of West Virginia, senior Democrat on the Appropriations Committee, to sponsor a rider to a minor hurricane relief bill stipulating that no congressional appropriation could be used to finance any contract or agreement found by the comptroller general to violate any federal statute. That would sink the Philadelphia Plan and give the GAO a potential veto over the expenditures and programs of all agencies in the executive branch.

Nixon knew that the GAO was an institution designed primarily to serve Congress. It was established in 1921 by the same Budget and Accounting Act that created the Budget Bureau to serve the president. Nixon resented Staat's GAO ruling and the Byrd rider as congressional interference with the president's constitutional responsibilities in contract compliance. Accordingly, he directed Attorney General John N. Mitchell to defend the Philadelphia Plan against the Byrd rider. To document the administration's defense of executive authority, Mitchell and the Labor Department's solicitor general, Laurence H. Silberman, issued "findings" that the flexible goals and timetables of the Philadelphia Plan were not quotas and deadlines and hence did not violate the Civil Rights Act. Silberman later admitted that the Labor Department's "findings" had followed, not preceded, the construction of the plan.[8] They were produced by hearings hastily arranged in Philadelphia in August 1969, two months after the revised plan had been issued in June. Nonetheless, Labor's post hoc findings proved important, in subsequent battles, in permitting federal courts to approve the plan as a remedy for documented past discrimination.[9]

Nixon's stout defense of the Philadelphia Plan was crucial to the survival of race-conscious affirmative action, which otherwise was unlikely to overcome the formidable barriers in the Civil Rights Act, in Congress, and in public opinion. The attack by organized labor, led by AFL-CIO president George Meany, ironically drew labor into an alliance with conservative southern Democrats and pro-business Republicans who normally opposed labor. Meany called the Philadelphia Plan "a concoction and contrivance of a bureaucrat's imagination," used by Nixon to offset criticism of his civil rights record.[10] Meany's ally in this battle in the civil rights movement, Clarence Mitchell, chief Washington lobbyist for the NAACP and a lifelong champion of constitutional color blindness, called the Philadelphia Plan a "calculated attempt coming right from the President's desk to break up the coalition between Negroes and labor unions."[11]

A key opponent of the Philadelphia Plan at this decisive juncture was Senate Minority Leader Everett M. Dirksen of Illinois, an architect of the Civil Rights Act of 1964 (because the Johnson administration needed Republican votes that Dirksen controlled to shut off the southern filibuster in the Senate). "This thing is about as popular as a crab in a whorehouse," Dirksen told President Nixon in the summer of 1969. "I myself will not be able to support you in this ill-conceived scheme."[12] Dirksen, who reminded the White House that he was the author of section 703(j) of the Civil Rights Act banning racial quotas, threatened to rally congressional appropriations committees to deny funding for the Philadelphia Plan.

In September, however, Dirksen suddenly died, weakened by lung cancer and felled by a heart attack. Leadership in the fight against the Philadelphia Plan fell to Judiciary Committee Chairman Sam Ervin (D-N.C.). Thus at a crucial moment, a master legislative tactician was replaced by a southern conservative who was associated chiefly with legislative defeats. Ervin, later a folk hero of the Senate Watergate investigation who lectured the Nixon administration for trampling on the Constitution, was noted in the Senate at the end of the 1960s as a loser of lost-cause votes in defense of racial segregation and southern filibusters. Dirksen's sudden replacement by Ervin produced an odd political alignment as conservative Republicans and southern Democrats, allied with their customary opponents, organized labor, rallied behind Ervin to defend the principle of color blindness, which most of them had steadfastly opposed as recently as 1964. On December 18, by a vote of 52 to 37, the Senate passed the Byrd rider. If enacted, it would enhance congressional power over the executive branch and kill the Philadelphia Plan in the bargain.

In reply, the Nixon White House summoned loyalist Republican representatives to block the Byrd rider in the House. It was a moment of strange political alliances. On December 22, House Republicans, led by their conservative minority leader, Gerald R. Ford, joined forces with liberal House Democrats, opposed by organized labor, and defeated the Byrd rider by a vote of 208 to 156. House Democrats supported the Byrd rider by a vote of 115-84. But House Republicans, rallied in a litmus-test vote by Nixon and resenting Democratic dominance of Congress, supported their president by a solid margin of 124 to 41. Because this was a vote against an obscure congressional rider, Republicans in Congress ran little risk that voters might retaliate against them for supporting racial preferences. Faced with the House vote, the Senate dropped its now hopeless proposal, and both houses quickly adjourned. "With the [Philadelphia Plan] battle won," Silberman observed, "we went on to spread construction plans across the country like Johnny Appleseed."[13]

Within a month, the Labor Department issued Order No. 4. This dull bureaucratic label disguised an aggressive regulatory power play. It extended the Philadelphia Plan's proportional hiring requirements from construction projects to all federal contractors. To qualify as bidders for government contracts, employers such as defense firms, builders, and suppliers were now obliged to submit written affirmative action plans, including detailed numerical goals and timetables for minority hiring that would remedy "underutilization." Underutilization meant worker distributions in all job classifications that failed to reach proportional employment for protected classes (African-Americans, Hispanics, Asians, Native Americans). In 1970, the Labor Department's contract compliance regulation covered

230,000 contractors, together doing $30 billion worth of business and employing more than 20 million workers—one-third of the entire U.S. labor force.[14] Employment standards imposed on these contractors by Washington contract compliance officials, as a requirement for receiving government contracts and grants, would set the new national standard. Labor's OFCC set the pace for 27 contract compliance offices scattered throughout the federal agencies. Thus the Nixon administration's rescue and sponsorship of the Philadelphia Plan in 1969, escorting it through the formidable barriers that had defeated its predecessor with little difficulty, was a breakthrough. The window of opportunity that this unexpected Republican-sponsored opening provided for race-conscious affirmative action enforcement was exploited with great speed and skill by Washington's new network of civil rights enforcement officials.

The New Social Regulation and Civil Rights Agency Capture

The ability of the minority rights interest groups to win control of the new agencies of civil rights enforcement established in the 1960s followed a traditional pattern in the politics of regulation that students of public administration called "clientele capture." The practice is as old as Jacksonian democracy, which set the American tradition wherein party patronage ruled the civil service and mission agencies were expected to cater to the needs of their organized constituencies: farmers, veterans, laborers, and business interests. By the 1960s, journalists referred to these arrangements as "iron triangles." They were three-way coalitions of mutual backscratching, operating in Washington and in state and municipal governments throughout America. The three points of the triangle were organized interest groups, which lobbied legislators to establish or expand programs beneficial to their members; legislative committees, which obliged the lobbyists by authorizing and funding programs for the mission agencies to manage; and government bureaucrats, who expanded their empire building service programs to benefit the interest groups. To complete the triangular cycle, interest groups supported the legislators. The American economy was growing, newly organized constituencies were eager to join the government benefits wagon, and it was all legal, more or less.

Capture of mission agencies such as Agriculture, Commerce, and Labor was regarded by students of American government as problematical but not serious. After all, the domestic mission agencies were organized to serve these large constituencies. Capture *was* a serious problem, however, with the federal regulatory agencies. Economists and consumer advocates in the

1950s complained that many independent regulatory agencies, established by progressives and New Dealers early in the century to regulate industries in the public interest, had been captured by the industries being regulated: the railroads, airlines, and truckers. By the 1970s, a bipartisan consensus had developed among economists that supported regulatory reform, under the banner of "deregulation," and during the Carter and Reagan administrations Congress significantly deregulated the railroad, airline, trucking, banking, communications, oil, and natural gas industries.

If deregulation was the solution for agency capture in economic regulation, it seemed happily unnecessary in the new agencies of social regulation established in the 1960s and 1970s to protect the environment, consumers, and transportation and workplace safety. For example, the EPA, the Occupational Safety and Health Administration (OSHA), and the Consumer Product Safety Commission (CPSC), all established by Congress during the first Nixon administration, did not seem threatened by capture. The reason is partly structural. Most forms of environmental, consumer protection, and transportation safety regulation are characterized by widely distributed benefits (clean air and water, safe drugs and highways) and narrowly concentrated costs (pollution abatement equipment, toxic waste disposal, air bag requirements). The concentrated costs of this kind of regulation are huge, and not surprisingly they prompt strong resistance from regulated industries. Automobile manufacturers and defense firms, for example, resent paying for benefits that add nothing to profit margins, and not surprisingly they are hostile to the agency's goals. But the regulation is popular with consumers and voters and hence popular with Congress and presidential aspirants. Moreover, because environmental and consumer protection regulation is cross-cutting and horizontal—covering pollution, for example, from all industrial sources, rather than single-industry and vertical, like economic regulation (airlines, communications, railroads, trucking)—it is a difficult target for capture.[15]

The new agencies of civil rights regulation, however, were different in ways that made them highly vulnerable to capture. Most important, the cost-benefit structure of civil rights regulation is the opposite of that found in environmental and consumer protection regulation. Benefits (jobs, promotions, admissions, contract set-asides) are narrowly concentrated among protected-class clienteles (racial and ethnic minorities, women, the handicapped). Costs, on the other hand, are widely distributed (government and corporate budgets). Regulatory agencies in this environment face a dominant interest group or coalition of advocacy groups favoring its goals. Such an environment is a lobbyist's dream. Regulatory officials dispense benefits through complex technical formulas (freight rates, communications frequencies, airline routes, minority employee manning tables) that are well understood by interest groups but are mystifying to the general public.[16]

By the 1970s, economists had formed a consensus that this pattern of client politics subverted the public interest in economic regulation. Regulated industries such as railroads and airlines had effectively captured "client agencies" (e.g., the Interstate Commerce Commission and the Civil Aeronautics Board). Together the regulators and the regulated industries formed a cozy partnership, restraining entry and competition and maintaining high prices and profits. In similar fashion in the 1970s, clientele groups representing the interests of minorities, women, and the handicapped (e.g., the NAACP, the Mexican American Legal Defense and Education Fund, the National Organization for Women, the American Coalition of Citizens with Disabilities) lobbied intensively and effectively to shape the regulatory agenda of agencies such as the EEOC, the OFCC, the OCR, the Voting Rights Section in the Justice Department, and their counterpart agencies in thousands of federal, state, county, and municipal governments.[17]

Capture is a problematical metaphor, a military term denoting total control. This rarely occurred in civil rights regulation, because the strength of the civil rights coalition—its mobilized base among blacks, feminists, Latinos, the handicapped—was also a source of division. During the 1970s, for example, the OCR was troubled by internal competition and jealousies between constituencies over agency priorities. African-American organizations pressed for priorities on school desegregation, feminists for equality in school sports expenditures, and Hispanics for bilingual education. On the whole, however, the coalition muted these differences, at least in public. All the civil rights constituencies agreed on the primacy of affirmative action. Because hard affirmative action was so controversial and was developed not in Congress, with public hearings and debate over its rationale, but in agency bureaucracies, the civil rights coalition needed to develop a theory of affirmative action plausible enough to challenge the powerful simplicity of constitutional color blindness.[18]

The Search for a Theory of Affirmative Action

A major advantage of the breakthrough civil rights laws of the 1960s was their grounding in the classic liberal theory of antidiscrimination and equal individual rights. The NAACP had trumpeted this doctrine since its founding in 1909 and, in its lawsuits against racial segregation, had been hammering it home since the 1930s. Even the vague language of soft affirmative action in the Kennedy-Johnson executive orders was grounded in nondiscrimination, augmented by ambiguous outreach programs, such as aggressive minority recruiting. Hard affirmative action, however, was necessarily grounded in the concepts of compensatory discrimination and group rights. It required preference for protected classes, not equal individual rights. It lacked a theory to legitimize its radical claims, so sharply at a variance with traditional liberal doctrine and with public opinion.

To supply such a theory, intellectuals in the civil rights movement fashioned a new body of theory during the late 1960s and early 1970s that would justify and indeed morally require the displacement of color-blind policies by minority preferences. The theoreticians of affirmative action, most of them based outside of government, were affiliated with universities (especially sociology departments and law schools), foundations (most notably the Ford Foundation), think tanks (Joint Center for Political and Economic Studies), public interest law firms (the American Civil Liberties Union), and single-interest lobbying groups (Minority Business Enterprise Legal Defense and Education Fund). The most striking attribute of the new theory of compensatory justice was its grounding not in the Constitution or statutes or in liberal traditions of equal treatment. Rather, the social force that justified the new doctrine of race-conscious affirmative action was *history itself*, in the form of past discrimination. As Lyndon Johnson told the graduating class at Howard University in June 1965:

> But freedom is not enough. You do not wipe away the scars of centuries by saying: Now you are free to go where you want, do as you desire, choose the leaders you please.

> You do not take a person who for years has been hobbled by chains and liberate him, bring him up to the starting line of a race and then say, "You are free to compete with all the others," and still justly believe you have been completely fair.[19]

Johnson was reading a speech written for him by two liberal staff aides, both young Harvard academics, Richard Goodwin and Daniel Patrick Moynihan. Johnson never returned to this theme, and his executive orders, like Kennedy's, emphasized color-blind nondiscrimination and soft affirmative action. But the Howard speech metaphor of the unfair footrace captured the essence of a latent theory that programs of social justice must compensate for past injustice.

History, in this view, endowed the present with deeply entrenched injustice. Effective reform must actively undo the baleful effects of past discrimination, not merely ban their further accumulation. The crippling legacy of history took the modern form of "institutional racism." The theory held that generations of racist thought and behavior had shaped institutional cultures and standards so profoundly that discriminatory results were perpetuated even in the subsequent absence of racial prejudice or discriminatory intent by contemporary individuals. A business organization or government agency, for example, even though devoid of bias on the part of management or employees, might nonetheless discriminate against minorities or women for inherited structural reasons: Senior officials were predominantly white, job tests and promotion criteria favored better educated employees, career incentives favored male employees, seniority disadvantaged recently hired workers, English language routines favored native speakers, the architecture hindered the disabled. Whereas discriminatory behavior was relatively easy to identify, its prejudicial intent was difficult to prove; institutional racism was subtle and difficult to identify in action, but was easy to demonstrate by its consequences. The results of institutionalized bias were seen as measurable by the statistical disparity between minority or female potential in the applicant pool (for jobs, promotions, appointments, awards, school admissions) and minority or female presence on the institutional rolls. Evidence of discriminatory intent, though required by the traditional code of color blindness that had shaped the Civil Rights Act, was held to be largely irrelevant.[20]

Compensatory justice was thus results-oriented. What counted was not discriminatory intent but adverse or "disparate" impact, the technical term civil rights lawyers developed to denote proportionately unequal results. The new results-oriented model for affirmative action enforcement did not fit the violation/remedy paradigm of Anglo-American law. In this paradigm, the juridic triad consisted of two contending adversaries (plaintiff or prosecutor versus defense) and a neutral judge, who presided over a fair trial, found a harm, identified a violator, and required a remedy. The traditional, violation/remedy model of jurisprudence had governed the structure of the civil rights legislation of 1964-68, and conformed to the negative and procedural principles of liberal nondiscrimination that underpinned the reforms of the 1960s. Civil rights discrimination, developed in the tort tradition of civil law, required demonstration of intent to harm. But intent was inherently difficult to prove, because the parties accused of harmful intent, usually employers, controlled the evidence needed for proof (hiring and promotion deliberations and their documentation).

For these reasons, not surprisingly, civil rights leaders in the late 1960s grew dissatisfied with the slow pace of antidiscrimination procedures with their quasi-judicial hearings, procedural guarantees (and hence heavy lawyering), and courtlike findings. Instead, they preferred the new social regulation of the 1960s as the model for affirmative-action enforcement.

Unlike the traditional economic regulation of the Progressive-New Deal tradition, which protected citizens from economic injury (price-fixing, restraint of trade, fraudulent securities, unfair labor practices) through "cease-and-desist" orders (stop discriminating) and make-whole relief (requiring hiring, reinstatement, or promotion with back pay), social regulation was forward-looking, seeking to reduce citizen risk of future harm. Its goal was to protect citizens from the hazards of polluted air and water, toxic food and drugs, unsafe transportation and workplaces.

By analogy, civil rights regulation in this analysis would remain ineffective as long as enforcement agencies followed the old, slow, quasi-judicial, "retail" approach. This meant investigating individual complaints through courtlike hearings, demonstrating not only discriminatory behavior but also discriminatory intent. Instead, civil rights regulators should set broad standards of compliance through an administrative process of notice-and-comment rule making, like the EPA. Employers who were told by the EPA to reduce toxic agents in their water or air effluent to so many parts per million by a certain date could also be told to increase their proportion of minority workers to certain percentages by certain dates.

This was what the Philadelphia Plan did for the nation's construction industry and what the OFCC's Order No. 4, issued in the winter of 1970, did for all federal government contractors. It was bound to be challenged in court.

Affirmative Action and the Federal Courts

Approval from the federal bench was essential to protect the new minority preference policies in the enforcement agencies from charges that they violated the Civil Rights Act itself. In the case of the Philadelphia Plan, the construction companies obliged by their collective bargaining contracts to hire workers sent by union hiring halls on a seniority basis were now threatened by the Labor Department with loss of contract if they didn't hire enough minority workers. Caught in the middle, they sued the Labor Department in federal court. The case, *Contractors Association of Eastern Pennsylvania v. Secretary of Labor*, was heard in the court of Judge Charles R. Weiner of the eastern district of Pennsylvania. Weiner, a Democratic, had been appointed to the federal bench in 1966 by President Johnson. A legislative leader for his party in the Pennsylvania state senate, Weiner had long experience in coalition-building with civil rights organizations and their leaders.

Attorneys for the contractors did not argue, on equal protection grounds, that the Philadelphia Plan was unconstitutional because the Constitution was color-blind. They knew that, despite popular belief to the contrary, the Supreme Court had never held that the Constitution was color-blind. The Court had not so ruled in *Brown v. Board of Education* in 1954. Nor did it do so in *Loving v. Virginia* in 1967, when the Court ruled unconstitutional on equal protection grounds a Virginia law banning interracial marriage. In *Loving*, the justices held unanimously that racial classifications in law were not unconstitutional per se, but they were "inherently suspect" and hence triggered strict judicial scrutiny. This stiff standard required a government authority to make a finding of constitutional or statutory violation and identify a compelling interest that justified a racial remedy. Strict judicial scrutiny, when applied by the 1960s, unfailingly struck down the challenged racial classification.[21]

By long tradition, however, the Court did not reach constitutional judgments when statutory grounds would suffice, and in the Philadelphia Plan lawsuit the contractors had available the full legislative history of the Civil Rights Act with its multiple rejections of racial classifications, ratios, quotas, and the like. The contractors claimed that the plan violated provisions in the Civil Rights Act making it unlawful for employers to refuse to hire, discharge, or otherwise discriminate against "any individual with respect to his compensation, terms, conditions, or privileges of employment, because of such individual's race, color, religion, sex, or national origin," or to "limit, segregate, or classify his employees in any way which would deprive any individual of employment opportunities or otherwise adversely affect his status as an employee, because of such individual's race, color, religion, sex, or national origin."[22]

Judge Weiner, however, agreed with the Labor Department that the Philadelphia Plan imposed no racial quotas. Instead, it set flexible goals and timetables, requiring for example that the percentage of minority iron-workers on all construction projects increase by stages, from 5–9 percent to 22–26 percent within a four-year period. Contractors who failed to reach these targets, Weiner pointed out, but who demonstrated "every good faith effort" to do so would not automatically lose their contracts. Consequently, on March 13, 1970, Judge Weiner upheld the Philadelphia Plan. Weiner's ruling rested chiefly on a narrow reading of congressional prohibitions, a broad reading of presidential authority in civil rights enforcement, and a contradictory mix of case law drawn not from employment contexts but from school desegregation litigation.[23] Weiner lectured the contractors from the bench. "Present employment practices have fostered and perpetuated a system that has effectively maintained a segregated class. That concept, if I may use the strong language it deserves, is repugnant, unworthy, and contrary to present national policy. The Philadelphia Plan will provide an unpolluted breath of fresh air to ventilate this unpalatable situation."[24]

The contractors were no more successful in appealing Weiner's ruling to the Third circuit. On April 22, 1971, a three-judge panel unanimously sustained Weiner's decision. The chief difficulty the judges faced was the language found in Title VI, which provided a statutory basis for the president's executive order program. In the first sentence, Title VI, sec. 601, lists its sole substantive command: "No person in the United States shall, on the ground of race, color, or national origin, be excluded from participation in, be denied the benefits of, or be subject to discrimination under any program or activity receiving federal financial assistance."[25] To disarm Title VI, the appeals panel simply decreed that its restrictions did not apply to the executive order program. Because the executive order program, originating in the "affirmative action" language of Kennedy's 1961 order, predated the Civil Rights Act, "the Philadelphia Plan does not purport to derive its authorization from Title VI."

To make such a claim in the early 1970s required extraordinary tunnel vision. Just as the Third Circuit judges were writing, the federal government was experiencing an explosion of social regulation. Of all statutes ever enacted by Congress, Title VI lay at the heart of this expansion in regulation from Washington. It provided the core mechanism and authority for contract compliance officials in federal agencies throughout the government to prevent discrimination against various protected classes in federally assisted programs. Prior to the enactment of Title VI, there was no OFCC, and the president's equal employment opportunity committee, run out of the vice president's office, largely confined its affirmative action initiatives to recruiting outreach for minority job applicants. Title VI was thus the crucial statutory enactment upon which the growth of hard affirmative action was subsequently based, beginning with the OFCC's Philadelphia Plan.

In 1964, when Congress first shaped Title VI, it was designed chiefly to protect African-Americans. In 1972, in Title IX of the education amendments, Congress used the exact language of Title VI, substituting only *sex* for *race*, to authorize the Office of Civil Rights in HEW to police gender discrimination in federally assisted education programs, which included all public schools and virtually all colleges and universities in the land. The following year, Congress did the same thing to bar discrimination against the physically and mentally disabled, once again cloning the proven language of Title VI and inserting it in the Rehabilitation Act of 1973.

The judges ruling on the Philadelphia Plan in 1970 and 1971 knew that the provisions of Title VI governed the president's executive order program, and that Congress in 1964 had elaborately stipulated a ban on minority preferences. They also knew, however, that a bill in Congress to explicitly bar the Philadelphia Plan, backed by the contractors association, had been defeated by the Nixon administration in December 1969. And they knew that other lower courts, without Supreme Court objection, had recently been approving race-conscious remedies in some EEO cases and especially in school desegregation litigation. Petitioned by the contractors to review *Contractors Association*, the Supreme Court refused to grant a hearing, a procedure followed when at least four justices requested it. Instead, the Court issued a one-line order in October 1971 affirming the finding of the appeals court. This allowed the Court to approve the Philadelphia Plan not only without confronting the elaborated nondiscrimination language in the Civil Rights Act but also without confronting the plan's conflict with the Court's own strict scrutiny standard in racial classification cases under the Constitution's equal protection clause. The Warren Court in *Loving* had held that racial classifications in the law triggered strict judicial scrutiny, a standard of review that was unfailingly fatal to the challenged classification. In *Contractors Association*, however, the lower federal courts disregarded strict scrutiny and the Supreme Court looked the other way. The Court would continue to dodge this awkward confrontation until the *Bakke* case in the late 1970s, by which time the Court was divided over affirmative action and forced to deal with its conflicts.

Although Chief Justice Earl Warren retired in 1969 and was replaced as chief justice by Nixon appointee Warren Burger, the Supreme Court in the early 1970s remained largely a liberal tribunal on racial matters, holding to its post-*Brown* tradition of unanimous rulings in southern desegregation cases. Not surprisingly, the pathbreaking shift from nondiscrimination to positive obligations in civil rights enforcement, seen in the Philadelphia Plan, followed the drama of school desegregation. The federal courts, embarrassed by a decade of tokenism following *Brown v. Board of Education* and encouraged by support from Congress and the executive branch in the Civil Rights Act, began in 1966 to demand from southern school officials not mere race-neutral behavior but rather "the organized undoing of the effects of past discrimination."[26] To redress the damage inflicted on an entire race down through the generations, the Supreme Court approved increasingly detailed school policies that stipulated the racial assignment of pupils, teachers, administrative staff, and the color-conscious construction of school budgets, judicial interventions that were similar in spirit to the minority hiring requirements of the Philadelphia Plan.

In the *Swann v. Charlotte-Mecklenburg County Board of Education* (402 U.S. 1) decision of 1971, the Supreme Court ruled, once again unanimously, that busing, racial balance quotas, and gerrymandered school districts were all appropriate methods for eliminating the vestiges of school segregation. When a North Carolina power company instituted tougher but race-neutral employment and promotion standards and tests that weeded out far more blacks than whites, the Supreme Court in *Griggs v. Duke Power Company*, 401 U.S. 428 (1971) ruled that the history of Jim Crow schooling in North Carolina had made the tests unfair even though the Civil Rights Act had specifically approved their use. In *Griggs* the Supreme Court, holding that the regulatory rulings of the EEOC expressed the intent of Congress, formally upheld the "disparate impact" theory of civil rights enforcement. *Griggs* completed the Supreme Court's shift from the equal treatment standards of antidiscrimination that underpinned the Civil Rights Act to the equal results standard of disparate or adverse impact law that, like the Philadelphia Plan, normatively rested on a model of proportional minority representation.

In 1974, the justices ruled unanimously, in the case of *Lau v. Nichols*, 414 U.S. 563, that public schools must make some positive effort to ensure that non-English-speaking students acquire language skills necessary to benefit from their schooling. Although the case involved Chinese-speaking students in San Francisco, and the Court did not specify bilingual education or any other method of instruction as a remedy, the *Lau* decision sharply accelerated the spread of bilingual education programs in the country's public schools, most of them involving Spanish. And once again, as in the case of the Philadelphia Plan, a controversial federal program based on racial and national origin classifications, and driven by civil rights enforcement officials in Washington, was nurtured by the political calculations of a Republican White House.

Bilingual Education as Latino Affirmative Action

The federal bilingual education program began in the last year of the Johnson presidency as a modest, noncontroversial initiative by Congress to authorize grants from HEW to school districts wishing to offer dual instruction in English and another language. Sponsored in the Senate by Texas Democrat Ralph Yarborough, who hoped to win Hispanic votes in a close reelection contest (which he lost), the Bilingual Education Act was not a separate statute, as the rubric implies, but rather was Title VII of the education amendments of 1968. The model program cited in the Senate hearings was the Coral Way school curriculum in Miami, where middle-class students, both Anglo and Latino, became proficient in each other's language. Supporters of bilingual education argued persuasively that monolingual Americans needed foreign language mastery to compete with the Soviets and China in the cold war and to compete successfully for overseas trade. Critics were few, and Title VII passed with scarcely any opposition. School participation was voluntary, the program was low profile, and Title VII's budget, by HEW standards, was tiny. In 1970, $21 million supported bilingual instruction for 52,000 students, 90 percent of them native speakers of Spanish.[27]

By the end of the 1970s, this modest wedge program had been converted into a nationally divisive issue of identity politics. The first step in this conversion was taken by the Nixon administration. It involved a shift from Nixon's first-year emphasis on supporting black capitalism and affirmative action programs to strengthen the black middle class, to wooing Hispanic voters in his reelection efforts. Faced with continued hostility from the NAACP and other African-American organizations, Nixon quickly lost interest in courting black voters. To appeal to white voters upset by school busing for racial balance, Nixon shifted school desegregation enforcement to the Justice Department and the federal courts. He fired Leon Panetta, the director of OCR he inherited from the Democrats, and appointed a Republican, Stanley Pottinger, to replace him.

School busing, effective though unpopular as a court-ordered remedy in the white South, was increasingly unpopular in the urban North, especially among European ethnic voters. To court their support for reelection, Nixon crusaded against school busing and even called for a constitutional amendment against it. Congress, responding to the same pressures, twice during the 1970s prohibited HEW (and thus the OCR) from including racial transportation provisions in the regulations accompanying federal school aid. Pottinger, as head of the OCR, thus needed a civil rights enforcement agenda to replace school integration. In 1972, Congress provided the OCR with one such fresh agenda, in the form of Title IX authority to enforce gender equality in the nation's schools and colleges. The other fresh agenda item, bilingual education, Pottinger devised himself, with support from the Nixon White House.[28]

In May 1970, Pottinger issued a set of regulations based on the OCR's Title VI authority. They were directed at "School Districts with More than Five Percent National Origin-Minority Group Children."[29] This encompassed 1,000 districts and more than 3.7 million children. The regulatory purpose was to combat "a number of common procedures which have the effect of denying equality of educational opportunity to Spanish-surnamed pupils," in violation of Title VI of the Civil Rights Act. The OCR directed school districts to take unspecified "affirmative steps to rectify" the deficiencies of LEP (limited English proficient) students. Bilingual education was nowhere mentioned. But bilingual/bicultural instruction was the remedy preferred by the OCR.[30]

Nixon's political aides were enthusiastic about using bilingual education as a wedge issue to woo Hispanic voters from their traditional Democratic loyalties. As inflation tightened the federal budget and threatened the president's reelection prospects, HEW budget cuts limited the growth of bilingual education grants. But OCR regulation offered program expansion and its political benefits at almost no cost to the federal budget. This was one political key to the expansion of the "rights revolution" in the 1970s. As unfunded mandates, social regulation ordered by federal agencies, but paid for by private employers and state and local governments, offered elected officials in Washington a way to spread benefits without paying for them.

Charles Colson, Nixon's chief strategist for courting ethnic voters, especially Catholics, urged the president in 1971 to take Pottinger's OCR directive one step further and "require that bilingual education programs be components of any educational institution receiving federal funds with more than 10 percent Spanish-speaking service population."[31] Nixon aides explored the feasibility of such a mandate, but ultimately concluded that it would require new legislation. The OCR, however, was heading this direction on its own. It was drawn by the normal bureaucratic instinct to increase agency authority, and impelled by the intensified lobbying of the newly mobilized Chicano nationalist groups, such as the National Council of La Raza, and supported by lawyers from MALDEF.

The OCR in the early 1970s in effect experienced an internal capture shift. The black agenda activists who had dominated the office between 1965 and 1970 were joined and to some extent displaced by a new cadre of Latino activists. Not content with the transitional model of bilingual education, which used native-language instruction as a bridge to English language proficiency, the Latino nationalists called for Spanish-based cultural maintenance programs of indefinite duration. La Raza Unida's 1967 founding statement captured the Chicano spirit of cultural nationalism and linguistic ethnocentrism: "The time of subjugation, exploitation, and abuse of human rights of La Raza in the United States is hereby ended forever," the manifesto proclaimed. "[We] affirm the magnificence of La Raza, the greatness of our heritage, our history, our language, our traditions, our contributions to humanity and culture."[32]

In 1971 OCR official Martin Gerry outlined an enforcement plan requiring schools to adopt "bilingual-bicultural program models" developed by the OCR following consultation with "outstanding Mexican-American and Puerto Rican educators, psychologists, and community and civil rights leaders." HEW Secretary Elliot Richardson told the Senate that the OCR would require "total institutional reposturing (including culturally sensitizing teachers, instructional materials, and educational approaches) in order to incorporate, affirmatively recognize and value the cultural environment of ethnic minority children so that the development of positive self-concept can be accelerated."[33]

The OCR nonetheless held back from fully mandating its multicultural agenda, cautioned in part by congressional criticism of HEW for interfering in local school affairs concerning such issues as racial teacher assignments and student dress codes. The OCR's green light came in 1974 with the Supreme Court's *Lau* decision. When the Court in *Lau* affirmed the OCR's authority but specified no required remedies, the OCR asked its consultants to draft compliance guidelines. The result was the Lau Remedies, a twenty-three-page document that the OCR and the U.S. Office of Education (USOE) jointly sent to thousands of school districts in 1975. Written in turgid, jargon-laden educationese, the Lau Remedies signaled the intentions of the education and enforcement bureaucracy that would form the heart of the new Department of Education, urged by President Carter and approved by Congress in 1979.

Substantively, the Lau Remedies were a preemptive strike against English-based teaching methods, such as English-as-a-second-language (ESL) and immersion techniques. They required native-language instruction in the basic courses (math, science, social studies) for elementary and intermediate-level students whose primary language was not English. "Because an ESL program does not consider the affective nor cognitive development of students in this category," the OCR directive explained, "an ESL program is *not* appropriate."[34] Instead, school districts must teach elementary and intermediate LEP children in their native language, using either transitional bilingual or bilingual/bicultural methods.

The 1975 remedies telegraphed an intrusive future, reaching beyond teaching methods to include instructional personnel and course content. They urged school districts to use "paraprofessional persons with the necessary languages and cultural background." The OCR remedies offered an employment bonanza for native speakers of Spanish as bilingual teachers and teacher aides. Even HEW Secretary Joseph Califano, arguably the leading liberal in the Carter cabinet (together with Vice President Walter Mondale), complained about the demands of the bilingual education lobby. "HEW's bilingual program had become captive of the professional Hispanic and other ethnic groups," Califano noted, with their "often exaggerated political rhetoric of biculturalism."[35] Between 1975 and 1980, OCR used the Lau Remedies to negotiate bilingual education requirements with more than four hundred school districts, concentrating on the major cities: Chicago, Houston, Los Angeles, New York, and Philadelphia.

The bilingual/bicultural programs spread under the Lau Remedies, not surprisingly, were controversial. Most Americans, polls showed, agreed with the *Lau* decision that it was unfair to teach children in a language they could not understand. The force-feeding, by a constituency-captured OCR, of only one method as remedy was quite another matter. In 1978 a four-year study by the American Institutes for Research, sponsored by the USOE, concluded that most of the Hispanic students involved were native speakers of English, that those who needed to learn English competence were not in fact acquiring it, that most bilingual programs were aimed at linguistic and cultural maintenance rather than learning English, and that the segregated Hispanic students who were already alienated from school simply remained so. Califano pointed out that "due in part to the misguided administration of bilingual programs, 40 percent of students whose first language is Spanish dropped out of school before earning a high school diploma."[36]

Many school districts resisted OCR pressures, some of them suing OCR in federal court. Plaintiffs charged that the Lau Remedies were mere policy guidelines and lacked regulatory authority. Under the *Lau* decision, OCR had the burden of proof to first find individual school districts not in compliance. The OCR, instead, cited the *Lau* precedent and used the Lau Remedies as a regulatory carte blanche. Yet the OCR never published the Lau Remedies for comment in the *Federal Register*, as required by federal regulatory procedures. A federal court in a 1978 lawsuit, *Northwest Arctic v. Califano*, ordered the OCR to go through the formal rule-making process to codify the requirements of school districts receiving federal aid—meaning almost all of them—in teaching LEP students. OCR's response was slow, partly because President Carter's departmentalization plan for education split the OCR, assigning one OCR to the new Department of Health and Human Services and the other to the new Department of Education.[37]

By 1980, the Carter administration was mired in controversy. Most of it flowed from the inflation-ridden, stagnant economy and the humiliating Iran hostage crisis. But part of the administration's unpopularity stemmed also from Carter's push for bilingual education. A federal program that forced non-English instruction on local schools was difficult to hide from voters. Carter had supported another federal program, however, that similarly linked government benefits to race and ethnicity, but did not arouse the same level of controversy. This was the minority contract set-aside program. Because, like the Philadelphia Plan, it dealt not with schools but with the obscure, complex world of government contracts, it attracted little immediate attention outside the Washington beltway. It was the last major affirmative action initiative of the 1970s.

Congress and Minority Contract Set-Asides

Before Jimmy Carter was elected president, Congress had been careful to avoid legislation endorsing racial or ethnic preferences. Carter himself had championed the Equal Rights Amendment during the campaign, but avoided the volatile affirmative action issue—the third rail of American politics. Democrats in Congress, however, were pressed by the Congressional Black Caucus to target relief for minorities hard hit by economic recession. With a Democrat occupying the White House in January 1977, Democratic leaders in the House developed a floor amendment strategy that would avoid the lightning rod of committee hearings and reports over the thorny issue of affirmative action. This approach promised to ease passage in Congress and smooth the path for a presidential signature.

The floor amendment strategy led to the enactment in May 1977 of the Public Works Employment Act, which established the minority contract set-aside program. The set-aside provision was offered as an amendment on the House floor on February 23, 1977, by Rep. Parren J. Mitchell (D-Md.), chairman of the Congressional Black Caucus. It was an amendment to a large public works appropriation measure, designed to jump-start the economy and provide employment for needy constituencies. Mitchell's amendment required that at least 10 percent of the $4 billion appropriation for public works contracts should go to minority business enterprises (MBEs). It stipulated that "minority group members are citizens of the United States who are Negroes, Spanish-speaking, Orientals, Indians, Eskimos, and Aleuts." At the time, Mitchell's amendment attracted little notice. In retrospect, it was a turning point in modern civil rights history. Congress's creation of MBE set-asides in 1977 is striking in three ways.

First, the set-aside initiative was a tour de force of policy entrepreneurship by leaders of the civil rights coalition in Congress. They included a rising generation of urban black Democrats active in the Black Caucus, such as John R. Conyers of Detroit and Augustus Hawkins of Los Angeles, working with white liberal allies such as Rep. Don Edwards of California, a senior member of the House Judiciary Committee, and aided by the sympathetic House leadership, including Speaker Thomas P. "Tip" O'Neill. They took skillful advantage of changing institutional circumstances of the 1970s, including the huge Democratic majorities elected in 1974, the weakening grip of senior southern Democrats on committee leadership, the proliferation of subcommittees and congressional staff, and the resurgence of congressional initiative in policymaking against an "imperial" presidency weakened by the Vietnam War and Watergate.

Mitchell and his colleagues laid the groundwork carefully. They created ad hoc and oversight committees and built a record of legislative findings that past discrimination left a legacy of institutional bias that crippled current efforts at minority participation. They concentrated on documenting the problem, not on shaping remedies. In 1972 the House Subcommittee on Minority Small Business Enterprise reported that minority businesses faced economic difficulties that "are the result of past social standards which linger as characteristic of minorities as a group." By 1975, this effort had produced similar findings by the House Subcommittee on SBA Oversight and Minority Enterprise, the General Accounting Office, and the U.S. Commission on Civil Rights. In January 1977, in the last days of the Ford presidency, the House Committee on Small Business concluded that "over the years, there has developed a business system which has traditionally excluded measurable minority participation . . . a business system which is racially neutral on its face, but because of past overt social and economic discrimination is presently operating, in effect, to perpetuate these past inequities."[38]

Second, in the field of government contracting, the civil rights coalition made a strong practical case for affirmative action remedies. Minorities faced formidable structural barriers to entry, even though government procurement had stressed nondiscrimination at least since 1961. Large, established firms held great advantages over new entrants in the form of experience in bidding, bonding, subcontracting, project performance, and reputation. Minorities were often excluded from lending or supplier networks and were unfamiliar with contracting agency protocols. In commercial enterprise generally in 1977, minorities (blacks, Hispanics, and Asians) accounted for 16 percent of the population, but formed only 3 percent of the nation's 13 million businesses and generated less than 1 percent of gross business receipts.

Third, by naming six groups as eligible for a 10 percent "share of the action," Mitchell's set-aside provision created a precedent that invited expansion. But the expansion was a double-edged sword. It strengthened the supporting coalition by adding new constituencies. On the other hand, it increased political vulnerability by calling attention to the problems of resentment inherent in proliferating protected classes. Set-aside payoffs were too attractive for other groups to resist. If speakers of a particular language or persons claiming a certain ancestry could win such entitlements, why not include other groups? If an arbitrary 10 percent set-aside was permissible, why not more? In attempting to blunt criticism that a minority set-aside remedy for past discrimination would create a racial quota, Congressman Mitchell in 1977 emphasized continuity with the SBA's section 8(a) program to assist "economically or culturally disadvantaged groups," a program begun in 1968 as a response to the urban riots. The SBA, pressed by applicants to define which groups were economically or culturally disadvantaged, had by 1977 developed a flexible, inclusive list: "Such persons include, but are not limited to, black Americans, American Indians, Spanish-Americans, Oriental Americans, Eskimos, and Aleuts."[39]

The MBE committee hearings and reports since 1972 had emphasized shared minority disadvantages and avoided distinguishing between particular groups. But the SBA 8(a) program, by aiding culturally *or* economically deprived groups, permitted including nonminority women and poor white men, even if only in token amounts. Mitchell's original intention had been to name only "Negroes and Spanish-speakers." But in justifying his set-aside as a logical extension of the 8(a) program, Mitchell borrowed the SBA list of approved minority groups. In a 6-3 ruling in 1980, the Burger Court upheld the set-aside provision in *Fullilove v. Klutznick*. The majority in *Fullilove* deferred to Congress, granting the legislative branch wide latitude in shaping social policy. In his dissent, however, Justice John Paul Stevens noted that Congress "for the first time in the Nation's history has created a broad legislative classification for entitlement to benefits based solely on racial characteristics."[40]

Congress gave Mitchell's minority set-aside provision overwhelming approval after only a perfunctory floor discussion, and the Carter administration then backed it with enthusiasm. The House, which held no hearings on the minority set-aside proposal, accepted Mitchell's House floor amendment by voice vote. Congress passed the public works bill with routine majorities, 335-77 in the House and 71-14 in the Senate, which also held no hearings. The Carter White House, criticized during its first year by black leaders for emphasizing budget balancing over full employment, seized the MBE set-aside as an opportunity to rally minority loyalty.

At a "10% MBE Meeting" on August 26, Carter aide Jack Watson warned national leaders from banking, surety, and construction firms that "if a general contract bidder does not line up MBEs for at least 10 percent of the grant funds, its bid will be disqualified."[41] On September 12 Carter appointed an Interagency Council for Minority Business Enterprise to expand MBE programs in all federal agencies. He also directed the Office of Federal Procurement Policy to require evidence of MBE participation prior to awarding contracts, and instructed all executive departments to double procurement purchases from minority firms within the next two fiscal years. At the same time, Carter won approval from Congress for a

reorganization of civil rights enforcement agencies that consolidated contract compliance for all federal agencies in the Labor Department's OFCC,
and increased its staff from 68 employees to 1,304.

Encouraged by the president's response, the Democratic leadership in
Congress pushed through a bill in 1978 that for the first time provided a
statutory basis for the SBA 8(a) program. Unlike the temporary public
works set-asides of 1977, the SBA bill established MBE set-asides as a permanent federal agency program. Approved by voice vote in both chambers, it required each federal agency to establish an Office on Small and
Disadvantaged Business Utilization to implement MBE procurement
requirements in the agency's contracts and grants.

The emergence of minority set-asides in 1977–78 demonstrates the two-
tiered nature of civil rights policymaking in the 1970s. Policies such as
racial school busing, college admissions, or abortion rights, in which Washington authority directly impinged on community institutions (schools,
universities, hospitals, clinics), engaged a broad public in debate and
brought elected officials under close scrutiny. Public disapproval of racial
school busing was so intense, for example, that Congress in 1977 passed
and President Carter signed an appropriations rider prohibiting HEW
from requiring school districts to pair or cluster schools to facilitate racial
integration. On the other hand, civil rights policies of a complex regulatory
nature, such as the Philadelphia Plan, the SBA 8(a) MBE program, or contract set-asides in government procurement, escaped the notice of most
voters. Regulatory politics was an inside-the-beltway game, where interest groups sought to join the game, not to break it up.[42]

In November 1980, Republican Ronald Reagan crushed Carter's bid for
reelection. Reagan brought to power in Washington a conservative insurgency that had been building momentum throughout the 1970s. As a presidential candidate, Ronald Reagan declared: "We must not allow the noble
concept of equal opportunity to be distorted into federal guidelines or quotas which require race, ethnicity, or sex—rather than ability and qualifica-
tions—to be the principal factor in hiring or education."[43] Reagan proposed to deregulate not only Washington's economic regulation, as Carter
had begun to do, but also its social regulation, including affirmative action
programs based on group rights that the Carter administration had
expanded.

Reagan inherited another legacy from the Carter administration, a blue-
ribbon commission on immigration, that reflected common concerns more
than disagreements. During the Carter years the "stagflation" afflicting the
American economy since 1973 had worsened, producing double-digit
inflation accompanied by low productivity and high unemployment.

These conditions strengthened public resentment of snowballing immigration. That immigration should be snowballing in the stagnant economy of the late 1970s was both worrisome and puzzling, given the assurances surrounding the 1965 immigration act that the reforms would not significantly increase the flow of immigrants. There seemed, in 1980, to be little connection between the two issues, affirmative action programs and an explosion of immigration. Both developments, however, were consequences of the civil rights reforms of the 1960s that were unintended, unexpected, accelerating in momentum, and increasingly controversial. Their common link was the American job market, which even in its stagnant state in 1980 was attracting immigrants in massive numbers, both legally and illegally. This in turn compounded the problem of affirmative action, which pitted native-born minorities against native-born whites, by adding a third competitor, immigrants of Latin American or Asian origin, who ironically enjoyed advantages over both.

5

The Return of Mass Immigration

The shift in federal civil rights policy, from an equal treatment basis in the 1960s to an equal result basis in the 1970s, demonstrates a modern trend toward unintended consequences in social legislation. The phenomenon of surprising results from policy changes is not unique to reforms of the 1960s. But so ambitious was the agenda of Great Society reforms in the 1960s, and so hurried was much of their planning and enactment during the vast legislative outpouring of 1964–68, that unintended consequences flourished. Historian Steven Gillon, in his book *"That's Not What We Meant to Do,"* discusses five such boomerang reforms since Franklin Roosevelt's New Dealers came to Washington in 1933.[1] Three of Gillon's examples are 1960s programs: the Community Mental Health Act of 1963, which de-institutionalized the mentally ill; the Civil Rights Act of 1964; and the Immigration Act of 1965. The latter two reforms, although effective in achieving their immediate, intended results, have become modern classics of unintended long-term consequences.

The Decline of European Immigration

As we have seen, the bipartisan sponsors of the Immigration and Naturalization Act of 1965 pledged that it would abolish the national origins quota system but not otherwise significantly change the number or composition of immigration to America. Initially the immigration reforms of 1965 appeared to work as intended. During the late 1960s and early 1970s, most immigrants came to America from southern and eastern Europe, as the law's sponsors had predicted. Immigration officials gave priority to working through a backlog of visa applications from relatives of American citizens living in the poorer nations of Europe's Mediterranean rim. Partly for this reason, every year between 1965 and 1975 the largest arriving group was Italian. Greece and Portugal were major sending countries as well, averaging more than 20,000 immigrants annually during the law's first decade. Only Poland, among the major contributing countries of the "Great Wave" era, declined in immigration numbers after 1965. There the communist government, fearing a brain drain and a propaganda loss, clamped down on exit permissions after 1965. Thereafter Poland never even filled the 6,524 annual quota it was given under the old national origins system.

Also confirming the immigration reformers' predictions, immigration from western Europe after 1965 declined as well. Partly this was because returning prosperity in the NATO countries and in Germany, Sweden, and Switzerland dried up immigration. By the 1960s, European recovery was producing labor shortages, often alleviated by importing large numbers of foreign guest workers, especially from Greece, Turkey, and southern Italy. Immigration to the United States from western and northern Europe also declined, however, because under the 1965 law, aspiring immigrants from these countries could often no longer obtain visas. For these countries, the large, unused visa quotas of the past were gone, replaced by a preference system that placed them at a disadvantage. The new preference system favored immediate family members. But few citizens of Germany or Britain had close family relatives in the United States. Moreover, by July 1968, when the new immigration system fully took effect, there was already a waiting list for visas for the two skills preferences—48,000 for third preference (scientists and professionals) and 34,000 for sixth preference (skilled workers). On July 1, 1968, visa applicants from northern and western European nations, previously accustomed to American visas on demand, went to the bottom of the preference lists.

Especially hard hit were visa applicants from Ireland, where a chronically weak economy made emigration to America attractive. But because most Irish immigrants had come to America before the Civil War, Irish-American family connections by the late twentieth century were rarely close enough to qualify for family reunification preferences. Also, most Irish workers were unskilled and hence were blocked by the U.S. Labor Department's entry permit standards. Under the new system, Labor Secretary Willard Wirtz explained to the White House in early 1968, "The best estimates are that Irish immigration will cease for two or three years" (such candid statements were not for public consumption). Members of Congress with large Irish-American constituencies began to propose special bills to provide more visas for Europeans. Emanuel Celler himself, disturbed by the steep decline of European immigration, introduced a bill to allow higher immigration from Ireland, Britain, and the Scandinavian countries, which he said had suffered from "unintentional discrimination" as a result of his own law. Efforts to provide relief for stymied European immigration built up enough pressure by 1972 for a bill to pass the House by voice vote that provided special visas to would-be immigrants from Britain, Ireland, Germany, the Netherlands, the Scandinavian countries, Czechoslovakia, Poland, and the Soviet Union. But the bill made no progress in the Senate, where equal representation for thinly populated rural states weakened the political clout of urban-ethnic concentrations. As a consequence of all these forces, immigration from Europe fell from 113,400 in 1965 to an annual average of 65,000 in the late 1970s.

The Surge of Immigration from Latin America and Asia

Legal immigration from Latin America and Asia, on the other hand, increased sharply after 1965. Latin American countries sent 88,400 immigrants to America in 1965, as compared with 113,400 from Europe and another 38,300 from Canada, most of the latter European in ethnic origin as well. By 1970, however, immigration from Latin America had grown by 30 percent, to 115,200. During the 1970s, legal immigration from Latin America totaled 1.8 million, more than 40 percent of total immigration to the United States. During the 1980s legal Latin American immigration doubled to 3.5 million, 47.6 percent of the decade's total. Immigration from Asian countries, only 20,700 in 1965, had grown by 1970 to 85,700. In only five years Asian immigration, starting from a lower base, had quadrupled, while immigration from Europe as a whole was rapidly declining. During the 1970s Europeans contributed only 17.8 percent of immigration to the United States, and during the 1980s this fell to 9.6 percent. Asian immigration during the 1970s totaled 1.6 million (36.4 percent of the total), and during the 1980s rose to 2.8 million (38.4 percent). Table 5.1 shows the sharp regional shift in immigrant origin from Europe to Latin America and Asia, and table 5.2 shows the dominant pattern of Third World immigration by the 1980s. What had happened to produce such surprising results in legal entry, with immigration from Europe drying up and immigration from Third World countries flooding in?

Table 5.1   Regional Origin of U.S. Immigrants, 1951–1990

Country of Birth	1951–60	1961–70	1971–80	1981–90
Europe & Canada	70.2%	45.9%	20.4%	11.2%
Latin America/Carib.	22.5%	39.0%	40.3%	47.2%
Asia	6.2%	13.4%	36.4%	38.4%
Africa & other	1.1%	1.8%	2.8%	3.2%

Source: 1996 Statistical Yearbook of the Immigration and Naturalization Service, 21.

Table 5.2   U.S. Immigration from the Top 15 Countries
of Last Residence, 1981–1990

Rank	Country of last residence	Immigrants
1	Mexico	1,655,843
2	Philippines	548,764
3	China	444,962 (includes Taiwan & Hong Kong)
4	Korea	333,746
5	Vietnam	280,782
6	Dominican Republic	252,035
7	India	250,786
8	El Salvador	213,539
9	Jamaica	208,148
10	Canada	156,938
11	Cuba	144,578
12	Haiti	138,379
13	Soviet Union	128,575
14	Colombia	122,849
15	Iran	116,172

Source: 1997 *Statistical Yearbook of the Immigration and Naturalization Service,* 26.

One factor was the "push" side of the push-pull equation that always drove world migration patterns. The postwar population explosion in Third World countries was a familiar topic of public inquiry, including studies sponsored by the Rockefeller Foundation and U.S. government agencies.[2] In Mexico, for example, the net annual population growth rate in 1960 was 3.5 percent, and Mexican women had an average of 7.2 children, one of the highest fertility indicators in the world. Testimony in the Feighan committee's immigration hearings between 1963 and 1965 had addressed population pressures as a factor driving immigration, particularly in nearby Latin American countries. Demographer Nathan L. Whetton of the University of Connecticut told the Feighan committee in 1963 that in Mexico, characterized by widespread poverty, large families, low literacy, urban overcrowding, and high joblessness, the population had increased by 78 percent between 1940 and 1960. "In the last ten years," Whetton told the committee, "there have been about 400,000 immigrants from Mexico into the United States, in addition to some 3 million braceros or farmhands coming in and out from the United States." Congressman Frank Chelf of Kentucky, questioning Whetton on the demographic numbers, pointed out that immigration from Mexico had been 60,589 in the decade 1941–50, but in the 1950s had jumped to 299,811. Whetton replied that immigration from Mexico in 1962 had exceeded 55,000; at that level and rate of growth, legal immigration from Mexico during the 1960s would exceed half a million.

The national media, however, paid little attention to the Feighan committee hearings, and the discussion of population trends in the immigration debate fell largely on deaf ears. Sam Erwin had raised the same questions in the Senate hearings, citing population pressures in his drive to bring Western Hemispheric nations within the immigration ceilings. Erwin's political leverage in 1965 stemmed from his position as chief Senate opponent of the immigration bill, and led the reluctant Johnson administration and the congressional leadership to agree to his demand that immigration ceilings include the Western Hemisphere. In both the House and the Senate, population issues were briefly aired, politely heard in committee testimony, and subsequent ignored. Because the American economy enjoyed an unprecedented run of expansion between 1940 and 1973 and showed strong employment growth during the mid-1960s, and because immigration had remained low for forty years, immigrants in the 1950s and 1960s were not generally resented as a source of unfair competition for American jobs, and Third World population trends were little perceived by the American public as a threat to economic well-being.

The "pull" side of the push-pull equation was, of course, the American economy itself, the robust job market and the fabled attractions of the Promised Land. So powerful was this magnet, especially among citizens of overpopulated, underdeveloped countries in Latin America and Asia, that immigration (illegal as well as legal) boomed even during the sharp economic downturn in the United States during the "stagflation" decade of 1973–83. Rising unemployment and worsening economic conditions during the Carter presidency brought increased criticism of immigration, especially the continuing flood of illegal entry across the porous Mexican border and by boat from Caribbean islands. But the immigration explosion, most of it legal, was sparked by policy changes in the 1965 law that mediated between the push factors overseas and the pull factors at home. Two policy changes in particular in the 1965 law produced consequences unforeseen by the reformers. Both involved family reunification provisions that, in hindsight, largely short-circuited the numerical ceilings that were politically essential to passing the bill. One involved family reunification preferences within the ceilings; the other functioned largely outside the ceilings. Together, they compromised the ceilings concept itself and reshaped the role of family ties and immigrant skills into entering wedges for chain immigration.

Preference Incentives for Chain Immigration

The numerical ceiling system that replaced the national origins quotas in 1965 was designed to produce an annual immigration of around 330,000.

This was the sum of a global ceiling the 1965 law set at 290,000 (170,000 from the Eastern Hemisphere, 120,000 from the Western—the latter ceiling effective in 1968), plus nonquota immigrants (spouses, minor children, and parents of U.S. citizens), and certain exceptions, such as special allotments for refugees from Vietnam, Cambodia, Laos, etc. By 1982, however, total legal immigration per year exceeded 594,000. This was twice the level predicted by the reformers of 1965. And most of it came from outside the ceilings. Immigration subject to the ceilings, for example, stood at 290,000 in 1982. But four-fifths of this (206,000) was consumed by family preferences. Moreover, by the mid-1970s approximately one out of every four aliens admitted for permanent residency was a nonquota immigrant, 90 percent of them admitted outside the ceilings on the basis of family kinships. How and why did this happen?

Congress began granting preferences to immediate family members in 1921 (including brothers and sisters of American citizens), seeking to balance increasing restrictions by easing entry of close relatives to avoid family breakup. Preferring permanent settlers to "birds of passage," Congress encouraged family unification. But in doing so Congress never debated what constitutes a family unit. Every act of immigrant admission in effect broke up a family and created a chain of potential "reunification" claims. Not surprisingly, family reunification became an effective rallying cry for immigration expansionists; family reunification was a mantra not subject to criticism in Congress. As Congress increased the weight of family preferences (as against occupational preferences) from 50 percent in 1952 to 74 percent in 1965, family preferences quickly overwhelmed occupation and skills preferences and undermined the annual ceiling system by driving nonquota admissions to levels exceeding the ceilings themselves. As immigration and naturalization rose, the new citizens claimed nonquota visas to bring in their parents, spouses, and children. As E. P. Hutchinson observed in his detailed history of American immigration policy, "The nonquota admission of relatives, like nonquota admissions as a whole, was in conflict with the policy of restricted immigration, for it opened the door to as many qualified aliens as chose to apply and were found to be admissible."[3]

Within the ceiling system, the chief culprit expanding chain immigration was the preference for brothers and sisters of U.S. citizens. It was included in the 1965 law as the fifth of seven preferences and limited to 24 percent of the preference visas. The potential of the brothers-and-sisters preference was quickly appreciated and exploited by immigration lawyers, consultants, and ethnic church organizations to become the preference system's major gateway to family chain immigration. Parents, spouses, and minor children clustered around the core of the nuclear family, but siblings in large immigrant families vastly expanded the kinship networks. By the 1980s, the brothers and sisters preference was eating up almost two-thirds of family preferences under the ceilings (see table 5.3). In 1985, the waiting list for immigration visas had climbed to 1.7 million, with 70 percent of the ceiling immigration (1,142,100) registered under the brothers and sisters preference.[4] By 1987, the visa waiting list exceeded 2 million. Critics began referring to the 1965 law as "the brothers and sisters act."

Table 5.3   U.S. Immigration Visa Waiting List
by Preference Category, 1985

Preference	Category	Totals
First	Citizen unmarried children	9,848
Second	Res. alien spouse & children	320,698
Third	Scientists & professionals	27,588
Fourth	Citizen married children	81,382
Fifth	Citizen brothers & sisters	1,142,107
Sixth	Skilled workers	49,383
Subtotal		1,631,006
Nonpreference		146,383
Total		1,777,389

Source: David E. Simcox, ed., U.S. Immigration in the 1980s (Boulder, Colo.: Westview Press, 1988), 19.

Ranked second in family reunification traffic under the ceilings was the second preference, for spouses and unmarried children of permanent resident aliens. Allowing immigrants to bring not only their spouses and children but also, once naturalized, their brothers and sisters from their country of birth produced a chain immigration effect that could bring to the United States entire villages and clans from south of the border or from overseas. In *Still the Golden Door*, immigration historian David Reimers provides a flowchart for chain immigration. It describes how a nonimmigrant student attending postgraduate school in the United States obtains a green card to work, achieves citizenship through naturalization, and uses the preference system to bring in eighteen family members within ten years. Each of these may then in turn exploit the family reunification preference system to extend the immigration chain.[5]

Yet this was only part of the story. By the 1980s, immigration that was exempt from the ceiling system typically exceeded ceiling-controlled immigration by a factor of 2. For example, in 1985 ceiling immigration was 264,000. But total legal immigration in 1985 was 570,000. A typical year's distribution of legal immigration in the 1980s would thus include 300,000

Figure 5.1

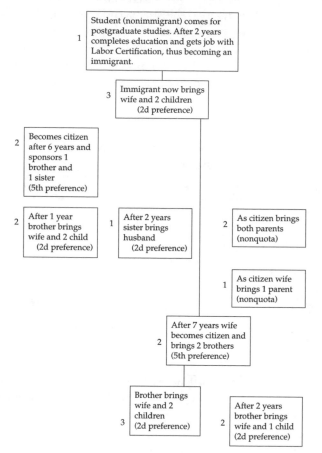

Source: David M. Reimers, Still the Golden Door (New York: Columbia University Press, 1992), 95.

ceiling-exempt immigrants. Approximately 100,000 of them would be refugees and asylees, and 200,000 would be immediate family members of U.S. citizens. Among the immediate family members granted visas, two-thirds were spouses, one-fifth were parents, and the remainder were the minor children of U.S. citizens. Thus when the family preferences within the ceilings were combined with the immediate family visas and refugees exempt from ceilings, the result was a powerful engine of chain immigration that would swamp the compromises and checks and balances negotiated by the immigration policymakers of 1965.

The key to chain immigration was knowledge of how the new system worked and enterprise on the part of a naturalized immigrant (U.S. citizen) or a legal permanent resident, the latter commonly possessing a "green card" permit to work in the United States Throughout history, emigrants seeking to leave their native land (as distinct from refugees fleeing disaster) have typically been enterprising risk-takers, living by their wits. Once in the United States, immigrants anxious to secure their status and bring over their families, had available to advise them, especially after 1965, a growing network of immigration specialists, especially the lawyers of the rapidly growing immigration bar. Immigrant lawyers, like defense lawyers, were dedicated to defeating the government. Immigrants hired immigration lawyers to obtain visas and green cards, win asylum or refugee status, avoid detention and deportation, and generally use the legal and administrative system to remain on U.S. soil, where the American constitutional tradition of *jus soli* provided significant legal advantages.

In the old-world tradition of *jus sanguine*, such as that found in Germany or Japan, citizenship was tied to the "blood" of a people and generally excluded outsiders. But in the Americas, where waves of conquest and settlement had built new nations, citizenship generally attached not to the blood but to the soil, or more to the point, to those resident on the soil. In settler societies with a colonial history (the Americas, Australia and New Zealand, South Africa), a citizenship law of the blood would favor precolonial or aboriginal inhabitants. In *Yik Wo v. Hopkins*, 118 U.S. 356 (1886), the Supreme Court declared that the Fourteenth Amendment, ratified in 1870, protected persons, not just citizens; it applied to "all *persons* within the territorial jurisdiction, without regard to any differences of race, of color, or of nationality." Between the 1880s and the 1940s, the Court generally deferred to Congress on citizenship rights, ruling, for example, in 1922 in *Ozawa v. United States* 260 U.S. 202, that Japanese were not white and therefore not eligible for citizenship. After World War II, however, Congress abandoned racial distinctions in citizenship law, and in 1952 the McCarran-Walter law ended racial exclusions in immigration law. The tradition of *jus soli* led the Supreme Court in 1982, in *Plyler v. Doe*, 457 U.S. 202, to rule unconstitutional a Texas law barring the children of illegal aliens from free public education.

To persons seeking entry into the United States, geographic proximity also conferred clear advantages, especially for immigrants from Mexico and the Caribbean. Would-be immigrants from Asia faced greater difficulties exploiting the 1965 immigration changes. This was partly because of geographic distance, and partly because most Asian immigration had ended before World War I and thus, like the Irish, Asians had few immediate relatives in the United States. The key was to get a foot in the door, and then leverage the system.

Patterns of Chain Immigration

Two main paths were developed to produce chain immigration. One, chiefly used by Asians, used preferences for educated or skilled immigrants to win a green card admitting a physician or nurse, engineer or technician. The settlement process often began with a nonimmigrant student or exchange visitor visa; American universities frequently provided the training needed to obtain green cards. Additionally, refugees provided the initial foot in the door. Between 1975, when the Republic of Vietnam collapsed, and 1985 the United States received for resettlement more than a million refugees, 800,000 of them from Southeast Asia. The skills path to chain immigration encouraged early naturalization to take advantage of the greater family reunification reach, especially the brothers and sisters preference, granted to U.S. citizens over permanent resident aliens. The original immigrant then used the family reunification mechanisms to bring to the United States their spouses, fiancés, children, parents, and brothers and sisters. Each of these in turn could repeat the process, producing an exponential or chain-reaction effect. It was a legal and effective strategy, although it drained source countries of their human resources investments. On the other hand, some countries (India, Korea, the Philippines) trained professionals in numbers beyond their domestic needs to prepare them for immigration to the United States. The result was an ever-expanding cycle of growth that drove the explosion of immigration, especially from Asia, following the Immigration and Naturalization Act of 1965. Chain immigration from Latin America was less reliant on skilled worker trailblazers, owing chiefly to quota-free immigration before 1968.

The most striking example of chain immigration following the 1965 changes involves the rapid growth of foreign-born medical professionals. Changes in American medicine, including the passage of Medicare and Medicaid in 1965 and the expansion of medical technology, services, and specialties, fueled an expansion in the American health care industry that brought 75,000 foreign physicians to the United States under the third preference by 1975. As American-trained physicians pursued lucrative, specialized practices serving mainly medically insured suburban populations, foreign-trained doctors were sought to staff hospitals in the inner cities and rural areas. By 1975, foreign-born physicians accounted for one-fifth of American physicians and one-third of hospital interns and residents. The most immediate effect of this powerful economic magnet for immigrant physicians was a "brain drain" of desperately needed medical professionals, especially from nearby Latin American countries. But over the longer haul the majority of these physicians came from Asia.[6]

The largest bloc came from the Philippines, a former American colony where medical schools commonly used English-language instruction and American textbooks. By 1980, 9,000 Filipino physicians were practicing in the United States, a number representing 40 percent of all Filipino doctors. The Philippines also led in sending nurses to America. During the 1970s the Philippines' fifty nursing schools, graduating 2,000 nurses annually to face an oversupplied domestic market, sent a fifth of their graduates to America. Ranked second in sending physicians was Korea. There Presbyterian missionaries had established American-model medical schools in the century before World War II, and the Korean war intensified Korean-American contacts in the 1950s, especially through war brides. Third was India, which trained and exported English-speaking professionals in the physical sciences and engineering as well as in medicine. Thailand, a country with little historic contact with the United States, jumped on the medical bandwagon in a dramatic way when in 1972 the entire graduating class of Chiangmai Medical School chartered an airplane and emigrated to the United States. China, including Taiwan and Hong Kong, supplied fewer medical professionals than the Philippines, Korea, or India, but sent increasing numbers of natural scientists, mathematicians, and computer scientists to American universities and private industry.

Between 1965 and 1975, the boom years of occupational visas, many immigrants from Asia and Latin America pursued less elite job markets: Chinese restaurant and garment workers, Korean greengrocers, Indian motel proprietors, Mexican agricultural and custodial workers. Occupational preferences, accounting for 60 percent of the quota ceilings in 1970, by 1978 had fallen to only 17 percent of total preference quota visas. By then, however, the chain immigration mechanisms had shifted to a second stage based on family preferences under the ceilings (known, confusingly before 1965, as "quotas"). By the 1980s, typically 70 percent of the ceiling immigration would be admitted under fifth preference (brothers and sisters of U.S. citizens) visas, and 20 percent would be third preference immigrants (spouses and unmarried children of permanent resident aliens). A third stage of chain immigration relied primarily on nonquota visas for the spouses, children, and parents of U.S. citizens. By 1978, for example, Filipino immigration averaged around 40,000 a year, almost half of it nonquota immigration, especially parents brought in after the original immigrant won naturalized U.S. citizenship. The chain migration cycle had thus reached a mature stage relying on both quota preference and nonquota provisions of family reunification and was self-sustaining.

Network Recruiting and Illegal Immigration

The second path to chain immigration, one used by all immigrant groups but especially characteristic of Latin American immigration, was network job recruiting. The term refers to job recruitment by word-of-mouth communication, both locally and across borders, using immigrant kinship and village networks. Unlike occupational visa immigration, with its tie to the ceiling quotas and its preference requirements for education and skills, network recruitment is a market-driven process independent of immigration rules or visa procedures. For self-evident reasons, the availability of American jobs and wage levels has long been the chief driving force behind illegal as well as legal immigration. Word-of-mouth networking identified the location of employers to obtain cheap and docile labor, and also provided nearby immigrant support communities.

Given the population pressures and the economic plight of Mexico, sharing a 2,000-mile border with the United States, networking recruitment has worked effectively with geographic proximity to extend Mexico's lead over all other nations as the largest single supplier of both legal and illegal immigrants. Given its geography and history, Mexico has always been a special case in U.S. immigration policy. Despite the huge American territorial acquisition in the treaty ending the Mexican-American War of 1846–48, Mexican-descended populations in the southwestern states were historically small. The Spanish-speaking population was tiny in the vast, dry territory that today forms the seven states of the Southwest—Arizona, California, Colorado, Nevada, New Mexico, Texas, and Utah. In 1824, the Spanish-speaking population of the Mexican province of Texas—a territory of 39,000 square miles that included most of present-day New Mexico as well as parts of Colorado—numbered only 3,000. With the exception of the California coastal rim and Santa Fe, the Spanish empire never established effective control over the lands dominated by the Indian tribes, especially the fierce Apaches and Comanches, whose military defeated Spanish colonial designs. By 1869, "ethnic Mexicans" were less than 2 percent (12,000) of the population of Texas (600,000). In California in 1900, Mexican-Americans numbered only 8,000. Large-scale migration of Mexicans to the United States was a phenomenon of the twentieth century.[7]

In 1900 the states of Texas, New Mexico, Arizona, California, and Colorado contained only about 100,000 people of Mexican birth. Between 1911 and 1920, revolution and warfare rocked Mexico, killing perhaps a million citizens and sending another million across the loosely supervised U.S. border. Mexican immigration increased after 1910, encouraged by a World War I contract labor program that ran through 1923 and was unaffected by the national origins quota legislation of the 1920s, because the quota system did not apply to the Western Hemisphere. In the late 1920s, as immigration from Europe plummeted and Asian immigration remained minuscule, immigration from Latin America increased—chiefly from Mexico, where the push of violence and depressed economic conditions joined a pull of American demand for cheap labor in southwestern agriculture, mining, and railroads.[8] By 1930, the total in the above states of Mexican-descended residents had soared to 1.25 million, about half of that number Mexican-born. During the Great Depression, Mexican migrants were unwelcome and local and federal officials deported an estimated 400,000. Many illegal border crossers were sojourners, young males who sought higher earnings in the United States and often returned to Mexico. But such labor migrations, whether illegal or through guest worker programs, thickened the networks leading to permanent migration.[9]

During the two decades of the Bracero program, 1943–64, Mexican immigration grew rapidly. During its peak in the 1950s, almost half a million Mexicans temporarily entered the United States yearly. Under the pull of network recruiting and family reunification, immigration from Mexico soared in the 1970s and 1980s. Legal immigrants from Mexico, about 40,000 in 1965, exceeded 90,000 yearly by 1978 and totaled 637,000 for the 1970s. These numbers were greatly exceeded, however, by the growth of illegal entry from Mexico. Annual apprehension of undocumented immigrants, 97 percent of them coming from (or through) Mexico, passed the million mark in 1979 (see table 5.4). The 1980 census estimated the number of illegal immigrants in the United States at 2.5 to 4 million, 77 percent from Latin America and 55 percent from Mexico.

Table 5.4   INS Apprehensions
of Undocumented Aliens

Year	Apprehensions
1964	86,597
1967	161,608
1970	345,353
1973	655,968
1976	875,915
1979	1,076,418
1982	970,246
1985	1,348,749
1988	1,008,145
1991	1,197,875
1994	1,094,717
1997	1,536,520

Source: *1997 Statistical Yearbook of the Immigration and Naturalization Service,* 171.

Mexico's economic dilemma was the need to create a million new jobs a year. Traditional high birthrates and falling death rates in Mexico produced an exploding labor force that could not be absorbed by an economy concentrating on irrigated agriculture and costly state-owned industries, including the capital-intensive petroleum and electricity sectors. Mexico's workers, characterized by low levels of education and training, especially in the displaced agricultural workforce, rose from 14.4 million in 1970 to more than 40 million in 2000. Through most of the 1970s, when the Mexican economy enjoyed a strong growth rate (4.38 percent annually, as against 2.74 percent in the 1960s and 3.23 percent in the 1980s), the Mexican labor force grew by about 750,000 a year, but new jobs approached only 400,000 a year. The result, not surprisingly, was continuing outmigration. By the mid-1980s, when Mexico's economy and currency had collapsed, annual INS apprehensions of undocumented Mexicans exceeded 1.5 million. The 2,000-mile U.S.-Mexican border had become a revolving door, with deported migrants routinely returning. Mexican officials, aggressively policing Mexico's southern border against entry by undocumented migrants from Central American countries, were notoriously corrupt along the U.S. border, practicing extortion on the illegal migrants. By the mid-1980s, more than 350,000 Mexicans were on the waiting list for U.S. immigrant visas. The American embassy in Mexico estimated, however, that 80 percent of the registrants were already living illegally in the United States.[10]

The Reform Movement to Curb Mass Immigration

The nation's political response to the return of mass immigration was shaped by a painful era of economic decline in the 1970s. This in turn quickened the growth of a national conservative movement that would send Ronald Reagan to the White House in the 1980s. The new Republican right of the 1970s was profoundly antistatist. Big Government, in its view, had crippled American enterprise by competing with the private sector, overregulating the economy, spreading bureaucratic waste, and driving up taxes. By slashing government agencies and social programs, the new right would quicken economic growth and at the same time defund the left, which at taxpayer expense had entrenched its philosophy in the social programs of the Great Society. But the conservatives' antistatist imperative excluded agencies that were instruments of national purpose and symbols of national sovereignty and determination (e.g., the Pentagon, the CIA, the FBI, and the Border Patrol). The new right's legacy of traditional values included unabashed patriotism, a nationalist counterpoint to the defeatist, post-Vietnam "malaise" that the Reagan conservatives condemned among Democrats. Consequently, Reagan Republicans embraced a rising public demand in the 1970s for the government to regain control of runaway immigration.

Nonetheless, the unique politics of immigration in America prevented immigration control from developing as a typical left-versus-right partisan issue. In the cross-cutting, bipartisan politics of the immigration issue, Republican business interests lobbied to expand immigration in cooperation with ethnic activists normally hostile to corporate agendas. On the other hand, labor unions and some African-American organizations, normally allied with ethnic-based civil rights groups under the umbrella of the Leadership Conference on Civil Rights, joined conservative and populist groups in working to control immigration and curb job competition from low-wage immigrant workers. These cross-cutting alignments held in the 1920s and were not fundamentally different even in the 1960s.

In the next two decades, however, as rising immigration convinced Americans that immigration was too high and strengthened demands for controlling the nation's borders, the politics of the immigration debate slowly shifted. The drive to restrict the influx of cheap labor began in the early 1970s as a reform pressed chiefly by the Democratic left wing, especially the unions. But as the two major parties polarized in the 1970s— Republicans to the right, Democrats to the left—regaining control of the nation's borders become a watchcry of the Reagan Revolution, a demand increasingly resisted by Democrats in Congress. Within the ranks of the Reagan administration, however, the conservative movement split. The libertarian wing of the Republican Party was attracted to the theory of free labor markets, even across national borders, as well as to the prospect of cheaper labor and weakened unions. Libertarian Republicans therefore defended the economics of mass immigration against traditional conservative calls for regaining control of the nation's borders. By the end of the 1980s, the issue had deeply split the Reagan and Bush administrations, while Democratic constituencies grew more unified (except for the recalcitrant unions) behind expanded immigration. As a result, major immigration laws passed in 1986 and in the 1990s dismayed the immigration control reformers by accelerating the immigration they were initially designed to curb.[11]

It is axiomatic in the politics of immigration that hard times encourage restrictionist demands. The economic distress of the decade following the OPEC oil embargo of 1973 gave American workers increasing reasons to resent job competition from low-wage immigrants. By the end of the 1970s, the unpopular Carter administration seemed helpless against the painful contradictions of "stagflation": declining worker productivity and real wages, high unemployment, a weakening dollar, rising trade and budget deficits, double-digit inflation, and long gas lines. Against this background, news reports featuring an influx of Haitian boat people and tens of thousands of refugees from the lost war in Southeast Asia raised the temperature of the immigration control issue. Between 1975 and the 1980s, more than 300,000 refugees from Vietnam, Cambodia, Laos, and Thailand were settled in American communities, often in circumstances featuring local resistance and cultural conflict. By the late 1970s, when unemployment reached 7 and 8 percent of the labor force, the INS reported that apprehensions of undocumented workers from Mexico alone was exceeding a million a year. In the wake of the humiliating Iran hostage crisis in 1979, Americans watched televised scenes of thousands of Iranian students on American campuses cheering for the Ayatollah. In the spring of 1980, Fidel Castro launched from the Cuban port of Mariel a flotilla of boats containing 125,000 refugees. The Mariel boatlift was welcomed by Miami's passionately anti-Castro refugee community. But it also flooded Florida with thousands of convicted criminals and mental patients who, flushed from Castro's jails, ravaged south Florida and soon filled federal lockups. By 1980, when urban drug wars and violent crime alarmed American voters, drug smuggling was dominated by networks tied to supply bases in Columbia, Jamaica, and other Latin American countries, and 25 percent of federal prisoners were convicted of drug crimes.[12]

In response to these events, public opinion shifted against mass immigration. Americans have traditionally been ambivalent about immigration, cherishing the Statue of Liberty ethos but fearing the strangeness of foreigners, especially in large numbers and in times of economic distress.[13] In an ABC News-Harris survey of May 26, 1980, 75 percent of respondents agreed with the statement that "it is wrong for us to let so many Cuban and other refugees into this country when we are having real economic troubles at home and unemployment is on the rise." Sixty-two percent agreed that "Castro made us look foolish when he forced the U.S. to take so many criminals, mental patients, and other misfits as refugees to the U.S." Polls showed opposition to the Cuban influx to be even higher among black respondents (73%/15%) than among whites (68%/24%). The alarm triggered by the Mariel boatlift echoed an accumulation of grievances, especially felt by conservative voters, against multiculturalist campaigns, chiefly led by Chicano organizations and implemented by federal civil rights enforcement agencies, to require bilingual/bicultural education in the public schools, bilingual ballots in federal and state elections, and even to count illegal immigrants in electoral redistricting procedures.[14] The tax revolt movement in California, gaining national attention with the passage of Proposition 13 in 1978, inspired studies by conservative groups emphasizing the heavy demands immigrants placed on local social services, such as schools, welfare assistance, and hospitals providing emergency and childbirth services, as well as on federal support programs such as food stamps and social security supplements. In Los Angeles County, where Hispanics had grown from 7 percent of the population in 1950 to 30 percent in 1980, and one-seventh of the residents were thought to be illegal immigrants, officials estimated they spent more than $100 million in fiscal 1980 on health care for illegal residents. An Urban Institute study found that when public school costs were included, Mexican immigrant households in Los Angeles County in 1980 cost almost twice as much in state and local government expenditures than they paid in taxes.[15]

The Shifting Politics of Immigration Control

As the immigration control issue strengthened in the 1970s, the first political response in Washington came chiefly from the Democrats, especially pro-labor Democrats in the House. The AFL-CIO, successful in halting the Bracero program in 1964, had played a more marginal role in shaping the 1965 immigration statute. That law, because it was chiefly a quick fix to dismantle the national origins quotas and replace them with a kinship-dominated visa preference system, did not attempt to reformulate the government's complex control system, a notoriously inefficient system last addressed in the McCarran-Walter Act of 1952. By the late 1960s, labor leaders were eager to organize the nation's low-wage migrant farm workers under the leadership of Cesar Chavez, the Mexican-American head of the AFL-CIO National Farm Workers Union, whose grape strike against California growers in the mid-1960s had become a cause célèbre among liberals. AFL-CIO leaders knew that success in organizing farm workers depended on stemming the flood of undocumented migrant workers from Mexico. In 1972 and 1973, House Democrats succeeded in passing bills outlawing the employment of undocumented workers. Both bills, however, were blocked in the Senate. There rural interests were overrepresented, growers concentrated their lobbying, and the Senate Judiciary Committee was chaired by a conservative planter from Mississippi, James Eastland.[16]

In 1977, President Carter responded to growing public concern over the influx of Vietnam War refugees, Caribbean boat people, and Mexican border crossings by proposing legislation not only to strengthen the Border

Patrol but also to prohibit employers from hiring undocumented workers. Because such statutes would require civil penalties for enforcement sanctions, including civil fines and possibly criminal penalties for persistent violators, they were called "employer sanction" laws in media shorthand. Carter's 1977 proposal included a carrot to balance the stick of employer sanctions, an amnesty provision for aliens illegally residing in the United States for at least seven years. Amnesty was a humanitarian gesture, intended to shift a vulnerable, "shadow" population to legal status, and intended also to appeal to the Democrats' growing Hispanic constituency.

Carter's immigration proposal soon bogged down in Congress, however. Part of a shower of proposals Carter sent to the Democratic-controlled Congress in 1977, it encountered resistance not only in the Senate but also in the House, where Speaker Thomas "Tip" O'Neill of Boston showed little enthusiasm. O'Neill feared the immigration issue's potential for splitting the Democratic coalition, pitting the party's traditional restrictionist constituencies (AFL-CIO, NAACP) against Latino and left-liberal constituencies (National Council of La Raza, MALDEF, the ACLU) and the Roman Catholic Church. The small but growing Hispanic Congressional Caucus objected that employer sanctions would increase discrimination against job seekers with foreign names or appearance. To defuse the issue and buy time, Carter agreed in 1978 to join Congress in establishing a select commission on immigration and refugee policy to study the issue and make recommendations. The blue ribbon commission, called the Hesburgh Commission after its chairman, Father Theodore Hesburgh, president of Notre Dame University, was directed to report to the president and Congress in 1981, thus quieting the divisive immigration issue through the 1980 elections.

Before 1979, the restrictionist forces lacked a major full-time lobbying organization. That year, a coalition of environmentalists and restrictionists formed the Federation of American Immigration Reform (FAIR) to support immigration control legislation. The effort was led by Dr. John Tanton, a Michigan ophthalmologist, Planned Parenthood and Sierra Club leader, and former national chairman of Zero Population Growth.[17] Other restrictionist organizations participated in the immigration reform debates of the 1980s and 1990s. These included the Carrying Capacity Network, Population-Environment Balance, and the Center for Immigration Studies, which were all Washington-based organizations, like FAIR, emphasizing the linkage between population, environmental, and immigration issues. Voicing more traditional conservative views was the American Immigration Control Foundation of Monterey, Virginia. But FAIR soon became the lead voice of restrictionist reform in congressional hearings and press reports.

The Federation of American Immigration Reform and Public Opinion

FAIR not surprisingly drew support from cultural conservatives, for example, those who valued assimilation and national unity in the traditions of western civilization. They responded to FAIR's mail appeals and predominated in its membership. But FAIR, especially at the level of its national board and staff, combined this with support from two kinds of liberal constituencies.[18] One was the traditional, working-class liberalism of organized labor, opposing guest worker programs and supporting employer sanction laws. To protect American jobs and wages and to combat illegal immigration, FAIR lobbied for a program of employer sanctions enforced through a verifiable worker identification card system, similar to those used in most European nations. FAIR ultimately argued, however, that the core of the problem was legal, not illegal, immigration, which should be capped, adjusted downward as unemployment rose, and revised in priorities to emphasize job skills, deemphasize family reunification, and curb chain immigration.[19] These proposals responded to present needs, felt by contemporary voting Americans threatened by high unemployment, downward pressure on wages, and rising job insecurity. FAIR's employer sanction and worker identification arguments were supported by the AFL-CIO and the American Legion, given tacit support by the NAACP and the National Urban League, and were consistent with the recommendations of the Hesburgh Commission.

FAIR's most distinctive appeal, however, derived chiefly from its other liberal constituency, the quality-of-life liberalism of the environmental movement. Theirs was an agenda of uncompromising government regulation to protect the environment, the opposite of the Reagan Revolution. Even conservatives on FAIR's board shared a commitment to national and worldwide population stabilization. FAIR's most visionary appeals spoke for constituencies yet unborn, and hence unorganized and unrepresented at the bargaining table—the grandchildren of the twenty-first century who would inherit the world shaped by the post-1960s policymakers. Jimmy Carter, in asking Congress for a new energy policy based on conservation and national sacrifices, was a crusader for this unborn constituency. Carter, however, found little sympathy among the jostling interest groups in Congress, inattentive by instinct to unborn, nonvoting constituencies.

In a spirit similar to Carter's conservationist energy proposals, FAIR called for the immigration debate to rise to a higher level of national goal setting and strategic planning that emphasized long-term national interest. FAIR urged lawmakers to shape immigration policy to the overarching needs of a national population and resources policy.[20] FAIR emphasized demographic projections of U.S. population growth into the twenty-first century, a trajectory that through mass immigration would reverse the population stability achieved by the 1970s. The result, FAIR argued, would be to severely overtax the nation's carrying capacity. New Americans by the tens of millions, and their children and grandchildren (and those of their brothers and sisters from overseas), would crowd the already over-taxed cities, fill the open spaces with suburbs, jam the highways with cars and trucks, poison the air with pollutants, and fill the lakes and streams with agricultural insecticides and industrial toxins. Such an expanding, growth-and-consumption-oriented America would poison its own nest. Increasingly, it would import and consume a hugely disproportionate share of the fossil fuels and minerals in the Earth's crust.[21]

FAIR's chief asset in the immigration control debates was public opinion. By the late 1970s American voters struggling with economic "stagflation" seemed no more receptive to FAIR's population and environmental arguments than they were to Jimmy Carter's energy conservation proposals. But most Americans were angry about uncontrolled immigration and unfair job competition from low-wage aliens. In response to Carter's 1977 immigration proposals, the Gallup poll found American opinion strongly backing strict immigration controls. An October 1977 Gallup poll found 77 percent of respondents favoring an employer sanctions law. Sixty-two percent agreed and 33 percent disagreed that all workers should carry an identification card. By a margin of 52 to 37 percent, moreover, Americans opposed Carter's amnesty provision to legalize undocumented workers living in the United States at least seven years. As the immigration control debates intensified, the Gallup poll asked the same three questions—about employer sanctions, worker identification cards, and amnesty—in 1980 and again in 1983. With the economy still showing high inflation and unemployment, public support for strict immigration control hardened. Gallup reported in 1983 that 79 percent of Americans wanted an employer sanctions law, 66 percent approved worker identification cards, and 66 percent opposed amnesty.[22]

The strong national consensus behind immigration control included minorities as well as whites. In a 1980 poll, Gallup found 66 percent of respondents agreeing that the government should halt all immigration when unemployment exceeded 5 percent. Among nonwhites the agreement was 79 percent. In 1983, when 79 percent of the national sample supported a ban on hiring illegal aliens, 62 percent of Hispanic respondents also agreed. In 1983, FAIR commissioned a poll by Peter Hart and Lance Tarrance—Democratic and Republican pollsters, respectively—to survey black and Hispanic opinion on immigration issues. The survey reported that 66 percent of Hispanics who were American citizens and 53 percent of those who were not citizens backed employer sanctions. Sixty percent of blacks and 57 percent of Hispanics opposed making illegal immigrants eligible for welfare. A majority of both groups agreed that "illegal immigrants hurt the job situation for American workers by taking away jobs."[23] In the early 1990s, the first comprehensive national survey of Hispanic-American opinion, the Latino National Political Survey, found that 80 percent of Puerto Rican Americans, 75 percent of Mexican-Americans, and 66 percent of Cuban-Americans wanted immigration to the United States reduced.[24]

The Simpson-Mazzoli Immigration Reform Bill and Its Opponents

The campaign during the 1980s to pass an immigration control bill, culminating in passage of the Immigration and Refugee Control Act of 1986 (IRCA), centered on a bipartisan package cosponsored by Wyoming Republican Alan K. Simpson in the Senate and Kentucky Democrat Romano L. Mazzoli in the House. Simpson, a member of the Hesburgh Commission, was the Republican point man on immigration control in the Senate, which Republicans captured in Reagan's landslide victory over Carter in 1980. Simpson's bill reflected the carrot-and-stick recommendations of the Hesburgh Commission, which linked tightened control of illegal immigration and an amnesty provision that would expand legal immigration. Like President Carter, the commission proposed employer sanctions accompanied by an amnesty program. The commission also recommended development of a reliable worker identification system and some measure of relief for growers of perishable crops whose labor supply would be reduced by sanctions and legalization. Nevertheless the Hesburgh report, despite its carrot-and-stick balance, reflected the national mood of resentment at the immigration invasion. "If it is a truism to say that the U.S. is a nation of immigrants," the report observed, "it is also a truism that it is one no longer, nor can it become a land of unlimited immigration."[25]

Simpson's main goal was to pass a workable employer sanctions law. He understood the political need to balance employer sanctions with some kind of amnesty provision, even though he personally opposed amnesty as a reward for lawbreaking. Simpson also resisted proposals by western and southern growers for a new agricultural guest worker program, and he supported ending the brothers and sisters preference in order to curb chain immigration. Simpson was joined, somewhat surprisingly, in his Senate efforts by Democrat Ted Kennedy, who emphasized the carrot provisions to grant amnesty and expand legal immigration, including "diversity" visas for groups little helped by family reunification preferences, such as the Irish. Simpson's co-sponsor in the House, Romano Mazzoli, was a moderate Democrat from Louisville who in 1981 became chairman of the House Immigration Subcommittee (which was part of the Judiciary Committee in both chambers). Like Simpson, Mazzoli was a relative newcomer to immigration issues. Unlike Simpson, a flinty westerner who was widely respected in the Republican-controlled Senate, Mazzoli was unpopular among House Democrats, who resented his tendency to vote against his party. Both men represented constituencies with few immigrants and hence were unusually free of narrow electoral interests in seeking reform.[26]

The new Reagan administration in 1981 embraced the spirit of the Hesburgh Commission report. But the leadership from the White House on immigration reform was ambivalent. On the one hand, President Reagan spoke of an "immigration emergency" in America. His attorney general, William French Smith, voiced the alarum of traditional conservatives that as a nation "we have lost control of our borders." Smith chaired an immigration policy task force during the first year of the Reagan administration and generally aligned his recommendations with the views of the Republican Party's traditional conservative constituencies. Reagan's senior White House staff, on the other hand, kept Simpson at a distance, fearing that employer sanctions would alienate Republican business interests. The libertarian, free-market, supply-side wing of the Reagan Revolution, represented by the *Wall Street Journal* and the Heritage Foundation, was pleased that mass immigration flooded the American labor market, dampening wage pressures and weakening the power of organized labor. Supply-side Republicans dominated the Office of Management and Budget and Reagan's Council of Economic Advisers. The White House paid lip service to supporting Simpson, but balked at worker identification proposals and favored the unpopular temporary worker program for growers. As a consequence, the White House did not play a leading role in the immigration debates of 1981–86.[27]

At hearings before the joint Senate-House immigration subcommittees in April 1982, witnesses addressed the specific provisions of the similar bills Simpson and Mazzoli had introduced in their respective chambers on March 17. Partly for this reason, spokesmen for the concerned interest groups avoided the broad themes of national well-being that gave weight to their advocacy. FAIR executive director Roger Conner, for example, emphasized at the hearings the harm mass immigration inflicted on the poor, minority Americans and working women by depressing wages and displacing native workers. Conner urged a 425,000 annual ceiling on legal immigration (noting that visas exceeded 800,000 in 1980). He supported employer sanctions enforced through a secure worker identity card, backed Simpson's call for an end to the brothers and sisters preference to curb chain immigration, and cautioned against a broad legalization program that would trigger massive subsequent family preference claims. But Conner's testimony, constrained by time and focus, did not press the environmental and population-based arguments that also animated FAIR's agenda.[28] The other witnesses supporting employer sanctions, such as the AFL-CIO's Lane Kirkland, similarly stuck to the specifics of the bill, although the NAACP's Althea Simmons did exclaim that the country "must decide how many people we can absorb."

Witnesses hostile to employer sanctions, especially the representatives of Hispanic organizations, similarly avoided making broad claims supporting high immigration—for example, positive claims that it was good for the economy, lowered the costs of goods and services, and balanced an aging workforce. Instead, the theme that linked Hispanic spokesmen in the Simpson-Mazzoli hearings was chiefly negative: Hispanics are victims of discrimination in America. Testimony by spokesmen for MALDEF, the GI Forum, the National Council of La Raza, and the League of United Latin American Citizens (LULAC) emphasized claims to racial discrimination that linked Hispanics, whether immigrants or natives, to the black civil rights model of protected classes. The Hispanic civil rights organizations were heavily financed by the Ford Foundation, whose president from the late 1960s through the 1970s was McGeorge Bundy, Harvard alumni veteran of the Kennedy White House and tower of the nation's eastern liberal establishment. In 1968 Ford had created MALDEF, as a Latino version of the NAACP, with a $2.2 million founding grant. La Raza, given a similar birthing grant of $630,000 by Ford in 1968, received $1,953,700 two years later. Between 1970 and 1999, Ford gave MALDEF $27.9 million and La Raza $21.5 million.[29]

In 1981 Ford started funding LULAC, the oldest Hispanic association. Noted since its origins in Texas in 1929 for espousing patriotism, political moderation, self-help ethic, support for English language mastery, and bourgeois civic boosterism, LULAC in the 1970s adopted the strident tone of Chicano nationalism common to La Raza and MALDEF. In 1983 the Ford Foundation, led by Ford's first African-American president, Franklin A. Thomas, began funding the National Immigration Forum, an umbrella association modeled on the Leadership Conference on Civil Rights, to coordinate lobbying against restrictionist organizations such as FAIR.[30] LULAC, although joining the racialized agenda of MALDEF and La Raza in the 1970s, retained its character as a membership-based organization rooted in the Hispanic (mainly Mexican-American) community.[31] But the constituency represented by MALDEF and La Raza was essentially the Ford Foundation and the tightly networking community of Latino political careerists.[32]

At the April 1982 hearings before the joint immigration subcommittees, LULAC's Tony Bonilla cited EEOC reports documenting that Hispanics, like blacks, were historic victims of discrimination in America. "The INS has been looked upon," Bonilla said, "as the enemy of the Hispanic, with no mercy, participating in indiscriminate raids of the workplace, participating in separation of families, and selective enforcement of the immigration laws." There was no Hispanic Caucus in the Senate, but in the House, under Democratic control since the early 1950s, the Hispanic Congressional Caucus was organized in 1976. Like its model, the Congressional Black Caucus, Hispanic Caucus members, with rare exception, were liberal Democrats.[33]

The Battle over the Simpson-Mazzoli Bill

The Simpson-Mazzoli bill began with considerable momentum in the spring of 1982, but then followed a tortured, four-year path to enactment. A pattern of passage in the Senate followed by death in the House was established early. On three occasions—1982, 1983, and 1985—the Senate passed Simpson's immigration reform bill, only to have Mazzoli's companion bill expire in the House. In 1982, the House Judiciary Committee passed a bill sponsored by Mazzoli, but it died in the closing hours of a lame-duck session. The following year, 1983, both chambers passed a bill, but Senate-House conferees could not bridge their differences. Disagreements on immigration issues, cutting across party and ideological lines, made consensus elusive. When IRCA finally passed in the fall of 1986, it was scarcely recognizable as the original Simpson-Mazzoli immigration control statute.

In the House, both the agribusiness lobby and the Hispanic Caucus opposed sanctions, although for different reasons. Neither growers nor the Hispanic caucus wanted to curb the flow of migrants from Latin America. But in formal testimony they emphasized less self-serving reasons. Employers resisted obligations to police the ban on hiring illegals, and Hispanic lobbies objected to civil liberties threats from a national worker identity card and to job eligibility requirements that might discriminate against minorities. Liberal Democrats opposed guest worker programs demanded by growers, and conservatives opposed the amnesty provisions as rewards for lawbreaking. Speaker O'Neill delayed bringing Mazzoli's bill to the floor until well into 1984, when the presidential election further polarized the debate, and economic recovery weakened restrictionist leverage. Democratic presidential nominee Walter Mondale promised Latino political leaders that he would veto employer sanctions. O'Neill pledged that the immigration bill would not reach the floor unless it had been rendered acceptable to Hispanic members of Congress. The Speaker even accused President Reagan of an election year plan to attract Latino votes by vetoing Simpson-Mazzoli. O'Neill compared the bill's worker identification provisions to practices of the Third Reich. "Hitler did this to the Jews," O'Neill said. "He made them wear a dog tag."[34] Although a deeply fractured House passed the bill 216-211 late in 1984, the Senate-House conferees remained far apart, and Congress adjourned without passing the bill, thus requiring proponents to start all over again in Reagan's second term.[35]

The resurrection and passage of Simpson-Mazzoli in 1985–86 was a story of compromise that produced a Pyrrhic victory for the champions of immigration control. Congress, exhausted by the six-year debate, passed IRCA on October 17, 1986, and President Reagan signed it into law on November 6. At the heart of the complex new law was a three-way bargain: an employer sanctions law for the immigration control reformers, an amnesty provision for the liberals, and a farmworker admission program for the growers. The latter ultimately provided for the legalization of about 1 million foreign workers to harvest perishable crops, with a provision for "replenishments" if legalization were to drain undocumented workers from the fields.[36] IRCA's huge agricultural worker program was an unambiguous victory for the growers and a defeat for virtually everybody else— Latino organizations and the Hispanic Caucus, the AFL-CIO, and FAIR, all of whom agreed that guest workers lowered wages and labor standards for all American agricultural workers.

The amnesty program, on the other hand, was a victory for the Latino, ACLU, and Catholic lobbies and, in its generosity and demographic implications, a defeat for FAIR. IRCA provided temporary resident status for aliens who had resided continuously in the United States since before January 1, 1982. At the time there were no reliable estimates of the numbers involved. With the illegal population conservatively estimated at 3-4 million in 1986 and growing by 250,000 to 300,000 a year, and with INS apprehensions for illegal entry still soaring (a record 1.7 million border violators were apprehended in fiscal year 1986), estimates of amnesty-eligible immigrants in 1986 hovered around the 2 million mark.

The crucial selling point of the legalization bargain in Congress was that it was a one-shot amnesty that would eliminate the country's "shadow population." According to this rationale, the new employer sanctions law, together with stiffened INS enforcement, would turn off the job magnet and end the widespread hiring of illegal migrants. As a consequence, the shadow population of fugitive illegals in America would wither away. For these reasons, Simpson and Mazzoli supported amnesty as a humanitarian gesture and a necessary price for winning employer sanctions, the heart of their bill. They knew that politically, without a carrot-and-stick approach that included some sort of amnesty provision, employer sanctions were unlikely to pass. But the result was an amnesty program that strengthened incentives to enter the country illegally and an employee sanctions program that turned out to be a sham.

Roberto Suro, in his 1996 study of American immigration policy for the Twentieth-Century Fund, found that IRCA's amnesty produced "the worst of both worlds." First, because IRCA's amnesty included only aliens who could document residence in the United States since 1982, it excluded approximately 40 percent of the aliens living illegally in the United States, according to INS estimates. This left intact large fugitive populations of undocumented workers in the sanctuary communities of the big American cities that continued to nourish the underground networks. Second, legalization produced a giant logjam in the system as 3 million people (far more than anticipated) gained legal status and thus won the right to sponsor relatives hoping to join them. The amnesty program's agricultural component, expecting 400,000 applicants, instead received 1.8 million "amid well-documented charges of massive fraud," Suro observed, "both by aliens and by many on the U.S. side, including some growers."[37] The amnesty thus created huge waiting lists of relatives in countries having the most immigrants in the United States, countries such as the Philippines, for example, where the waiting time for siblings of U.S. citizens by the 1990s was more than forty years, or India and Mexico, where the wait exceeded twenty years. Not surprisingly, these relatives commonly ignored the law and made their way to the United States anyway, either illegally or on temporary visas they overstayed.

In the wake of IRCA, community workers and demographers noticed that the amnesty seemed to transport almost entire source-country villages to the United States. The pattern was not entirely new; townships in the vicinity of Fuzhou, in China's Fujian Provice (opposite Taiwan), for example, had begun exporting many of their young men to America and Europe long before IRCA.[38] But IRCA's amnesty triggered a wave of migration that transported intact families. Many of their members were newly legalized, but others, in effect, were acting as illegal replacements for undocumented migrants newly amnestied by IRCA. The rapidly expanding market in international immigration was resilient. It reacted quickly to legalize through amnesty its supply of new undocumented workers, taking advantage of family reunification provisions, and thus building pressure for future amnesties. In California, for example, community workers noticed that Mexican immigrants often came from the same villages in Mexico. The *Los Angeles Times*, marking ten years under IRCA's amnesty, described how the village of Granjenal, an empoverished Mexican farm community more than a thousand miles southeast of San Diego, had been emptied by a mass exodus following the passage of IRCA as amnestied migrant workers sent for their families to come to Santa Anna, California.[39] In 2000 the INS released a study showing that IRCA's amnesty, far from eradicating the "shadow population" of illegal aliens, brought in a replacement cohort of illegal immigrants that roughly equaled the number amnestied. Between 1987 and 1997, 2.7 million people received lawful permanent residence (green cards) through IRCA amnesties. But during the same period the former illegals had been replaced by new illegal settlers, the INS study concluded, leaving the unauthorized population at roughly 5 million, just as before amnesty.[40] IRCA's amnesty provision was thus successful in legalizing millions of undocumented immigrants, an intended consequence. But it failed to eradicate America's shadow population of illegal immigrants, instead providing incentives for its renewal and expansion.

The greatest failure of IRCA, however, was that the jobs magnet lying at the heart of the American economy's global gravitational field was scarcely altered by the IRCA reforms that originally were designed to shut it down and protect American workers. By 1986, the compromises the reformers felt politically forced to accept in the sanctions provisions promised to neutralize IRCA's new sanctions machinery. As FAIR's Roger Conner lamented: "We wanted a Cadillac, we were promised a Chevy, and we got a wreck."[41] It would be a few years before they learned how bad a wreck they got.

The Failure of Employer Sanctions

The opponents of employer sanctions had built a broad, left-right coalition and used it to construct a package of antidiscrimination amendments that effectively paralyzed the new law's employment verification system. The antisanctions coalition included, on the right, the U.S. Chamber of Commerce, the National Association of Manufacturers, the National Council of Agricultural Employers, the United Fruit and Vegetable Association, the

National Restaurant Association, and the Associated Builders and Contractors—in sum, the nation's major employer organizations, eager to maintain the flow of hardworking, low-wage, union-resistant immigrant labor. On the left, opponents of sanctions included many liberal organizations active in the civil rights coalition, for example, the ACLU and the American Immigrant Lawyers Association. Church-related groups included the U.S. Catholic Conference, the National Council of Churches, and the American Jewish Committee. The core of sanctions opposition was provided by Latino organizations: MALDEF, La Raza, LULAC, the GI Forum, and the Hispanic Congressional Caucus. Ably orchestrating the antisanctions coalition was the National Immigration Forum, the umbrella organization established in 1982 by Rick Swartz, funded by the Ford Foundation, and modeled after the Leadership Conference on Civil Rights.

Despite survey evidence that Hispanic opinion was mixed and a majority appeared to favor less immigration, Latino political leaders maintained an effective solidarity behind immigration expansion. Elected officials, such as the eleven congressmen in the Hispanic Caucus in the mid-1980s, had much to gain and little to lose by expanding the flow of Hispanic immigration, illegal as well as legal. Electoral redistricting following the 1990 census would sharply expand the number of elected officials, staff, and political patronage available to further Latino careers in public service. The Reagan and Bush Justice Departments shrewdly and quietly cooperated, urging federal judges to require "majority minority" jurisdictions in electoral redistricting to maximize the election of minority candidates. For Republicans, this would pack minority voters into inner-city districts won by Democrats, leaving the surrounding suburbs ripe for Republican capture.[42] Black elected officials, threatened by growing Latino populations in or near their districts, were eager to appease Hispanic constituencies. For this reason the Black Congressional Caucus, unlike the NAACP, showed solidarity with Hispanic members of Congress on immigration issues as early as the 1970s.

The Hispanic-led antisanctions coalition, warning that employers fearing sanctions would discriminate against foreign-looking and foreign-sounding workers, proposed a package of antidiscrimination amendments to Simpson-Mazzoli. Given Speaker O'Neill's pledge to satisfy Hispanic Caucus demands in the Simpson-Mazzoli bargaining, the restrictionist coalition, led by Simpson, accepted a complex series of compromises in the interest of passing the bill. As a result, IRCA imposed a contradictory set of obligations on employers. In addition to facing fines for hiring illegals, employers faced fines for discriminating against foreign-looking workers in the process of attempting to verify employment eligibility. How did this occur? Sanctions opponents were successful in stripping away Simpson-Mazzoli's original provision for a secure national identity card system to verify worker eligibility. Opponents even managed to insert in the bill a ban on subsequent implementation by the executive branch of an identity card program without approval by joint resolution from Congress. For worker verification purposes, opponents substituted instead a list of seventeen documents (subsequently increased to thirty) that applicants might show to establish their identity and eligibility. These included not only passports (even if expired) and temporary resident cards, but also a driver's license, school ID card, nondriver's state ID card, U.S. Social Security card, voter registration card, birth certificate, I-20 form given by colleges to admit foreign students, and similar documents, many of them easily obtained by illegal residents. IRCA prevented employers from requiring different documents or more than two from those the list specified, or from refusing to accept "documents that appear to be genuine."[43] To police such discrimination, IRCA established a new watchdog agency in the Justice Department, the Office of Special Counsel for Immigration Related Unfair Employment Practices.

The result was a contradiction within the employer sanctions law that short-circuited its main purpose, which was to bar jobs to illegal immigrants. It was a classic Catch-22, but for employers it was not a damned-if-you-do and damned-if-you-don't situation. In public comments, employers complained about such contradictory obligations and about the paperwork required. But privately, most employers were pleased. The new system was a bother, but it left them free to observe the pro forma obligations, accept from applicants at face value two documents shown from the menu of thirty, and then hire whomever they wished. IRCA required of employers only a "good faith effort" at compliance, not a careful screening; indeed, a careful screening risked penalties for discrimination. As the vice president of the National Council of Agricultural Employers, Sharon M. Hughes told Congress in subsequent testimony, employers "are hesitant to refuse to accept uncommon documents about which they are uncertain. . . . Employers are charged with a per se violation of the Act if they require more or different documents than are required or refuse to accept tendered documents that appear on their face to be genuine." If employers scrutinized employment documents "too carefully," Hughes said, they faced significant fines.[44]

IRCA required the General Accounting Office to study employer compliance with the sanctions program and the antidiscriminations provisions and report to Congress. In March 1990 the GAO sent Congress its final report. Most of its findings were unexceptional. IRCA had apparently reduced illegal immigration, compliance did not unnecessarily burden employers, and the INS and Labor Department generally carried out their compliance duties in a satisfactory manner. The GAO found no discrimination in 90 percent of the sample of 461,000 employers the GAO surveyed, although there was scattered evidence of discrimination, most of it reflecting employer misunderstanding of IRCA's requirements, e.g., checking documents only concerning foreign-looking job applicants, hiring only U.S. citizens.

Most striking, however, was the evidence in the GAO report of massive fraud and evasion. Aliens apprehended by the INS were often well documented. They "commonly have counterfeit or fraudulently obtained documents," the GAO reported, usually Social Security cards or one of the various INS alien work eligibility cards (20 million old cards were still in circulation). In August and September 1989, the INS ran a check on 222 apprehended aliens. Of these, 127 falsely claimed permanent residence, 39 falsely claimed authorization to work, and 12 falsely claimed U.S. citizenship. To document their claims, the apprehended aliens produced 166 Social Security cards, 81 percent of which were fraudulent, and 110 alien registration cards, 98 percent of which were fraudulent. These two cards accounted for 76 percent of all employer verifications. The GAO quoted one unidentified employer: "The '86 immigration law is unworkable. Documents are easily counterfeited. . . . The going price for a set of counterfeit documents, that includes a SS [Social Security] card, INS work card and an Arizona driver's license, is $300–500."[45]

The Growth of Immigration in the 1990s

In 1986, five of the eleven members of the Congressional Hispanic Caucus voted yes in the final IRCA tally. This surprised some political observers. In hindsight, however, the yea votes confirmed an effective process of wearing down the reformers and defanging their key proposals. Given the goals of the Hispanic Caucus, IRCA provided for them the best of both worlds, responding to the public demand for an employer sanctions law, yet producing a nonfunctional system. As the American economy expanded after 1983 and the Mexican economy collapsed, immigration expanded on all fronts. Amnesty under IRCA greatly expanded visa claims under both the family preference and nonceiling quotas. IRCA's new special agricultural worker program brought in hundreds of thousands of Mexicans to thicken transborder networking. The success of the immigration lobby in neutralizing IRCA's centerpiece, the employer sanctions law, quickened congressional pursuit of expanded legal immigration to benefit organized interest groups. These measures included stays of deportation and expanded political asylum for designated refugee groups (from Cuban, Haiti, El Salvador, the Soviet Union, Tibet, Hong Kong), diversity visas for underrepresented groups (Ireland, Africa), and, increasingly popular with business groups and Republicans in 1990, new temporary worker programs in skilled fields to nourish the booming electronic industry. To appease state and local officials distressed by the fiscal burden of providing heavy welfare and medical services to illegal immigrants, Congress in IRCA and subsequent immigration statutes authorized large reimbursements from the federal treasury. These authorizations, however, were rarely matched by subsequent appropriations in an era of chronic budget deficits in Washington, which lasted until the late 1990s. The passage of IRCA thus whetted rather than sated congressional appetites for immigration bills, which increasingly took on a Christmas tree appearance.

Such an expansive political environment could be changed abruptly by economic recession, which threatened economic security and quickened populist impulses to cut back immigration. This had happened in the late 1970s, when rising resentment of mass immigration in hard times had fueled the reformers backing Simpson-Mazzoli in the early 1980s. It happened once again in the early 1990s, when rising economic discontent spoiled the reelection bid of President Bush and fueled resentment against immigrants in states with high immigration, above all in California, which received about a third of them. Yet the immigration legislation of the 1990s, while maintaining the carrot-and-stick approach seen in IRCA, including a readiness to beef up the Border Patrol and curb immigrant crime and welfare program abuse, increasingly emphasized immigration expansion. Why?

Part of the explanation is partisan. In the 1986 congressional elections the Democrats regained control of the Senate and routinely overrode the vetoes of a president weakened by the Iran-Contra scandal. Social legislation passed by the Democrat-led Congress during 1987–90 included a civil rights restoration bill, legislation strengthening the bargaining power of labor, a renewed and strengthened Clean Air Act, and statutes expanding food stamps, providing aid to the homeless, and protecting against catastrophic illness. In 1989, House Democrats ousted Romano Mazzoli from his chairmanship of the immigration subcommittee and replaced him with a Connecticut liberal, Bruce A. Morrison, keen to expand immigration.[46] In 1990, Congress passed a law that in theory placed a cap on annual levels of immigration, but did so at a level even higher than current visas. It raised annual immigration from 500,000 to 700,000 and significantly increased visa allotments for education and skills, including diversity visas for underrepresented countries and a new temporary worker program, H-1B, to bring in highly skilled workers for electronics and software industries. On the slim, "stick" side of the ledger, Congress in 1990 streamlined deportation procedures for criminal aliens and approved an INS increase of 1,000 Border Patrol officers. The 1990 bill also established a nine-member commission on immigration reform to report to Congress by 1994 on the effects of current immigration law.[47]

The Politics of Immigration Resentment in California

Overall, however, the 1990 law was vigorously expansionist. Annual legal immigration soared after IRCA into the 1990s: 601,516 in 1987, 1,090,924 in 1989, 1,827,167 in 1991. In addition to this flow across the border, in 1991 alone, 1,123,162 in-country immigrants were legalized under IRCA amnesty provisions, 909,159 of them special agricultural workers. By 1992, however, the national economy was in recession. When the end of the cold war flattened California's defense economy in the early 1990s, resentment soared against immigrants, especially illegal migrants, for displacing native-born workers, lowering wage levels and conditions, burdening social welfare and health services, and flooding the public schools with children illegally in residence. Of the nation's estimated 5-6 million undocumented population, California contained 2 million, more than half of them from Mexico and Central America. In 1994, these tensions boiled over into electoral politics in two ways. First, a loose coalition demanding a crackdown on illegal immigrants sponsored Proposition 187, a voter initiative that would exclude the children of illegal aliens from the public schools and deny illegals access to social welfare benefits and nonemergency medical services. Second, Republican Governor Pete Wilson, running for re-election, endorsed Proposition 187, made it a partisan issue, infused its lagging campaign with Republican money and professional expertise, and exploited it as a wedge issue against his Democratic opponent, Kathleen Brown.[48]

The electoral result in November 1994 was passage of Proposition 187 and reelection for Wilson, both by substantial margins. But both causes were tarnished, even in victory. Wilson, during his years in the U.S. Senate, had sponsored IRCA's provision for special agricultural workers—"Wilson workers," they were called, not without irony. Wilson's flip-flop in 1994, from patron of Mexican migrants to their scourge, sang of expediency, especially when he explained that he expected Proposition 187 to pass and then be declared unconstitutional in federal court.[49] And declared unconstitutional it was, not surprisingly, since by denying schooling for illegal children it clashed with the Supreme Court's 1982 ruling in *Plyler v. Doe*.[50]

Proposition 187 was ill designed in another respect. By requiring school teachers, social service workers, and other public employees to report suspected illegal aliens, it seemed to impose a police surveillance role on the state's civil servants. Proposition 187, like so many California initiatives, was a crude blunderbuss of a device, one badly designed for public policymaking but an effective outlet for public frustration. Californians voted 59-41 to pass Proposition 187. Among Asian voters, the split was similar, 57-43 in favor. Although the Catholic Church opposed Proposition 187, non-Hispanic Catholic voters supported it 58-42. Blacks by a slight majority also voted in favor. Only California's Hispanic voters, although initially favoring Proposition 187, shifted against it as the campaign progressed.

The Victory of the Expansionist Left-Right Coalition

Against this backdrop of rising, recession-driven opposition to immigration, Congress passed another major immigration bill in 1996. And once again, as had happened a decade earlier, recession-aided momentum by reformers was largely overcome by a left-right coalition of immigration expansionists.[51] Evidence of restrictionist momentum in the 1990s included, in 1994, Proposition 187 in California, Governor Wilson's reelection, and the Republican capture of both houses of Congress. Political leaders speaking out for curbing immigration abuses included President Clinton in his January 1995 State of the Union address, Senate Republican leader and 1996 presidential nominee Robert Dole, House Speaker Newt Gingrich, Labor Secretary Robert Reich, House Immigration Subcommittee Chairman Lamar Smith of Texas, Senate Immigration Subcommittee Chairman Alan Simpson (replacing Kennedy), and Senator Diane Feinstein, a California Democrat, who supported Simpson's call for a national identity card for American workers. The Commission on Immigration Reform, chaired by former Democratic congresswoman Barbara Jordan of Texas, in 1994 recommended reducing legal immigration levels, eliminating the brothers and sisters preference, tightening sponsorship requirements, and curbing illegal alien use of programs such as Medicaid and

Social Security payments for the elderly poor.[52] "Come to America for opportunity," said Gingrich in an impassioned floor speech. "Do not come to America to live off the law-abiding taxpayer."[53]

By 1996, however, the economy had improved, and the new Republican Congress elected in 1994 proved receptive to the same expansionist pressures as had its Democratic predecessors. Many Republicans of libertarian persuasion, following the *Wall Street Journal*, called for open borders and a free flow of labor as well as capital in the globalized economy. President Clinton, sensing the mood swing, switched from supporting the Jordan Commission's proposed cuts in legal immigration to opposing them. Conservative Republican leaders in Congress, including Rep. Richard Armey and Senators Phil Gramm of Texas and Spencer Abraham of Michigan, opposed measures to tighten employer sanctions enforcement or reduce the flow of immigrant workers. They spoke for the right-wing anchor of the left-right coalition, the libertarian Republicans whose supporters now included the CATO Institute, Americans for Tax Reform, Ralph Reed's Christian Coalition, and the heavy artillery of the high-tech economy— Microsoft, IBM, Cypress Semiconductor, in addition to Proctor and Gamble, Walt Disney, and the National Association of Manufacturers (NAM). With this phalanx of the right added to the Latino-led coalition on the left, Americans found the ACLU lobbying with the National Rifle Association to disarm employer sanctions and increase legal immigration.[54]

Under these circumstances, Congress on the eve of the 1996 presidential election passed legislation that camouflaged an expansionist victory with punitive measures aimed at abuses by illegal immigrants that were marginal to the core problem. The 1996 legislation, titled rather grandly by the Republican Congress the Illegal Immigration Reform and Immigration Responsibility Act and the Antiterrorism and Effective Death Penalty Act, followed the standard model of curbing illegal immigration by enlarging the Border Patrol and beefing up the INS budget. But it was targeted against specific abuses: terrorist entry, illegal alien smugglers, convicted criminals, immigrant abusers of welfare and social services, and the delaying tactics of immigration lawyers who jammed federal court dockets with deportation appeals. The 1996 legislation stiffened penalties for smuggling aliens and using false documents, streamlined asylum hearings, and blocked judicial review of appeals in deportation proceedings. The reforms included tightened requirements for immigrant sponsorship to curb growing reliance on food stamps and federal disability payments by legal immigrants. In both the immigration and welfare statutes of 1996, Congress specified that Social Security benefits were not to be paid to illegal immigrants.

The core problem driving illegal immigration, however, lay elsewhere—in a nonfunctional employer sanctions law that left the American jobs magnet unaltered, and ultimately in high levels of legal immigration, which like a rising tide, pulled armies of kin and countrymen in its wake. In 1996 the expansionist coalition in Congress defeated restrictionist attempts to repair the employer sanctions law. The restrictionist proposal, sponsored by Simpson, for a national toll-free line to verify worker identification with Social Security and INS records was neutralized by the left-right coalition, which transformed it into a feckless three-state experiment that was voluntary for employers.

Expansionists in 1996, successful in confining reforms to relatively narrow abuses and defeating restrictionist attempts to enforce the employer sanctions law, thus left intact, like a default setting, the high-immigration levels and incentive programs inherited from IRCA and the 1990 amendments. Immigration levels continued to exceed the million-a-year mark into the twenty-first century. By the late 1990s, immigration was averaging 1.2 million a year, 800,000 legal and 400,000 illegal. Congress ignored the recommendations of its own advisory panel, the Jordan Commission, to cap annual legal immigration at 550,000, cap refugees at 50,000, expand employment skills visas, and limit family reunification preferences to parents, spouses, and minor children. Congress also ignored the Jordan Commission recommendation that businesses pay a fee to fund job training for native workers in areas of high immigrant demand, such as computing hardware and software. Indeed, importing more such high-skilled immigrants became a business priority following the 1996 law, one aggressively sponsored by the Republican chairman of the Senate Immigration Subcommittee, Spencer Abraham of Michigan, a freshman senator of Lebanese extraction.

By the late 1990s, the surging U.S. economy had reduced unemployment to forty-year lows. Robust worker productivity and full employment elevated real income levels for all ethnic groups, dropping poverty rates to twenty-year lows; median household income in 1999 reached record highs of $27,910 for African-Americans, $30,735 for Hispanics, $44,366 for non-Hispanic whites, and $51,205 for Asian-Pacific Islanders. Households in the bottom fifth of the income scale, victims of a widening wage gap since the 1970s, narrowed the gap for the first time as their household earnings in 1999 rose by 5.4 percent, the largest of any quintile. In this environment, resentment of immigrant job competition weakened, and employers demanded increased immigration to fill jobs, especially those requiring high levels of education and skill.[55]

By the late 1990s, the bipartisan coalition demanding increased immigration had grown on both its left and right flanks. On the left, the greatest change was the reversal by organized labor of its historic restrictionist stance. The change was signaled in 1995 by the election as president of the 13-million-member AFL-CIO of John J. Sweeney, former head of the Service Employees International Union. Sweeney pledged to reverse labor's long decline in membership, from representing 35 percent of the U.S. workforce as union members in the 1950s to 13.8 percent in 1995. Sweeney's strength was organizing low-paid service workers, such as restaurant, hotel, janitorial, and home-care workers, jobs heavy with immigrants. In 1999, Sweeney's organizing drives among such workers increased union membership by 265,000. In the spring of 2000, Sweeney persuaded the AFL-CIO to embrace immigrant workers, oppose employer sanctions, and support amnesty for illegal immigrants. "We are on the side of working people everywhere," announced AFL-CIO executive vice president Linda Chavez-Thompson, whether "they came to this country 400 years ago on slave ships, 100 years ago through Ellis Island in New York harbor or a year ago across the Mexican border."[56]

Labor's defection was a severe blow for the restrictionist coalition, already weakened by tepid support since the 1960s from its other traditional supporter on the left, African-American leaders and organizations opposing immigrant competition with black workers. This left the restrictionist coalition, led by FAIR, overbalanced on the traditionalist conservative right, its left wing reduced principally to environmentalist supporters. Meanwhile the expansionist coalition recruited prominent bipartisan leaders, including Jack Kemp, the Republican vice presidential candidate in 1996, and Democrat Henry G. Cisneros, secretary of Housing and Urban Development in the Clinton administration. The coalition in the late 1990s also assembled a powerful array of business lobbying organizations, including not only the U.S. Chamber of Commerce and the National Association of Manufacturers, but also Americans for Tax Reform, the National Retail Association, the National Restaurant Association, and the American Hotel and Motel Association. High-tech firms including Apple, Intel, Microsoft, Sun Microsystems, and Texas Instruments, coordinated by the Information Technology Association of America, contributed more than $22 million in political campaigns to both parties, building support for more temporary workers. Ethnic organizations joining the lobbying for immigration expansion and amnesty included the National Asian Pacific American Legal Consortium, the National Coalition for Haitian Rights, and the Arab-American Institute.[57]

Not surprisingly, the politicians responded, especially to the generous importunities of the computer industry. In 1998, Congress increased the allowance of H-1B temporary high-skill worker visas from 65,000 to 115,000 a year. In October 2000, during the presidential campaign, Congress increased H-1B visas for temporary workers with college degrees and special skills to 195,000 a year for three years, each valid for a period of six years, renewable after three years. President Clinton supported the bill, as did presidential candidates Albert Gore and George W. Bush, both of whom courted immigrant voters during the campaign. The vote in the Senate on the temporary worker expansion bill was a bellwether 96-1, and the House quickly passed the bill on a voice vote. Employers admired the H-1B program because the temporary workers were bound to their employers in a kind of indenture and employers were not obliged to pay them the prevailing wage. Nearly half of the visas went to workers from India, and the second highest number went to workers from China. In most cases, the workers were already in the United States, pursuing advanced degrees at American universities.

By the year 2000, then, mass immigration was no longer an issue of persistent controversy in American political life. Economic prosperity had muted the complaints of a public still distressed by high levels of illegal immigration. Between 1965 and 2000, approximately 35 million immigrants had come to America. Their many attributes, their numbers and origins, strengths and weaknesses, had been so widely debated by Congress in the reform drives of the 1970s and 1980s that by the 1990s, the debate had assumed familiar, formulaic contours and almost predictable rhythms. By the late 1990s, political advantage in Washington had clearly shifted to the expansionists. Immigration issues were not static. They were changing with the globalized economy, as transportation and communications changes sped large population shifts and immigration smuggling became a lucrative world industry. But overall in America, the well-rehearsed dance of legislation for immigration policy held few surprises.

One element of the 1990s public debate, however, was new. That was the complaint, heard especially in the context of the political and cultural combat in California over Proposition 187 in 1994 and Proposition 209 (affirmative action) in 1996, that four-fifths of the new immigrants, because they came from countries in Latin America or Asia, could claim the right of affirmative action preferences over native-born white Americans in job hiring and promotions, government contracts and loans, and college and university admissions. This meant that approximately 26 million immigrants coming to America since 1965 could claim affirmative action preferences on the basis of historic discrimination they had never experienced. How could this be? Virtually all parties to the congressional debates over civil rights and immigration policy in the 1980s and 1990s studiously avoided the topic of affirmative action for immigrants. Yet civil rights enforcement officials, when asked whether wealthy immigrants from Hong Kong or Argentina were eligible for American affirmative action programs, acknowledged that all persons of Asian ancestry or Hispanic national origin are eligible. The next chapter tells the tangled story of how, when, and why this extraordinary policy came to be.

6

The Strange Convergence of Affirmative
Action and Immigration Policy

In the early 1990s, when a sharp recession increased unemployment and threatened job security throughout the United States, newspapers began publishing stories about immigrants participating in affirmative action programs.[1] The issue was especially controversial in cities with large immigrant populations, such as Chicago, Houston, Los Angeles, Miami, New York, and Washington, D.C. Civil rights leaders, anxious to protect affirmative action programs from criticism, avoided discussing the issue, as did immigrant rights leaders. Government officials responsible for affirmative action programs, unable to avoid comment, generally reiterated agency guidelines on eligibility, a response which affirmed, often in obfuscating bureaucratese, that immigration status was generally not relevant to affirmative action eligibility.

These stonewalling strategies by beneficiary groups and agency officials were often successful in deflecting criticism and sidetracking the issue. Affirmative action programs were a confusing mix of federal and local, public and private, court-ordered and agency-mandated. Journalists were rarely able to ferret out specific information about how many immigrants were benefiting from which programs. Larger issues, moreover, dominated the news in the early 1990s: the end of the cold war, the winning of the Persian Gulf hot war, the Bush-Clinton-Perot presidential contest, the controversies over national health care insurance and gays in the military, the Republican sweep of Congress in 1994. Affirmative action for immigrants was an emotion-laden issue, especially during recession, but it was not generally a page-one news item. Resentment of immigrants, though strong in the heavy immigration states of Arizona, California, Florida, Illinois, New York, and Texas, was not a powerful grassroots force in most other states.[2]

Among policy intellectuals, however, the issue was troublesome. This was especially true among the more independent-minded academics and think-tank policy analysts whose opinions were not ideologically predictable. Lawrence Fuchs, former MALDEF board member and executive director for the Hesburgh Commission, wrote in the *Washington Post* in 1995 that immigrant inclusion in affirmative action programs "is an historical accident for which there is no possible justification."[3] Noting that "affirmative action was aimed specifically at redressing the grievances of African Americans," Fuchs said, "There was never a comparable historical justification for including others as designated beneficiary groups because of ethnicity."[4] David Reimers, a leading historian of American immigration who supports liberal immigration policies and is critical of immigration restrictionists, wrote in his 1998 book on the anti-immigration movement in America that he could see no reason to involve immigrants and their children in affirmative action programs.[5] Harvard sociologist Nathan Glazer, whose 1975 book *Affirmative Discrimination* marked him as a leading critic of race-conscious affirmative action, changed his mind in the 1990s. By then he defended affirmative action for African-Americans, but *only* for African-Americans. "The fact is that blacks, not Hispanics or other groups, have posed the key dilemma for American society since its origins."[6]

Many black social critics and policy intellectuals, not surprisingly, have agreed that race-conscious remedies were developed to compensate for America's unique history of slavery and segregation. The spread of affirmative action programs to other racial and ethnic groups was seen as broadening and strengthening the civil rights coalition, yet at the same time it weakened the logic of affirmative action's original, black-centered rationale. Black civil rights leaders generally held steadfast in their defense of affirmative action and muted whatever concerns or resentments they held, especially about growing Hispanic and Asian demands on affirmative action programs, in the interest of maintaining coalition solidarity.

Boston University economist Glenn Loury, a prominent African-American critic of affirmative action, had softened his opposition to race-conscious remedies for black Americans by the 1990s. He opposed "color-blind absolutism" because logically it must reject targeted outreach efforts that are legitimate and desirable, such as prison wardens and urban police targeting black recruits.[7] But Loury also objected to affirmative action's reliance on racial preferences. Because preferential hiring policies lower the hiring threshold, they reward only marginal blacks and harm only marginal whites, Loury argued. As a consequence, the outside reputation of most blacks is lowered and that of most whites is enhanced. Such policies thereby "erode the perception of black competence." They do nothing to mitigate the plight of the inner-city underclass, and they represent "a concession of defeat by middle class blacks." Loury supported a middle road of "developmental" as opposed to "preferential" affirmative action. Loury's version of soft affirmative action would use different criteria for admitting or hiring black and white candidates and would tailor training, internships, and summer workshop programs to enhance black performance, but use common standards of performance evaluation. Loury's analysis, however, remains largely confined to the traditional black white dyad. He mentions Asians as an overrepresented group, with whites, in the fields of math and science, thereby legitimizing developmental affirmative action for blacks.

Harvard sociologist Orlando Patterson was even more ambivalent about which groups merit what kind of affirmative action and why. In *The Ordeal of Integration* (1997), Patterson argued that affirmative action for Afro-Americans (his preferred term) and women should be "phased out" over the next fifteen years (he didn't explain how), to be replaced by a class-based program. But he found insupportable the blanket protected-class status for Latinos and Asians. "It is ridiculous," Patterson stated, "that all persons of so-called Hispanic ancestry are considered disadvantaged minorities." On the other hand, Patterson's formula for affirmative action eligibility, beyond Afro-Americans and women, illustrates the treacherous sand beneath hard affirmative action's rationales. First-generation Mexican-American and black immigrants should be excluded, Patterson explained. But "their children and later generations should be eligible," he added, "in light of the persistence of racist discrimination in America." Additionally, all Asians should be excluded, "except Chinese-Americans descended from pre-1923 immigrants."[8]

The Tangled Origins of Official Minority Designation

The growing debate in the 1990s over which minority groups deserved affirmative action preferences, and why, raised questions about how, why, and when various groups were included or excluded in the first place. There were few answers. The cavalcade of books on the civil rights revolution either never asked such questions or threw no light on the answers. Scrutiny of the hearings and debates surrounding the nation's revolution in civil rights policy since the 1950s produced abundant discussion of the brutal legacy of slavery and caste that arguably created a unique burden that justified affirmative action for black Americans. But the record showed almost no discussion of why other minority groups in America were included (for example, Chinese, Argentinians, Pakistanis, Cubans, Spaniards, Portuguese) or excluded (Jews, Italians, Jehovah's Witnesses, Mormons, Palestinians, Iranians).[9]

The answers to the why, when, and how questions could not be found in the public record of elected officials in shaping civil rights policy. Instead, the answers had to be teased out of reports and archival documents left by rather obscure government bureaucrats who did not answer to voters for their decisions. The story these documents reveal about the way official minorities were designated is one shaped not only by the country's history of past discrimination but also by the vagaries of chance, historical accident, logical contradiction, and inadvertence. Above all, none of the career civil servants and appointed officials who shaped the outcomes had any awareness that they were sorting out winners and losers in a process that, by the end of the twentieth century, would grant preference in jobs, government contracts, and university admissions to government-designated official minorities, including approximately 26 million immigrants from Latin America and Asia who came to the United States after 1965.

The process began in 1941, when President Franklin D. Roosevelt by executive order established the Fair Employment Practices Committee (FEPC), a small, temporary agency created under wartime emergency powers. The FEPC's charge was to police discrimination on account of race, color, creed (meaning religion), and national origin. The FEPC expired with few successes at the end of the war. But the momentum of liberal nondiscrimination was continued at the state level under the leadership of New York. In 1945 New York passed the State Law against Discrimination, enforced by a State Commission against Discrimination, New York's version of an FEPC. The law banned discrimination in private as well as government employment on account of race, religion, and national origin. By the end of the 1940s, race and national origin were inseparably linked in the law of antidiscrimination. By 1960, almost all urban-industrial states in the North and West had established antidiscrimination commissions similar to New York's with cease-and-desist enforcement powers.

Similarly, although FEPC bills in Congress between 1946 and 1964 could not overcome Senate filibusters by southern Democrats protecting segregation and conservative Republicans objecting to government control of business, Presidents Truman, Eisenhower, and Kennedy all signed executive orders creating FEPC-like White House-level committees to police discrimination by government contractors. When President Johnson signed the Civil Rights Act of 1964, which established the EEOC and provided a statutory basis for the presidents' executive order programs in contract compliance, he joined Congress in affirming the ruling principle of nondiscrimination. It rested on liberalism's command not to discriminate on account of race, color, religion, or national origin (in Title VII, on employment discrimination, the Civil Rights Act additionally prohibited discrimination on account of sex). In all this statutory and executive order language, there was no mention of particular groups—not even of "Negroes," the prime group behind the civil rights revolution. In the liberal doctrine of equal individual rights, the goal was to ensure that all Americans enjoyed the full exercise of the *same* rights. The way to achieve that goal, in classic liberalism's negative command, was to stop doing harm.[10]

How, then, did particular groups get singled out under the nondiscrimination law? The record shows two paths leading to specific group identification. One was primarily political, the other administrative. The political path, more visible but less determinative in this process than the administrative path, involved the national investigations and reports of advisory bodies. The most important of these were the President's Committee on Civil Rights, appointed by President Truman in 1946, and the U.S. Commission on Civil Rights, established by the Civil Rights Act of 1957. Truman's committee, like all civil rights inquiries and reports in the postwar era, emphasized discrimination against black Americans. But the Truman committee's 1947 report, *To Secure These Rights*, also described discrimination against other groups. The report noted the wartime evacuation and internment of Japanese-Americans, citizenship limitations on Chinese and Japanese, voting restrictions on American Indians, and school segregation and jury duty restrictions on Mexican-Americans. The Truman committee briefly mentioned incidents of past bias against whites— against Jews in particular, and against Italians during World War II. But *To Secure These Rights* marked a shift away from the concerns over religious discrimination that had characterized New York's pioneering campaign, for example, against Jewish quotas at Ivy League colleges and bias against Catholic immigrants, toward an emphasis on color. "Groups whose color makes them more easily identified are set apart from the `dominant majority' much more than are the Caucasian minorities," the report observed.[11]

The hearings and reports of the Civil Rights Commission, beginning in the late 1950s, continued this shift. The commission concentrated in the early years on African-Americans and segregation in the South, then shifted after 1965 to emphasize nationwide discrimination against blacks and Latinos. Advisory panels such as the Truman committee and the Civil Rights Commission served important political needs in the national campaign against discrimination. They sought to identify victims of discrimination in order to convince the nation of the pervasiveness of abuses and the need for reform. Discrimination "on account of" race and national origin was an abstract sin. Segregating black Americans, denying them the vote, and murdering civil rights workers were palpable offenses that stirred the emotions and fueled reform.

Nonetheless, the advisory bodies had no regulatory or enforcement authority, and their efforts in the decade following the *Brown* decision concentrated increasingly on black civil rights. More important to our story about the origins of affirmative action for immigrants were the decisions of obscure government officials providing staff support in the fledgling civil rights compliance bureaucracy. Needing information about employment patterns to support the work of the president's contract compliance committees, they designed forms for government contractors to fill out showing how their employees were distributed by race, ethnicity, and sex (but not by religion, an attribute of individuals that was barred to government inquiry by the First Amendment).

Since the concept of group rights was alien to the civil rights bureaucracy until the end of the 1960s, the career civil servants designing survey forms for the contract compliance committees had no notion that their rather amateurish efforts would have such far-reaching consequences. Sociologist John Skrentny has called attention, for example, to the decisions of one David Mann, director of surveys for Eisenhower's contract compliance committee and later for Kennedy's committee as well.[12] In 1956, Eisenhower's committee asked government contractors to count their "Negro," "other minority," and "total" employees. For contractors with large numbers of "other minority" employees, the survey questionnaire added that "the contractor may be able to furnish employment statistics for such groups" including "Spanish-Americans, Orientals, Indians, Jews, Puerto Ricans, etc." Contractors were not provided with definitions to guide their count of such groups. Since employment records presumably did not list the employees' religious affiliation, it was unclear how a contractor's visual inspection might identify Jewish workers, how they should define Spanish-Americans, or how employers might distinguish between Spanish-Americans and Puerto Ricans. Presumably, employers were given wide latitude by the form's permissive invitation—contractors *may* be able to furnish further information—and by the enigmatic "etc."[13]

This was a clumsy beginning. The only minority group that contractors were required to identify in the 1956 form was "Negroes." But once minority groups started getting named on the government's civil rights compliance forms, the ethnic organizations kicked into play. LULAC, the GI Forum, and the Mexican-American Political Action Committee argued that Hispanics had suffered discrimination and deserved equal billing with blacks on the government's new form. The Latino organizations recruited support from Mexican-American members of Congress—representatives Henry Gonzales (Texas), Joseph Montoya (New Mexico), and Edward Roybal (California), all Democrats. By 1962, when President Kennedy's contract compliance committee revised the early survey questionnaire into Standard Form 40, "Spanish-Americans" were included with "Negroes" as obligatory reporting categories. A similar campaign led by the Japanese-American Citizens League, and supported by two Asian-American legislators from Hawaii, Republican Hiram L. Fong in the Senate and Democrat Daniel K. Inouye in the House, persuaded Mann to add "Orientals" as a required category on the standard form. Mann also added American Indians to the standard form, even though Indian groups had not lobbied. Jews, on the other hand, were dropped from the form. Some black groups had objected to their inclusion, and Jewish organizations did not contest the matter.

Thus by 1965, when the newly established EEOC used the contract compliance committee's Standard Form 40 as the basis for constructing its own form, the EEO-1, the government had produced a de facto list of official minorities that employers were required to count and report. Workers were assigned to five ethnic categories: Negro, Spanish-American, Oriental, American Indian, and White. Because the Civil Rights Act, which created the EEOC and provided in Title VI a statutory basis for the presidents' executive order programs in contract compliance, prohibited discrimination on account of race and national origin, none of the five groups could legally be discriminated against in 1965, including whites. But whites, alone among the five groups, were not considered a minority.

Thus when the ghetto riots of 1965–68 prompted federal agency officials and judges to speed black job recruitment by devising race-conscious affirmative action programs such as the Philadelphia Plan, the government already had at hand a list of four official minorities. Although individual ethnic organizations lobbied federal officials to pay more attention to their group, there is no record of civil rights leaders addressing the issue of which groups to include on the EEO-1 form, no hearings or record of discussion by the presidents' contract compliance committees or by the EEOC, and no record of minority rights or women's organizations asking for race-conscious or gender-specific remedies. Instead, as John Skrentny pointed out in *The Ironies of Affirmative Action*, the initiative in both the earlier minority-counting projects and, later, in developing race-conscious affirmative action programs came from appointed federal officials and served their political needs.

The exploding racial crisis triggered by the Watts riot of 1965 provided alarmed and harried government officials in the new civil rights enforcement agencies with an irresistible path to spreading remedies by shifting from nondiscrimination to underutilization as an enforcement model. The EEOC, stripped by the Dirksen compromise in the Civil Rights Act of the authority to order employers to stop discriminating, and attacked as timid and ineffective by impatient civil rights organizations, turned eagerly to underutilization analysis as a way to appease its complaining clients. By 1968, the EEOC had largely dropped discussion of nondiscrimination in favor of underutilization. Instead of identifying specific acts of discrimination and proving that they were intentional—a slow, uncertain process even for state fair employment commissions that could punish offending employers, which the EEOC could not—utilization analysis allowed the EEOC to infer discrimination from employment statistics supplied by employers on the EEO-1 form. By 1970, the EEOC had developed a "disparate impact" theory of discrimination, as described in chapter 4, that disregarded intent and inferred discrimination from statistical underutilization of minorities in the workforce. In 1971, the U.S. Supreme Court in *Griggs v. Duke Power Company* upheld this approach, deferring to the EEOC's expertise in employment policy.

Compliance officials at the Labor Department followed the same path. In 1969 the OFCC revised the Philadelphia Plan, though it was revived with only black workers in mind, drew on the EEO-1 form's list of official minorities—"Negro, Oriental, American Indian, and Spanish Surnamed Americans"—to establish the Labor Department's own form of underutilization analysis. The OFCC held hearings to document discrimination against black workers in Philadelphia's construction trades. But there is no record of hearings or discussions about identifying other minorities, beyond black workers, for statistical reporting purposes.[14] In 1970, the Labor Department issued Order No. 4, extending the Philadelphia Plan from the construction industry in Philadelphia to all federal contractors.

During these tumultuous years of urban riots and violence commissions, a third federal agency, the Small Business Administration (SBA), used the new bureaucratic concept of official minorities to reshape its programs. Established in 1953 in the Commerce Department to help small businesses recover from natural disasters such as floods and hurricanes, the SBA broadened its program scope in the 1960s to include helping economically and socially disadvantaged small businesses succeed. This was consistent with the Great Society's war on poverty and equal economic opportunity programs. In 1968 the SBA, responding to appeals from the Kerner Riot Commission for special outreach programs to build economic opportunity in the inner cities, established the 8(a) program. Deriving its title from section 8 of a 1958 law that authorized the SBA to contract with other federal agencies and to subcontract the work to small firms, the 8(a) program channeled procurement contracts to small businesses owned by "economically or culturally disadvantaged individuals." The SBA thus acted as an agent for 8(a) certified companies, seeking out available government contracts and persuading other agencies to set aside procurement work for these companies. Aimed at the black ghettos, the SBA's 8(a) program nonetheless did not define what it meant by economic or cultural disadvantage. Given this vague foundation, the 8(a) program developed slowly, its focus unclear. Black and Hispanic organizations criticized the program as cumbersome and ineffective, charges not new to the SBA, which since its inception had been criticized in GAO reports and newspaper accounts as inefficient.[15]

In response, the SBA reached out to the new and growing civil rights constituencies to bolster its support in Congress. In 1973 the SBA published new regulations for the 8(a) program in the *Federal Register*. Henceforth, the status of cultural disadvantage would be *presumed* for all program applicants identifying themselves as black, Hispanic, Asian American, or American Indian.[16] Since the beginning of the 8(a) program, the status of economic disadvantage had been easy to achieve. SBA guidelines, sensitive to the need for broad middle-class participation in SBA programs, set income and other economic eligibility threshholds so high that only wealthy individuals were excluded.[17] Thus the key to eligibility for the 8(a) program's federally subsidized grants, loans, and procurement contracts was culturally disadvantaged status. The concept of "presumptive eligibility" was conferred automatically under the 1973 regulations by official minority group status. Section 8(a) was a Minority Business Enterprise (MBE) program. This meant that white Americans alone had to demonstrate, through "clean and convincing evidence," that they had suffered "chronic or ethnic prejudice or cultural bias." Because the 8(a) bureaucracy, like counterpart bureaucracies at the EEOC and OFCC, was unsympathetic to nonminority claims, participation by whites in the 8(a) program never reached even 1 percent of participating firms.[18]

The Policy Implications of Official Minority Designation

By 1973, when the leading federal agencies in civil rights enforcement had consolidated their shift from nondiscrimination to an underutilization model of affirmative action, they already had at hand a list of four minority groups on whose behalf the new model would be applied. What were the most significant attributes and consequences of the process that identified official minorities, a process that evolved unevenly in fits and starts over three decades? First, it was not an open process of public policymaking. The democratic model of policymaking features elected officials who hold public hearings, debate policy goals, argue the strengths and weaknesses of alternative means, cast their votes on the record, and are held accountable by voters. Instead, the government's minority sorting quest was a closed process of bureaucratic policymaking. It was largely devoid not only of public testimony but even of public awareness that policy was being made. There are areas of policymaking that may arguably be shielded from open forums, even in a democracy. Examples might include national security and defense or economic decisions such as interest rate changes by central banks. But the civil rights of Americans is surely not such an issue area.

Second, the closed, in-house nature of the government's deliberations narrowed the goals of policy from meeting broad public needs to meeting the more immediate political needs of the agency. Closed deliberations facilitated sheltered bargaining between agency officials, constituent groups, and members of Congress, bargaining that is neither unusual nor inherently improper but that often marks the "iron triangle" dealmaking associated with the client model of politics, where clients "capture" agencies that regulate their industry or sponsor their benefit programs.[19] Before 1965, the government's rather clumsy search for useful survey categories seems innocent enough. When nondiscrimination and equal individual rights were the agreed anchors of policy, getting one's ethnic group added to a questionnaire promised little in benefits beyond elevated visibility and prestige. But the subsequent shift, during the Nixon administration, to hard affirmative action and adverse impact claims radically changed the stakes of policy. It is not surprising that the agencies shaping the new definition of official minorities in America—the EEOC, the OFCC, the Office of Civil Rights in the Department of Health, Education and Welfare, the 8(a) program bureaucracy in the SBA—became largely captured bureaucracies whose policies rewarded the protected classes that the official minority designations recognized. For these agencies, hard affirmative action was a risky gamble that paid rich dividends by serving multiple agency goals. It radically enlarged the policy repertoire of the agencies. It allowed them to appease volatile, radicalizing constituencies, quieting criticism by directing a robust new stream of benefits to reward racial and ethnic clientele groups. Best of all, by requiring private firms and other government agencies to pay the cost of the new benefits to minority constituencies (jobs, promotions, government contracts), it freed the civil rights bureaucracy from the necessity of persuading Congress to provide appropriations to pay for the benefits.

Third, the agencies provided no rationale to justify their racial and ethnic categories. Dealing with inherited notions of race that were being abandoned in science and social science, government officials drew up questionnaires that reflected assumptions they took for granted. No explanations were provided. What was a race? Were Spanish-Americans a race? Should a list of minorities suffering discrimination in America include Jews, Catholics, Mormons, Jehovah's Witnesses? Were Portuguese-Americans Spanish-Americans? Were persons from the Middle East or North Africa "white"? How should the government categorize persons of racially or ethnically mixed ancestry? Not having to answer questions like these in public made it easier for government officials to adjust their lists pragmatically, winnowing the official minorities down to four by 1965. By that year the new EEO-1 form, by isolating four minority groups that corresponded to the racial color coding of American popular culture—black, yellow, red, and brown—reified a cluster of assumptions about American society that agency officials, shielded from public debate by their closed process, simply took for granted. This was a fourth important attribute of the long process that identified official minorities: It reified assumptions that hindsight reveals to be profoundly problematic.

One implicit assumption was that membership in a minority group carried a presumption of disadvantage in American society. Other attributes of minority individuals that might reflect socioeconomic success, such as income, wealth, and educational achievement, were disregarded. Minority status, in effect, trumped socioeconomic class. A second implicit assumption was that all minority groups were equal in their disadvantage. Although the paradigmatic disadvantaged minority group was indisputably, in 1950s parlance, the Negro American, there was no implication that civil rights remedies could differ for blacks, Hispanics, Asians, or American Indians. As John Skrentny observed, "[G]overnment officials operated within a policy paradigm that led to the mostly unreflective equation of the histories and sociologies of different groups." [20] Third, the government listing of enumerated minority groups, which erased the lines separating official minorities from each other, drew a bright line separating official minorities from all other Americans. By 1965, when the EEO-1 form asked employers to use visual identification rather than employee records or queries to assign workers to EEO categories, the white ethnics and religious groups had all been excluded.

Finally, the government officials making these decisions from the beginning privileged the rights claims of African-Americans. This privileged claim was politically crucial, yet paradoxically, it gave African-Americans no legal advantages over other minorities. Politically, black claims came first; all other minority groups played a distant tag-along. This assumption was almost universally shared by postwar liberal reformers. When speaking of "the" Civil Rights Movement, one meant the black movement. Presidents Kennedy and Johnson, when pressing the civil rights bills of the mid-1960s, rallied Americans exclusively to the justice claims of African-Americans. The early EEOC, in its race-centered commitment to mission, resented the demands by feminist groups for aggressive enforcement of gender equality, even though one-third of EEOC complaints charged sex discrimination.[21] Historically, the assumption of African-American primacy seemed self-evident. Politically, it provided the moral power behind the breakthrough legislation of 1964–65. Subsequently, it also provided the rationale for adopting race-conscious remedies under affirmative action, speeding government-subsidized jobs to rioting urban blacks. But it coexisted uneasily with the assumption that all official minorities were equally disadvantaged and were entitled to the same remedies in civil rights enforcement.

By 1965 the four official minority groups were officially designated in the EEO-1 form. By 1970, with the Labor Department's release of Order No. 4, the four groups were given protected class status in the federal government's affirmative action remedies. This locked into place a set of unexamined assumptions underpinning the affirmative action rights of official minorities that would not stand up under close analysis. By equating the disadvantage of all four minority groups, the assumptions were reductionist. They ignored the historical and cultural differences separating not only the four minority groups from each other but also the especially wide differences within the overarching categories of Hispanic and Asian. They also ignored distinctions of economic class, excluding poor whites but not wealthy minorities. They recognized, by excluding upwardly mobile ethnic whites (Jews, Irish and Italian Catholics, Greeks and Armenians) the changes brought by time, but were blind to such changes among the official minorities themselves, even if the changes reflected future success by affirmative action remedies. Furthermore, by assigning all employees to one of five racial and ethnic categories, the official minority list also denied the reality of racially mixed individuals, a rapidly growing category in an age of mass immigration. Although most African-Americans were racially mixed, owing to widespread miscegenation, the federal government's racial designations reinforced the racist one-drop rule, developed under the South's slavery regime to define as Negro anyone with one drop of black blood. Finally, when the official minority scheme was linked to affirmative action requirements, it employed the rationale of past discrimination to justify race-conscious remedies for a new generation of minority individuals who never lived under slavery or segregation laws but who presumably suffered from their cultural legacy. This compensatory ratio- nale, however, made no sense for the 26 million immigrants from Latin America and Asia who arrived after 1965.

Asian-Americans and the Problem of Protected Minority Classes

In *Equal Employment Report No. 1* (1966) the EEOC showed, in its first report based on the EEO-1 form data, that black and Hispanic Americans were severely underrepresented in white-collar jobs. The EEOC demonstrated, based on a nationwide survey of 43,000 employers and 26 million work- ers, that "the chances of a man with a Spanish surname" becoming a man- ager or official "are only one fifth as good as that of a member of the major- ity group; and for Negroes, the figure is one twelfth."[22] The report also demonstrated that Asian-Americans had a higher occupational standing than did European ethnic groups, even in 1966. "More than 1 out of every 4 Oriental men is a professional compared to 1 out of every 11 Anglos (and 1 out of 100 among Negroes)," the report said, and "the chances of an Ori- ental male being a technical worker are twice as high as the chances of an Anglo worker." Not surprisingly, the EEOC ignored the question of dis- crimination against Asians and concentrated its efforts elsewhere. In 1970, a U.S. Civil Rights Commission report stated that the EEOC had set its pri- orities on African-Americans, Hispanics, and women.[23]

Politically, these priorities made sense, responding as they did to EEOC complaint patterns and to pressures from mobilized black, Chicano, and feminist groups. But accumulating evidence of Asian socioeconomic suc- cess confounded the model of nonwhite, protected-class minorities, with its presumption of group disadvantage. The economist Thomas Sowell, using census data for the 1960s, calculated the average family income of the major racial and ethnic groups as of 1969. In Sowell's study, the rank- ing of social mobility, as reflected in an index of median family income, is surprising, especially as a snapshot of the 1960s.[24] Table 6.1 shows Japan- ese-Americans ranking second and Chinese-Americans ranking fourth among the fifteen groups. For groups subject to severe and prolonged dis- crimination in America, from the Civil War to the 1940s, this was a stun- ning performance. The low ranking of American Indians, blacks, Puerto Ricans, and Mexicans, on the other hand, supported EEOC priorities.

Asian success raised questions about including Asians as protected minorities even at the EEOC itself. Herbert Hammerman, chief of the EEOC's reports unit, urged EEOC chairman Stephen Schulman in 1967 to

Table 6.1   Median Family Income of Ethnic
Groups in the United States, Ranked by
Percentage of the National Average, 1969

Ethnic Group	Median Family Income
Jewish	172%
Japanese	132%
Polish	115%
Chinese	112%
Italian	112%
German	107%
Anglo-Saxon	105%
Irish	103%
National average	100%
Filipino	99%
West Indian	94%
Cuban	80%
Mexican	76%
Puerto Rican	63%
Black	62%
Indian (American)	60%

Source: Thomas Sowell, The Economics and Politics of Race (New York: Morrow, 1983), 187.

remove Asians and American Indians from the commission's forms. Both groups were small, Hammerman argued. Asians showed little evidence of current discrimination or harm from a legacy of past discrimination, and Indians on reservations were not covered by the Civil Rights Act's Title VII, which established the EEOC. "No one disagreed," Hammerman recalls, "not even the chairman."[25] But Schulman declined to remove any group from the list, explaining that he was unwilling to take the political heat that such a move would generate.

Schulman was right about the politics of minority listing. Organized minority groups competing for official recognition were quick to punish government officials for treating their group less favorably than others. In 1978, when Congress in the Small Business Investment Act provided a statutory basis for the SBA's 8(a) program, the law omitted Asian-Americans from the list of minorities (blacks, Hispanics, and Native Americans) considered presumptively "socially and economically disadvantaged."[26] Responding to this omission, Asian-American groups hammered the SBA, which within a year reinstated them among the presumptively eligible groups. Yet there was something bizarre about awarding taxpayer-subsidized business grants and loans to members of the country's top income strata on the grounds that all members of the group were presumed to be socially disadvantaged. Nonetheless, the SBA, in its administrative reinstatement of Asians in 1979, was able to expand the scope of "Oriental" Americans from its traditional meaning in the EEO-1 form (Chinese, Japanese, and Filipinos, the major pre-1920s immigrant groups) to include a wide array of newly recognized immigrant groups. These included Americans from Vietnam, Korea, Samoa, Guam, the U.S. Trust Territory of the Pacific, the Northern Marianas, Laos, Cambodia, and Taiwan.

These were the new, post-1965 immigrants, called "Asian Pacific Americans" in the SBA's revised 8(a) program eligibility list. The SBA's new listing, like most previous such designations by government agencies, was made without formal hearings. Though the SBA provided no rationale for the changes, the agency was following administrative guidance recently provided by the Office of Management and Budget (OMB). In 1977 the OMB issued a directive standardizing racial and ethnic categories for the entire federal government. OMB Directive No. 15 of May 1977, while disclaiming that the classifications were "scientific or anthropological in nature," defined five official racial and ethnic groups.[27] An Asian or Pacific Islander was a person "having origins in any of the original peoples of the Far East, Southeast Asia, the Indian subcontinent, or the Pacific Islands." Blacks were persons "having origins in any of the black racial groups of Africa." Whites were "persons having origins in any of the original peoples of Europe, North Africa, or the Middle East." An American Indian or Alaskan Native not only was a "person having origins in any of the original peoples of North America," but additionally was one who "maintains cultural identification through tribal affiliations or community recognition." These were the federal government's four official racial categories. Because Hispanics could be of any race (polls showed that most Hispanics considered themselves white), the OMB defined a Hispanic as "a person of Mexican, Puerto Rican, Cuban, Central or South American or other Spanish culture or origin, regardless of race." True to the government's tradition of closed deliberations in such matters, the OMB held no hearings and confined its discussions to federal interagency committees.

OMB Directive 15 was full of vague, problematical terms it did not define. What was the meaning of such ambiguous phrases as "having origins in," "maintains cultural identity," "community recognition," and "Spanish culture"? Who was to decide? Was Portuguese a Spanish culture? Where and how (and why) should the line be drawn, in racial or cultural or geographic terms, between "white" Middle Eastern countries and neighboring Asian countries such as Afghanistan and Pakistan, or between white North Africans and blacks elsewhere in Africa? As the census shifted, following the 1960s, from enumerator designation to self-identification in regards to race and ethnicity, Americans of racially and ethnically mixed backgrounds would complain that the government forced them to choose one parent over the other.

For the SBA, however, the OMB categories provided greater flexibility than the SBA's redundant 1973 list of presumptively eligible minorities, which named "blacks, American Indians, Spanish-Americans, Asian-Americans, and Puerto Ricans." And the 1978 law gave the SBA wide discretion to determine presumptive eligibility in response to petitions from groups seeking inclusion in the 1980s. One such petition, submitted by an enterprising immigrant from Indonesia, captures the political dynamics of the minority designation process in the 1980s—when, ironically, affirmative action programs experienced robust growth during the presidency of Ronald Reagan.

Immigrant Participation in Minority Business Set-Aside Programs

In 1988, the SBA received a letter from an Indonesian-born woman who owned a small business in California. We know about her petition, and about the SBA's 8(a) petitioning process following its provision by Congress in 1978, only from documents obtained in the 1990s through the Freedom of Information Act.[28] In her letter to the SBA requesting 8(a) certification, the Indonesian woman (the SBA did not reveal her name) made a strong case for herself. She recounted how she had office experience in Indonesia, but language and cultural barriers in America forced her to work her way upward as a house cleaner, dishwasher, and waitress. Eventually she gained English competence, started her own business, and became a naturalized citizen. Then, following the lead of many of her business competitors, she sought the benefits of SBA minority set-aside contracts.[29] Up to that point, hers was a typical immigrant success story in America.

The SBA, however, turned her down. Indonesian-Americans were not named as "members of a designated group," the SBA replied. So the Indonesian woman petitioned for 8(a) eligibility for all Indonesian-Americans. Following linguistic clues in SBA documents, she switched the tone and theme of her appeal, from the story of immigrant success in America to an emphasis on discrimination and racial oppression: "My color is yellow like other Indonesians I know," she wrote. "Asian Pacific Americans have suffered the chronic effects of discriminatory practices for a very long time, over which they have no control, and Indonesian Americans most definitely included have suffered economic deprivation. This has impacted all the Indonesian Americans I know in a most negative way. Good jobs are scarce regardless of talent. Language and color are a barrier to both employment and a good education. Indonesian-Americans have no business history."

In point of fact, Indonesians had an impressive record of business success in America. In 1989, there were only about 20,000 Indonesians in America. Despite the recency of their arrival, on average they were better educated and more prosperous than most other Americans. Nonetheless, in response to the Indonesian businesswoman's second petition, the SBA, making no reference to socioeconomic data, added Indonesians to the Asian Pacific American cluster as presumptively eligible for 8(a) minority set-aside contracts.

Indonesia's inclusion on the SBA's 8(a) presumptive eligibility list marked a decade of group petitioning that began in 1979 with a petition by a Brooklyn organization on behalf of Hasidic Jews. During the 1980s the SBA accepted four petitioning groups and rejected another four. The Hasidic petition in 1979 and the Indonesian petition in 1989 straddle the decade of SBA decision-making like bookends, clarifying the political ground rules that determined winners and losers. On behalf of the Hasidics, a major Washington law firm presented a seventy-three-page petition backed by eighty-six letters of support including those by two U.S. senators, New York Republican Jacob Javits and Connecticut Democrat Abraham Ribicoff, and other prominent members of Congress. The ultra-orthodox Hasidim were described in the petition as strange in appearance and language, victims of anti-Semitism and, many of them, immigrant survivors of the Holocaust. The SBA's general counsel, Edward Norton, urged acceptance. Norton wrote Stuart Eizenstat, President Carter's chief aide for domestic policy, that Congress in its SBA statute in 1978 made it "clear that the 8(a) program is not exclusively a racially preferential program."[30] The final conference committee report accompanying Congress's 1978 SBA statute even referred to a "poor Appalachian white person" as an example of cultural bias that might justify inclusion in the 8(a) program.

The SBA, however, turned the Hasadic Jews down. Why? The SBA's official explanation cited constitutional concerns. Granting "disadvantaged" status to a religious group, the SBA concluded, might violate the First Amendment by establishing an impermissible religious classification. This was a legitimate concern, although antidiscrimination law since the 1930s had protected Americans against discrimination on account of religion and creed. The White House senior staff, however, identified the real opposition to granting presumptive eligibility to Jews as coming from African-American leaders who resented competition for affirmative action benefits from other minority groups. Such competition diluted the set-aside contracts and other race-conscious preferences originally intended as remedies for past discrimination against black Americans. There was "significant under-lying hostility," White House aides noted, "to inclusion of persons of other racial minorities and Hispanics in section 8(a) programs among black con-tractors."[31] Most important, however, was the opposition of Congressman Parren Mitchell, sponsor of the original minority set-aside provision in 1977. Not only was Mitchell chairman of the Congressional Black Caucus. He also chaired the House Subcommittee on Housing, Minority Enterprise, and Eco-nomic Development, which controlled the budget and programs of the SBA.

Having rejected the Hasidic Jews in 1980, the SBA next, in 1982, consid-ered a petition on behalf of Asian Indians. SBA guidelines required peti-tioners to provide evidence of several factors, including "evidence of long-term prejudice and discrimination in American society suffered by an overwhelming majority" of the petitioning group, and evidence of "past and present effects of discriminatory practices" that together "have resulted and continue to result in substantial economic deprivation for an overwhelming majority" of the group, including "substantial impedi-ments in the business world." This would seem to be a tall order for Asian-Indian Americans. They were overwhelmingly a post-1965 cohort of immi-grants. In 1990, of the 815,000 persons of Indian descent in America, most (450,000) were born in India, and most of these (56 percent) had come to America since 1980. In 1980, the percentage of college graduates and man-agers or professionals among Asian Indians was 52 and 49 percent, respec-tively, while for all Americans it was 16 and 23 percent. In 1989, Asian Indi-ans had the highest median household income ($48,320 in 1989 dollars) of all immigrant groups in the country. (The median for foreign-born Amer-icans in 1989 was $28,314, and the median for European-born immigrants was $30,892.) The SBA, avoiding socioeconomic data and comparisons, added India to the presumptively eligible list in February 1982. The fol-lowing August, the SBA granted presumptive eligibility to persons from Pakistan and Bangladesh, even though no one from those countries had petitioned the SBA.

In its petitioning process during the 1980s, the SBA faced the impossi-ble task of rationalizing an incoherent and contradictory program. At its heart was the concept of presumptive group eligibility. This coveted status brought government benefits based on ancestry to individuals and groups that often were highly advantaged in income and education. Before 1980, the SBA was not required to provide any rationale supporting its eligibil-ity decisions. It thus was partly shielded from complaints that the govern-ment was favoring high-income groups on the basis of ancestry or skin color. The formal petitioning process of the 1980s, however, required at least a summary justification for acceptance or rejection, and this pulled the agency into awkward contradictions.

In 1981 the SBA rejected a petition on behalf of women contractors on the grounds that "presumptive group `social disadvantage' is primarily intended for the traditional `minority' groups and should not be extended to the broader class of `women.' "[32] Yet the SBA offered no definition of "traditional minority groups," and the congressional language of 1978 contradicted this claim. In 1989, the SBA rejected a petition by Iranian-Americans. In doing so, SBA officials reasoned that Iranians had not demonstrated long-term discrimination in America. Also, they were "too narrow" as a group, basing their claim on country of origin rather than on cultural affinity. Yet the SBA granted presumptive eligibility to numerous groups composed mostly of post-1960s immigrants from one country, including Bhutan, Burma, Indonesia, the Marshall Islands, Nepal, Sri Lanka, and Tonga. The SBA's notice of rejection to Iranian petitioners included language suggesting that the agency's real motive was fear that a domino effect might lead to including ancestral claims from Afghans, Syrians, Iraqis, or Turks. Having included Pakistan in its Indian subcontinent logic, the SBA in effect drew a red line at the border with Afghanistan. This action blocked future claims from Middle Eastern immigrants, including Arab-Americans who, even more than the Iranians, encountered prejudice and discrimination in America. But the SBA's ethnocultural line-drawing at the Khyber Pass, coming from an agency not noted for this expertise, made no sense in terms either of Middle Eastern cultural anthropology or of American history and law.

Behind all of this geocultural maneuvering lay the apprehensions of black leaders such as Parren Mitchell that new claimants to affirmative action benefits would threaten the primacy of African-American interests. Mitchell, who had omitted Asians and American Indians in his original minority set-aside proposals in Congress, had included Hispanics. To do otherwise would have ruptured the civil rights coalition. But as President Carter's White House aides had noted, black contractors resented competition from the rapidly growing Hispanic minority. In fiscal year 1981, black-owned firms won almost two-thirds of the $1.8 billion distributed by federal agencies through the 8(a) program. But blacks by 1990 no longer constituted a majority of the minorities. Immigration had raised the Hispanic share of the four official minorities in the American population from 32 percent in 1980 to 37 percent in 1990. Correspondingly, the black share had fallen from 57.3 percent to 48.5 percent. During the same decade, the Asian-American population had doubled, from 3.6 million to 7 million.

In 1981, black contractors had dominated the 8(a) program, which was

Table 6.2   Minority-Owned Businesses Certified by the
Small Business Administration as Eligible for the 8(a)
Minority Business Enterprise Program for Fiscal Year 1981

Owner	Businesses	Percentage
Black	1,418	62.6
Spanish-American	451	19.9
Asian	164	7.2
American Indian	133	5.9
Puerto Rican	38	1.7
Eskimo and Aleut	4	.2
Other	56	2.5
Total	2,264	100

Source: General Accounting Office, *The SBA 8(a) Procurement Program*
(Washington, D.C.: Government Printing Office, 1981).

still relatively small (see table 6.2). During the 1980s, however, affirmative action programs expanded rapidly throughout America following a brace of favorable Supreme Court decisions. In 1978 in the *Bakke* case the Court ruled against a fixed minority quota in university admissions, but approved the use of race as a factor in affirmative action efforts to redress past discrimination and enhance institutional diversity. In 1979 the Court in *Weber* approved race-conscious employment policies by private firms and labor organizations, and in 1980 the Court in *Fullilove* approved the minority contract set-asides included in the 1977 public works law.[33] Given a green light by *Fullilove*, minority contract set-aside programs spread rapidly throughout the country's city, county, and state governments.

The Political Dilemma of Minority Set-Aside Programs

From the beginning, minority set-aside programs offered major strengths to the coalition of organized minority groups offset by persistent weaknesses. The strengths included justice claims, political camouflage, and financial wallop. Regarding social justice, Congressman Mitchell noted, when introducing his 10 percent set-aside amendment in 1977, that minorities were 18 percent of the population but received less than 1 percent of federal contracts. Government contractors everywhere were largely a white male cohort with long experience and close agency ties. Political camouflage, needed by legislators eager to please civil rights and minority organizations while avoiding punishment by voters for supporting racial quotas, was provided by the bureaucratic obscurity of the government's procurement process. Voters did not understand the complexities of government contracting and agency regulation. Finally, government procurement budgets were huge and produced an immediate impact in redistributing tax dollars. During the 1980s, at the federal level alone, Congress added MBE requirements for procurement budgets in the large mission agencies that included 5 percent for defense procurement, 8 percent for NASA contracts, and 10 percent for transportation projects. By the end of the 1980s, federal agencies were awarding $8.7 billion in MBE and (after 1987) WBE contracts.

The weaknesses of minority set-asides were chiefly two. First, they were indubitably racial and ethnic quotas, and hence were politically controversial. As government benefits tied to ancestry, they violated the classic liberal creed that Americans possessed equal individual rights. As dollar volumes grew and set-asides spread across the country, controversy grew with them. Nonminority contractors were barred by their ancestry or their skin color from even bidding on contracts paid for by taxpayer dollars, including their own.

Second, and less obviously, set-aside programs produced a common set of flaws in implementation. The most severe problem was the concentration of set-aside contracts on a few successful firms. Agency officials, needing to spend a large amount of money on minority procurement contractors every fiscal year, found very few minority contractors able to do the job. Four-fifths of all certified minority firms had no employees, their personnel roster consisting solely of the owner of the enterprise. As a consequence, agency set-aside contracts were typically concentrated on only a few firms large enough and sufficiently experienced to meet the terms of the contract, providing construction, street paving, computer services, military uniforms, or other goods and services. In 1990, for example, only fifty firms, representing less than 2 percent of the certified minority firms in the 8(a) program, accounted for 40 percent of the $4 billion awarded. Such firms, not surprisingly, were often profitable and owned by wealthy entrepreneurs. Moreover, such firms never seemed to "graduate" from the set-aside program, weaned from the incubator and ready to compete in the normal marketplace of competive government contracting.[34]

The problem of dominance in minority set-aside programs by a few successful firms, identified in GAO reports in the late 1970s, not only persisted but worsened as procurement set-asides expanded in the 1980s and 1990s.[35] Almost all the contracts were awarded on a no-bid or "sole source" basis; in fiscal 1991, for example, only 1.9 percent of the 4,576 contracts in the 8(a) program were awarded on a competitive basis. This short-circuited the government's standard bidding protocol for federal procurement, a system proudly built at the beginning of the twentieth century by Progressive reformers fighting the rampant corruption of the Gilded Age. Not surprisingly, the combination of billions of dollars in set-aside contracts, reliance on self-designation for classifying minority business enterprises, and hasty administration of large dollar-volume contracting, produced widespread fraud. The prospect of lucrative, sole-source contracts tempted business owners to make phony claims of minority control. Finally, immigrant entrepreneurs, 80 percent of them either Hispanic or Asian, were naturally attracted to the business opportunities offered by minority set-aside programs. A 1995 GAO report showed that, of the top twenty-five firms receiving 8(a) contracts, only three were black-owned. Most of the 8(a) MBE firms were legitimate. But in cities across America in the 1980s and 1990s, set-aside programs developed a bad press from stories featuring government-subsidized, high-profit businesses owned by minority individuals of lofty income, many of whom were immigrants.[36]

Affirmative Action for Immigrants in America's Cities

The most notorious example of minority set-aside abuse in the country was the Wedtech scandal during the Reagan presidency. Wedtech was a South Bronx company whose board chairman, John Mariotta, won 8(a) eligibility as a Puerto Rican and majority stockholder. Wedtech's procurement contracts with the Defense Department brought Mariotta wealth and fame, then conviction and imprisonment in 1988 on federal racketeering charges. Mariotta, born in Spanish Harlem to Puerto Rican immigrant parents, never finished high school. Yet he built the tiny machine shop he inherited from his father into a multimillion dollar enterprise that manufactured cooling systems and auxiliary engines for the army. The rags-to-riches Mariotta became a poster child for the Reagan administration, the Latino entrepreneur whose business acumen and MBE contracts were helping to save the South Bronx. To send lucrative contracts Mariotta's way, top presidential assistants Edwin Meese III and Lyn Nofziger interceded with Pentagon officials on Wedtech's behalf.[37]

In Reagan's second term, the Wedtech Corporation collapsed into bankruptcy. Hearings in Congress and a federal racketeering investigation under U.S. Attorney Rudolph Giuliani in New York revealed widespread fraud and bribery.[38] New York congressman Mario Biaggi, a Democrat whose district included the South Bronx, went to jail along with Mariotta and several others on charges of conspiracy, extortion, and bribery. Meese resigned as attorney general after an investigation by independent counsel James C. McKay of Meese's role in influencing Wedtech contracts and other interventions on behalf of friends and associates. McKay concluded that Meese "probably violated" criminal law, but he declined to prosecute.[39] Nofzinger was indicted and convicted in federal court of influence peddling, but won a reversal on appeal. Mariotta's claim to majority ownership of Wedtech turned out to be fraudulent from the start. Mariotta served as minority front man behind a scam guided by two immigrants, Romanian-born Fred Neuberger and Mario Moreno, a Colombian. But Neuberger, as a Jew, did not qualify as an 8(a) minority; Moreno, who did, was a salaried executive vice president, not an owner. In 1975, when Wedtech (then called Welbuilt) first applied for the 8(a) program, Neuberger and Mariotta both owned 50 percent interest in the struggling machine shop; to win 8(a) certification, Mariotta agreed to claim two-thirds ownership. The SBA's program bureaucracy, notoriously lax in monitoring such claims, accepted Mariotta's misrepresentations at face value.

In several important respects, the Wedtech scandal was atypical of the rapidly expanding world of affirmative action programs in the 1980s and 1990s. White House connections were unusual in the early years of the set-aside programs—although this would change as contract values soared in the 1980s, bolstered by large new set-aside requirements in appropriations for defense, transportation, and NASA. National attention in the media was also unusual. In Wedtech's case, the media attention included two books by journalists and a Mariotta interview on CBS with Dan Rather.[40] More typical of the problems found in MBE programs nationwide, and demonstrated in the Wedtech scandal, was a pattern of abuse that included dominance of contracting dollars by a small number of larger and financially successful firms, fraudulent equity ownership claims by applicants seeking affirmative action eligibility, and fiscal inefficiency and waste from no-bid contracting.[41]

The growth of federal set-aside programs in the 1980s should not obscure the larger story behind minority set-aside growth in state, county, and municipal governments in America, including growing participation by Asian and Hispanic immigrants. The Supreme Court's 1980 *Fullilove* decision, giving the green light to minority contract set-asides, coincided with the emergence of minority political power in the nation's major cities. Black mayors won election in Atlanta, Baltimore, Charlotte, Chicago, Cleveland, Detroit, Los Angeles, Newark, New York, New Orleans, Richmond, Philadelphia, and Washington. When the Supreme Court in *City of Richmond v. Croson* (1989) sharply narrowed the scope of minority set-aside programs below the federal level, more than 230 government jurisdictions—states, cities, counties, and special districts—had established set-aside programs.[42] In Richmond, Virginia, the set-asides followed the election of a black majority to the city council in 1977 and the installation of the city's first African-American mayor. In 1983, the Richmond City Council established a 30 percent dollar-value quota for minority contractors on all municipal contracts, a provision the Supreme Court overturned six years later in the Croson decision as arbitrary and lacking any documented relationship to past discrimination it was to remedy.[43]

In Washington, D.C., a city already controlled by a black-majority city council and a black mayor when Congress in 1977 added the 10 percent minority set-aside provision to the public works bill, MBE set-aside requirements were established in 1978. Following Croson, lawsuits filed throughout the country by excluded white contractors—including a suit by Arnold O'Donnell, owner of O'Donnell Construction in Washington—began to reveal the normally obscured inner workings of the set-aside programs. Like the federal programs, and largely for the same reasons, the city programs were dominated by a small number of successful firms, often owned by wealthy immigrants.

In Washington, the O'Donnell lawsuit revealed that in fiscal year 1990, 41 percent of the District's contracts, about two hundred thirty-seven million dollars, went to minority-owned firms. Between 1986 and 1990, although more than 500 firms were certified by the city for MBE contracts, 80 percent of the city's road and sewer contracts had gone to only four firms. The largest of the four, Fort Myer Construction Co., was owned by Jose Rodriguez, an immigrant from Portugal. Rodriguez had come to America when he was eighteen, founded his company in 1972, and competed successfully for construction contracts in the era before MBE set-asides. In the 1980s, Fort Meyer became a leading player in the District's set-aside contracting. In fiscal year 1990, for example, Fort Myer received about half of Washington's $64 million in road and sewer contracts. Another of Washington's top four MBE companies, Capitol Paving, was owned by Rodriguez's brother, Francisco Rodriguez-Neto. Capitol Paving received $7.4 million or 12 percent of the District's set-aside road and sewer contracts in 1990. Together, the two wealthy immigrant brothers from Europe, certified as Hispanic by the District's MBE program, received 63 percent of the city's road and sewer contracts.[44]

In Florida, another set of immigrant brothers, Alphonso and Jose Fanjul, exploited MBE set-aside opportunities even though they presided over a fifth-generation sugar dynasty with a net worth estimated by Forbes magazine in 1995 at $500 million. The Fanjuls, whose family wealth came chiefly from Cuban sugar plantations, fled Castro's revolution in 1959, bringing with them Spanish passports and retaining Spanish citizenship in order to avoid U.S. estate tax laws. By the 1980s the Palm Beach-based

Fanjul estate included more than 400,000 sugar cane acres in Florida and Caribbean Islands, a 7,000 acre luxury resort in the Dominican Republic, and major holdings in Florida real estate, banking, and finance. U.S. protectionism and price supports for sugar paid the Fanjuls' Flo-Sun Corporation $65 million in 1995. To protect this subsidy and other helpful U.S. and Florida policies, the Fanjuls contributed hundreds of thousands to both political parties, including the presidential campaigns of George Bush and Bill Clinton and the Florida gubernatorial campaign of Jeb Bush.[45]

In the early 1990s, the Fanjul-controlled FAIC Securities company took advantage of new federal and state set-aside programs to build minority business enterprise in securities underwriting. As a Hispanic-owned firm, FAIC qualified for essentially risk-free underwriting profits on hundreds of millions in Fannie Mae and Miami Airport bonds. Participation in minority set-aside programs by the "Sultans of Sugar," as the Fanjuls were often called in the press, was ethically questionable, but it was indubitably legal on its face. However, the story of affirmative action for multimillionaire Cuban immigrants with Spanish passports, and associated reports of a Securities and Exchange Commission investigation of political contributions and public contract awards, brought the Fanjuls more negative publicity than the profits were worth, and in 1995 they withdrew from minority set-aside underwriting.[46]

Competition between Immigrants and African-Americans for Affirmative Action Jobs

Horror stories about millionaire immigrants do not typify the governments' minority contract set-aside programs. But they do illustrate the tendency of MBE programs to benefit large successful firms, an increasing share of which were owned by Hispanic and Asian Americans, many of them immigrants. Nonetheless, affirmative action programs that apply to business owners are inherently limited in their reach. The nation's mass-based affirmative action arena was in employment, not business ownership. In job discrimination law, the standard for minority hiring was set from the beginning by the EEOC and the OFCC. By 1971 these agencies had won federal court approval for a disparate impact model of EEO enforcement based on an assumption that, absent discrimination, minorities should be proportionally represented in each firm's workforce.

The shift from nondiscrimination to affirmative action, however, brought with it an increase in ambiguity. This was partly because it was unclear just what affirmative action meant, and partly because the Civil

Rights Act and American public opinion ruled out stark racial quotas. To circumvent the Civil Rights Act's ban on racial quotas, the Nixon administration and its successors emphasized flexible "goals and timetables" in affirmative action hiring plans, not "quotas and deadlines," inviting employers to set their own targets. An employer's "good faith effort" in minority hiring might therefore deviate modestly from the precise benchmark numbers that the Census Bureau produced for each labor market, showing the percentage of available workers who were African-American, Hispanic, Asian Pacific Islander, etc. Thus an employer hiring in an urban labor market that census data showed to be 24 percent black, 17 percent Hispanic, and 9 percent Asian would be expected by the EEOC to employ a workforce in which close to half of the workers were minorities. But because EEO law protected minorities (and women), not just blacks, and because the government denied using proportional representation quotas, the internal mix of minority employees within a company was not closely policed. This flexible standard eased the government's vulnerability concerning quota hiring. But it also opened a window of opportunity for businesses, under the banner of diversity, to hire Hispanic and Asian immigrants in preference to native-born black workers.[47]

The shift to diversity-based employment practices marked a fundamental transition in American business. Initially, this change sped the hiring and promotion of African-Americans. By the 1980s, however, it had shifted employment emphasis toward Hispanic and Asian workers, especially immigrants. The process was driven by expanding federal civil rights protections, extended by Congress to minorities and women in the early 1960s, then to older workers in 1967, to the handicapped in 1973, and to Vietnam war veterans in 1974. At the same time, the government's employment rights protections were extended by Congress beyond job discrimination to include safety and health risks (the Occupational Safety and Health Administration, OSHA, established in 1970) and employee benefits (the Employee Retirement Income Security Act, ERISA, passed in 1974). In response, large employers shifted from traditional systems of personnel management to expanded systems of "human resources" management that institutionalized, professionalized, and integrated business practices in affirmative action, safety, health, and benefits.[48] Corporate legal departments, alarmed by the sharp rise of EEO lawsuits in the 1970s, exaggerated the threat of litigation and urged employers to adopt comprehensive affirmative action plans.[49]

It was this change, the embrace of affirmative action by American big business, that dismayed conservatives when the Reagan administration declined to rewrite the affirmative action executive order in the early 1980s.

American corporate managers, following the expansive logic of the human resources management paradigm, reconstituted the EEO/affirmative action office as the "diversity" center. They justified employment policies in terms of economic efficiency: In a globalizing economy, greater employee diversity brings new ideas, cross-cultural perspectives, and language abilities that in turn bring design, production, and marketing advantages. In human resources parlance, "diversity" came to replace "affirmative action" as the code word for efforts to integrate the workforce.[50]

One consequence of this shift by management to a diversity rationale was the support it provided employers for hiring immigrants. Sociologist William Julius Wilson, surveying employment practices in a representative sample of 179 firms in the greater Chicago area in 1987–88, was "overwhelmed" by the willingness of Chicago employers to talk with his interviewers "in a negative way about blacks."[51] Three-fourths of the employers surveyed expressed some negative views about black workers, especially inner-city black men. They were seen as lazy, dishonest, undependable, and lacking in a work ethic. Employers strongly preferred Hispanic and Asian workers, seeing them as hardworking, dependable, and honest.[52] Wilson's survey only confirmed patterns of behavior and belief about employer preferences that many black leaders had been quietly complaining about since the 1970s, when the unexpected force of Latin American and Asian immigration first began to be felt.[53]

By the 1980s, social scientists were studying ethnic network recruiting, documenting the tendency for language, kinship, and community ties to convert certain American job fields into immigrant enclaves.[54] This process was especially advanced in restaurants, hotels, janitorial services, and furniture manufacturing. By the 1980s, ethnic networks, word-of-mouth recruiting, and business preferences were combining to drive Hispanic and Asian employment up and keep black employment down. One study, noting that affirmative action regulations do not distinguish between American-born minorities and immigrant minorities, concluded that because hiring was commonly done through existing employee networks, "African Americans are becoming increasingly excluded, even in their own neighborhoods."[55]

The EEOC, alarmed by these trends, was determined to stop them. EEOC employment reports for 1980, a recession year, showed unemployment levels of 14.3 percent for blacks and 38.5 percent for black youth, as compared with 8.9 percent for Hispanics and 16.4 percent for Hispanic youth. In 1979 the EEOC, accustomed to winning in federal court, filed suit against a company in Chicago, seeking a landmark ruling against employers who failed to hire blacks in proportion to their availability in the relevant labor pool. The EEOC's target was the Chicago Miniature Lamp Works.

Located in a largely Hispanic and Asian neighborhood on the north side of Chicago, Miniature manufactured small incandescent and neon lamps. Most hiring was done in low-paying, entry-level jobs that did not require prior experience, a particular educational background, or special skills. Miniature recruited primarily by word-of-mouth, a process that even without advertising produced enough applicants to hire one person for every fifteen that applied. Because the jobs required minimal English language fluency, they were attractive to persons who did not speak English as a primary language. Between 1978 and 1981, Miniature hired 146 entry-level workers, only 9 of them (6 percent) black. Between 1970 and 1981 Miniature employed between 202 and 396 entry-level workers, with employment of blacks ranging from 4.5 to 6.5 percent, Hispanics from 40 to 66 percent, and Asians from 0 to 16.5 percent.

The EEOC, pointing out that blacks constituted 36 percent of entry-level workers in the city of Chicago but only 6 percent of Miniature's workers, charged Miniature with racial discrimination against African-American workers. The EEOC's case rested almost entirely on statistics comparing Miniature's hiring of entry-level black workers and their availability in the city of Chicago. In 1985 the trial court ruled against Miniature. Applying disparate impact analysis developed in the 1970s, the district court found that "the statistical probability of Miniature's hiring so few blacks in the 1978–1981 period, in the absence of racial bias against blacks in recruitment and hiring, is virtually zero."[56] By relying on community word-of-mouth networks, the court ruled, Miniature had unlawfully excluded blacks from the hiring process. Miniature appealed.

That same year, 1985, the EEOC sued Consolidated Service Systems, a janitorial and cleaning business in Chicago. Like Miniature Lamp Works, Consolidated relied primarily on word-of-mouth recruiting to fill low-paying, low-skill jobs. Owned by a family of Korean immigrants named Hwang, the company hired mostly Korean workers. From 1983 to 1987, 73 percent of the applicants and 81 percent of the hires at Consolidated were Korean. The EEOC, noting that Cook County was less than 1 percent Korean, charged Consolidated with discriminating against black workers. The district court, however, dismissed the suit, and both parties appealed. Given the customary delays of the appeals process, this meant that more than a decade would elapse before the EEOC's drive to increase black employment, relative to that of competing minorities, would clear the appeals process. For the EEOC, this was a fateful delay.

The EEOC began its campaign to protect black workers from the surging tides of immigrant competition during the Carter presidency, when federal court rulings continued to support the claims of the civil rights coalition. By the early 1990s, however, the judicial appointments of presidents Reagan and Bush had reshaped the federal bench in a conservative direction. The Reagan-Bush appointees were more sympathetic to business needs and less sympathetic to government regulation. In 1991, the Seventh Circuit Court of Appeals overturned the trial court's ruling against Miniature Lamp Works. The three-judge panel ruled unanimously that the district court improperly used the entire city of Chicago as the relevant labor market, and ignored legitimate factors in hiring, including relative commuting distance and lack of an English fluency requirement. "Without probative evidence of discriminatory intent," the appeals court held, "Miniature is not liable when it passively relies on the natural flow of applicants for its entry-level positions."[57]

In 1993, another Seventh Circuit panel ruled against the EEOC in the Consolidated Service Systems case. As in the Miniature case, the appeals court found that Mr. Hwang's word-of-mouth recruiting method was simple, straightforward, and effective. "It would be a bitter irony if the federal agency dedicated to enforcing the antidiscrimination laws," Judge Richard Posner wrote for the court, "succeeded in using these laws to kick these people off the ladder by compelling them to institute costly systems of hiring."[58]

The EEOC lawsuits provide a window on the rising economic competition between blacks and immigrants. Another view was provided by news reports in the 1980s of black-Hispanic tension and violence concentrated on the Cuban influx in the Miami area, especially in Liberty City. In 1992, the most destructive urban riot in the nation's history broke out in Los Angeles. Triggered by the jury acquittal of Los Angeles policemen accused of beating an African-American suspect, Rodney King, the 1992 riot was explained by black leaders as a rerun of the Watts protest riot of 1965, exploding again to protest American civil rights failures. But subsequent study confirmed that on the contrary, the Los Angeles eruption was in many respects an intramural, immigration riot, as blacks attacked Asian businesses and street warfare broke out between Latinos and blacks. Half of the arrested rioters were Hispanic, and most of the torched businesses were Korean-owned.[59] Hispanic organizations in Los Angeles increasingly had complained that blacks used affirmative action to entrench themselves in the civil service bureaucracy. With half of Angeleans foreign-born and more than 40 percent speaking Spanish at home, Hispanic rights organizations demanded that affirmative action preferences reflect the city's new demographics.[60] In the wake of the Los Angeles riot, Congressman Luis V. Gutierrez (D-Ill.), a Puerto Rican elected in 1992 in a newly formed Hispanic-majority district in Chicago, requested a General Accounting Office study of affirmative action hiring in the U.S. Postal Service. The report the

GAO prepared for Gutierrez in 1993 showed that blacks were heavily over-represented and Hispanics underrepresented in the Postal Service.[61] In the GAO study, a representation index of 100 indicated demographic parity between groups (blacks, for example, holding 15 percent of jobs in the area civilian workforce and also 15 percent in the Postal Service).

In Chicago, the GAO found, the representational index for blacks in postal service jobs was 439, meaning they were overrepresented in postal jobs by a factor greater than four. For Hispanics the index in Chicago was 33 (an index lower than 50, according to the EEOC, showed extreme underrepresentation). The index for Asians in Chicago was 56. For whites, it was 20. In Los Angeles, the Postal Service index for blacks according to the GAO study was 646. For Hispanics it was 42. For Asians, the index in Los Angeles was 145. For whites, it was 16. Nationwide, the representational index for Postal Service employment was blacks 204, Asians 169, whites 85, Hispanics 76.

The GAO study offers only one small window, a rare empirical glimpse into the demographic consequences of affirmative-action programs, in this case one of the oldest and largest (678,000 postal employees in 1993). In this program, complaining Hispanic organizations had the strongest case for underrepresentation. But they had the weakest claims to a compensatory remedy originally intended for the descendants of African slaves. The GAO study illustrates both the advantages blacks enjoyed from political entrenchment in affirmative action bureaucracies and the disadvantages blacks encountered from market forces in a global economy with heavy immigration.

Economists debate the overall effect of immigration on the American economy, but most agree that from the 1970s to the mid-1990s, large-scale immigration by low-skilled workers reduced job opportunities and pay for working-class African-Americans.[62] Sociologists, more than economists, have studied immigrant displacement of native-born workers through ethnic network recruiting in job fields such as construction, garment and furniture production, hotel, restaurant, janitorial, and agricultural employment.[63] By the 1990s, however, the emphasis of study on immigration in the labor force had shifted toward high-skilled employment fields, especially those supporting the fast-developing electronics industry and university engineering and science. Controversy over affirmative action in higher education admissions and employment grew in the 1990s, especially in California. Asian groups protested preferential treatment for blacks and Hispanics, and African-American groups complained that Asians, including many immigrants, displaced blacks in graduate education, in employment in the booming electronics and software industry, and in minority business set-aside contracts as well.[64]

From Entry-Level to Highly Skilled Immigration

As the U.S. economy recovered from the recession of the early 1990s, employers looked abroad for more skilled and educated workers to service the economy's rapidly expanding high-technology sector. Critics of American immigration policy had argued persuasively that the needs of the surging high-tech economy were poorly served by the mass importation of low-skilled, uneducated workers. In the 1980s, one-third of male immigrant workers were school dropouts. To attract top international brainpower, American universities had taken the lead in recruiting abroad, filling classroom seats added during the 1960s and emptied by the "baby bust" of the 1970s, and recruiting graduate students and faculty in science and engineering. By 1990, of the 13.8 million students enrolled in U.S. postsecondary education, 1.5 million were foreign-born. Nearly a third of all students who earned their doctorates in the sciences—and more than half of all students who earned their doctorates in engineering—in this country between 1991 and 1995 came from other nations. As of 1993, 37 percent of engineering professionals and 27 percent of math and computer science professionals were foreign-born.[65]

Although most foreign-born graduate students studied in the United States under temporary student visas, not immigration visas, reports from the National Science Foundation (NSF) showed that in 1995, 63 percent of all foreign graduate students planned to settle in the United States. Graduate students from developing countries, sent to study in the United States and return home to help build their nation's economies, found ways to remain in the United States. According to NSF data, in 1995, 59 percent of graduate students from India and 57 percent of those from China remained in the United States upon completion of their degrees. They commonly won permanent residence by using their skills to obtain green cards and secure jobs in American industry, government, and higher education, often winning postdoctoral appointments in the process. At Harvard in 1991, for example, 46.4 percent of postdoctoral appointees in the science, engineering, and health fields were noncitizens. University professors and supervisors in industry generally found foreign graduate students and newly minted Ph.D.s to be hardworking, well trained, uncomplaining, and willing to work for modest compensation.[66]

Not surprisingly, American universities recruited abroad for faculty as well as for students. The practice was not new. Witness the roster of distinguished European scientists engaged in the Manhattan Project to develop the atomic bomb. Neither was it particularly controversial. It seemed appropriate for American universities, globally dominant in the postwar era, to recruit abroad for faculty brainpower. American Nobel Prize winners in physics, chemistry, and medicine, interviewed on television, often spoke with a foreign accent. Complaints against the practice arose chiefly from students in classes taught by nonnative speakers of English (including graduate teaching assistants) and from some African-American leaders resenting foreign displacement of blacks in graduate school and faculty appointments.

Both complaints reflected particularly the success of Asians on American campuses. In 1997, for example, Asians constituted 13.2 percent of the full-time faculty at the University of California, Berkeley and 69.7 percent of the minority faculty. At the University of Michigan, where affirmative action hiring between 1987 and 1992 had increased African-American representation on the faculty from 3 to 4.4 percent, and Asian representation from 4.9 to 6.1 percent, the faculty senate nonetheless raised objections. Of the minority faculty listed by the university, the faculty senate found that 56.1 percent of the Asian-Americans were not American citizens. Nor were 23.3 percent of the Hispanic faculty and 18.8 percent of black faculty.[67]

Sorting out citizens from noncitizens, native-born from foreign-born, and immigrant from nonimmigrant is no less difficult on American campuses than elsewhere in the American economy. The EEOC, both in the EEO-6 form it used to monitor institutions of higher education before 1993, and in the IPEDS form it used subsequently, obscured the data by excluding immigrants with green cards from the reporting of foreign nationals. Colleges and universities themselves typically ignored distinctions between foreign nationals and U.S. citizens, a practice that maximized their minority counts of students, faculty, and staff. At Stanford, for example, an affirmative action incentive plan awarded departments half of a new faculty position for every full-time minority appointee. But when the *San Jose Mercury News* reported in 1993 that most of Stanford's minority faculty members were foreign-born, the administration retargeted Stanford's affirmative action plan on underrepresented minorities. These were identified as African-Americans, Mexican-Americans, Puerto Ricans, and American Indians. But Asian-Americans were excluded on the grounds that they were already well represented on campus. The University of California, Berkeley had adopted a similar policy for student admissions in the 1980s, but reverse discrimination complaints by Asian-American groups had fueled a controversy that led the University of California regents in 1995 to abandon affirmative action preferences.[68]

The controversy over affirmative action at the University of California drew worldwide attention. Stanford's struggle over minority preferences had a lower profile but involved the same problem: Should universities include all four official minorities in affirmative action programs, as required in federal law, or exclude Asians because they were not underrepresented in university admissions and faculty appointments? Stanford's retargeting, with its Asian exclusion, proved upsetting to members of the affirmative action establishment, which had built its coalition on the federal government's color-coded minority designation of black, brown, yellow, and red. Federal law included Asian Pacific Islanders as minorities, and the "people of color" formula encouraged nonwhite solidarity. Robert Rubin, of the Lawyers' Committee for Civil Rights in San Francisco, warned that Stanford was bound under Title VI of the Civil Rights Act to affirmative action for Asians as a protected minority. Gazella Summit, president of the American Association for Affirmative Action, said of Stanford's narrowed formula, "They would be leaving themselves open [to a lawsuit] in my opinion." Stanford quietly dropped its retargeting plan.[69]

Stanford is an apt example of the interplay between immigration and affirmative action at the high-skill end of the spectrum, because it is surrounded by Silicon Valley, the national heartland of the high-tech economy that Stanford helped pioneer. In 1998 the *San Francisco Chronicle* published a series, The Digital Divide, on low levels of black and Latino employment in Silicon Valley firms. The *Chronicle* obtained employment records for thirty-three Silicon Valley firms under the Freedom of Information Act (twenty-one of the fifty-four firms receiving the Chronicle requests declined to participate). The reports based on this somewhat skewed sample showed that whites were 56 percent of the Bay Area workforce but held 61 percent of the high-tech firm jobs. Blacks and Latinos were 8 percent and 14 percent of the area workforce, respectively, but held only 4 percent and 7 percent of the jobs, most of them in production rather than in management or professional staff. Asians, 21 percent of the Bay Area workforce, held 28 percent of the jobs. Although Asians were the most overrepresented group in Silicon Valley employment, the *Chronicle* played up the traditional white/nonwhite dyad. The story quoted Amy Dean, executive officer of the South Bay AFL-CIO Labor Council: "Silicon Valley is very much a tale of two cities—and the community of color is being left behind."[70] The *Chronicle* thus missed the main story behind the numbers, which was one of Asian immigrant success, a story that confounded the affirmative action premise upon which the *Chronicle*'s Digital Divide series was based.

The *Wall Street Journal*, a cheerleader for Asian-American entrepreneur success but no fan of affirmative action, reported on 21 September 1999 that from 1995 to 1998, 29 percent of Silicon Valley startup firms were formed by Chinese or Indian migrants. In 1998, Indians or Chinese headed 2,775

Silicon Valley high-tech firms, employing 58,000 people, with total sales of $16.8 billion. The *San Francisco Chronicle* series, relying on data from Silicon Valley's larger, more established firms, such as Apple Computer, Intel, Oracle, and Sun Microsystems, in all likelihood underestimated Asian participation. Few observers credit affirmative action with a significant role in the Asian success story in Silicon Valley. Yet equally dramatic evidence of Asian achievement is provided by the nation's largest single affirmative action program, in terms of tax dollar totals, the federal government's SBA's 8(a) contract set-aside program for designated minorities. During the 1990s, Asian-Americans sped past Latinos to become the top beneficiaries in California of the SBA's $6 billion MBE program.

From 1990 to 1996, the percentage of SBA contract dollars awarded to Asian-Americans in California quadrupled, while the share awarded to Hispanics decreased by almost half. In 1990, Asian-Americans received 12 percent of SBA contract dollars nationwide, compared with 30 percent for Hispanics and 35 percent for blacks. By 1996, the nationwide share of contract dollars for Asians had risen to 28 percent while the Hispanic share had fallen to 26 percent and the black share to 34 percent. In California, where the breakdown of the minority population in 1996 was 61 percent Hispanic, 22 percent Asian, 15 percent black, and 1 percent Native American, the MBE contract dollar breakdowns were Asians 40 percent, Hispanics 33 percent, blacks 23 percent, and Native Americans 2 percent.[71] Proportionally, by 1996 Asian entrepreneurs in California were receiving almost twice their population share in federal MBE tax dollars and Hispanics were receiving little more than half.

As the twentieth century came to a close, the last thirty years characterized by large-scale immigration and by affirmative action programs for designated minority groups, the interplay between these two sprawling developments, neither of them intended by the lawmakers shaping the civil rights and immigration legislation of the 1960s, had illuminated the strengths and weaknesses of both. Who were the main winners and losers in this long-running contest of politics and policy, and why?

7

Conclusion

At the heart of this book is a story about the surprising development of two of the great legislative victories in civil rights and immigration policy won by American liberal reformers in the 1960s. Both reforms were grounded in the liberal theory and constitutional doctrine of equal individual rights, and both were driven through Congress by essentially the same cadre of liberal elites. By 1970, moreover, both appeared to be achieving their intended consequences: destroying the racial caste system in the South and abolishing the national origins quota system. By 1975, however, it was clear that both reforms were leading to unintended consequences. In civil rights policy, enforcement methods shifted from nondiscrimination and soft affirmative action to the minority preference remedies of hard or race-conscious affirmative action. Immigration, both legal and illegal, soon surpassed pre-World War I levels in annual entry, with more than three-quarters of the immigrants coming from countries in Latin America and Asia. Although the civil rights and immigration reforms of the mid-1960s were widely approved throughout the United States by 1970, even among southern whites, polls showed that by 1980, both affirmative action and mass immigration were unpopular in the eyes of most Americans.[1] Nevertheless, the civil rights and immigration coalitions showed skill and persistence in fending off attempts made during the Reagan presidency to curb immigration and hard affirmative action. Despite the political success of the conservative movement and the "Reagan Revolution," both statutory and regulatory provisions for affirmative action programs and legal immigration levels generally expanded through the 1980s and 1990s, as elected officials at national, state, and local levels in both parties proved reluctant to offend the well-organized constituencies of the rights revolution.

In response to the policy reversals seen by the 1970s, the national debate over affirmative action came first. From the urban race riots of the 1960s to the *Bakke* decision of 1978, Americans argued about institutional racism and reverse discrimination and paid little attention to immigration, which in any event seemed to have little to do with affirmative action. When the boatlift refugees from Cuba, Haiti, and Vietnam brought attention to soaring immigration in a faltering economy, the immigration issue for the first time surpassed affirmative action as a controversial issue on the national legislative agenda. During the 1990s, economic distress and political protest in high immigration states such as California raised new questions about affirmative action that had not been debated in the 1970s. Why were millions of immigrants—including illegal immigrants—in job competition with native-born Americans given special protection through affirmative action preferences? The success of the rights revolution coalition in committing American government to affirmative action and high immigration policies had demonstrated the political strengths of these policies. Their convergence in the 1990s, however, increasingly demonstrated their substantive weaknesses. From this three-decade process, immigration emerged greatly strengthened and affirmative action significantly, perhaps even mortally, weakened.

Strengths of Affirmative Action

To identify the most important achievements of hard affirmative action since the 1960s, one should begin with the federal officials who led the shift to race-conscious affirmative action following the inner-city riots of 1965–68. Their main goal was to speed redistribution of jobs and income to African-Americans. And this, by and large, they accomplished. The Philadelphia Plan rather quickly demolished the holdout barricades in the AFL's lily-white craft unions. Government agencies quickly reduced underutilization of minorities in public employment. By 1980 the EEOC, the Labor Department, and the federal courts had firmly established disparate impact theory as the norm in American employment law. Contract set-aside programs at the federal, state, and local levels helped open the networks dominated by established government contractors. The combined effect of hiring and promoting "by the numbers" in government, industry, unions, and the nonprofit sector, together with minority set-asides in government contracting and minority preferences in college and professional school admissions, contributed substantially to the extraordinary tripling of the black middle class since the 1960s.[2]

It is important not to overestimate the role of race-conscious remedies in this achievement. The most dramatic narrowing of the nation's racial income gap occurred before 1973, the year of the OPEC oil embargo that marks the end of the postwar era of robust economic growth in the United States. By far the most effective engine of racial justice in the postwar era was economic growth combined with rigorously enforced nondiscrimination law. Expanding race-conscious affirmative action thus coincided with the sharp economic downturn of 1973–82, years of stagnant real wages and high unemployment that produced counterpressures and widened the income gap between rich and poor, and between blacks and whites as well, that had been narrowing prior to 1973. Also, part of the gap-closing between the incomes of white males and the various protected classes in EEO enforcement is explained by the success of soft rather than hard affirmative action.[3] The chief example of this (and of its limits as well) is the rising employment and earnings of women, the largest single beneficiary class of modern EEO policy. Feminist organizations routinely supported affirmative action. But the affirmative action that most effectively benefited women as a class was the soft variety, with its emphasis on nondiscrimination enforcement plus targeted outreach. With the exception of small-scale participation in Women's Business Enterprise programs, organized feminist groups, most of them founded in the crusade for the Equal Rights Amendment, rarely sought or benefited from gender preference policies.[4]

Despite these caveats, and despite persistent misunderstanding and muddled debate caused by public inability to distinguish between soft and hard affirmative action, substantial credit must be given to race-conscious affirmative action programs for expanding the black middle class. This achievement is anchored in government employment, where African-Americans disproportionately staff the nation's civil service jobs. But more broadly, the spread of minority preference programs in college and professional school admissions in the 1980s and 1990s opened career doors to a generation of black and Hispanic students whose grades and test scores had previously disqualified them.

Beyond these important practical achievements, the theory of affirmative action made sense of American history in ways that liberalism's abstract theory of equal individual rights did not. Liberal theory centered on the social contract, a bargain of convenience voluntarily undertaken by humans possessing inherent equal rights. American history, however, showed vast stretches wherein the rights of Native Americans, blacks, women, Asians, and other groups were not recognized, followed by bursts of recognition and liberal reform that embraced the newly included groups, but that found them hobbled by generations of deprivation. This was the message preached by President Lyndon Johnson, in a Howard University commencement address in June 1965, when he described the unfair footrace between the hobbled and the hale.[5] To provide a theoretical rationale and a structural justification for affirmative action's heresy of racial preferences, academic sociologists developed a theory of institutional racism. It explained how institutions as they evolved often embedded racist (and sexist) beliefs in their rules and traditions. As a consequence, institutions could perpetuate racist behavior even if all individuals and policies within the institutions were free of bias.[6]

Mere color-blind nondiscrimination, in this analysis, could not achieve racial justice in the absence of the compensatory race-conscious remedies of hard affirmative action. Classical liberal theory, unlike academic sociology, offered no remedy to help compensate for the unequal burden of past discrimination. Race-conscious remedies, on the other hand, promised not equal procedures but equal results, enforced by numerical goals and deadlines. Not only did this approach seem more realistic to beneficiaries but it dovetailed nicely in the 1960s with contemporary theories of compensatory education. Poor children, stunted by mean environments, merited enriched learning environments to catch up. More important, compensatory remedies fit comfortably within the modern framework of social regulation, where a new generation of watchdog agencies—the EEOC, the Environmental Protection Agency, the Occupational Safety and Health Administration, the Consumer Products Safety Commission—set numerical standards of performance to protect Americans from social risk and harm. This common setting of social regulation located affirmative action programs in the context of the modern administrative state and thus strengthened their legitimacy.[7]

Weaknesses of Affirmative Action

Set against these and other qualitative assets of affirmative action are its greatest liabilities. First among these is the persistent belief by a majority of Americans that minority preferences are unfair. They violate the American creed that all citizens possess equal individual rights. It is unfair, the majority believes, to deny a job, promotion, contract, or other government benefit to one person and award it to another on account of their race, gender, or ethnic ancestry. Public opinion surveys since the 1960s have persistently shown four out of five whites rejecting race-conscious affirmative action.[8] By 2000, college students by the same margin opposed giving preferential treatment to minority applicants in admissions.[9]

Majority opposition to affirmative action is not confined to white males or even to whites. Survey research shows that while women have not differed from white men in holding this belief, even though women are a protected class in the minority rights revolution. Asians, too, share these attitudes, despite their protected class status. A 1988 Field poll reported that while 56 percent of California blacks favored "special preferences" for minorities in hiring and promotions, only 36 percent of Hispanics and 15 percent of Asians agreed.[10] According to a 1993 poll conducted by the California Policy Seminar, two-thirds of Asians opposed affirmative action.[11] Forty percent of the nation's 12 million Asian-Americans live in California, where they have the highest median income and proportion of college graduates of any ethnic group and the lowest welfare rate among minorities. Hispanics, especially Mexican-Americans, the largest Latino group, have been ambivalent, torn between traditional attitudes that resist racialized politics and political leaders who emulate the black activist racial model.[12] Given the similarities in education, income, and attitudes between whites and Asians, and the ambivalence of Hispanics about racial identity and minority preferences, it is evident that defenders of affirmative action have failed to convince most Americans that minority preference policies are fair. There is no "people of color" consensus behind affirmative action. Black and Latino political leaders have maintained solidarity with national liberal elites in support of affirmative action; indeed, among affirmative action's major achievements must be listed effective political support by a coalition skilled at persuading legislative and agency officials. At the grassroots, however, black Americans remain largely isolated in approving race-conscious measures.[13]

Another weakness of affirmative action has been its failure to benefit the poor, especially the black underclass in the inner cities, whose rioting in the late 1960s led alarmed federal agency officials to develop the program in the first place. Despite affirmative action's origins in ghetto riots, its clientele has been middle-class. The benefits of minority preference programs reflect this middle class orientation. They include college and professional school admissions, small business government contracts, and appointment and promotion in civil service jobs, school classrooms and administrative staff, armed services careers, the U.S. Postal Service, higher education and medical services staff, industrial and service sector trade unions, human resources and personnel management posts, and civil rights organizations staff. Taking advantage of affirmative action required middle-class skills: education, organization, lobbying, and litigation. All this was alien to the world of the "truly disadvantaged," in sociologist William Julius Wilson's term: the school dropouts of the inner city with arrest records, the drug pushers and addicts and teenage mothers with little work discipline and few marketable skills.[14] Like most government benefit programs—farm subsidies, college tuition aid, veterans benefits, medical care for the elderly, housing deductions—affirmative action rewarded well-organized constituencies. There were some spillover benefits for poor minorities from affirmative action, for example, minority quotas for inner-city police and firefighting forces. On the whole, however, for poor blacks as well as for poor whites, affirmative action has been at best economically irrelevant and at worst harmful.

Affirmative action programs were further burdened, in the process of implementation, because sponsoring governments had no experience running benefit programs where participation was based on selected ancestry. As affirmative action expanded, these practical problems led to complaints about corruption, waste, and unfair implementation by civil rights enforcement agencies. Concerning program corruption and abuse, as minority business enterprise (MBE) programs spread in the 1980s, the news media reported fraudulent business ownership claims, including bogus executive titles conferred on formerly low-ranking minority employees or on owners' wives to make firms eligible for affirmative action programs. In most affirmative action programs, claims of ancestral lineage were seldom verified. Often officials acting on applicant self-classifications, such as employers or college admissions staff, welcomed the minority traffic and refused to question minority status claims. The number of individuals claiming American Indian ancestry, for example, declined for generations and then zoomed sharply upward after 1970. Claims of Native American ancestry became a rarely challenged ticket to college admissions and other affirmative action benefits.[15] Self-identification without verification tempted many white Americans, including persons of Middle Eastern and North African origins, to claim Hispanic as well as American Indian ancestry. Such incidents, when discovered, made good copy for human interest stories. But because the rewards were large and the checkpoints were few and weak, affirmative action fraud tainted the entire enterprise with a persisting stigma.

Incentives for policing corruption were especially weak in the municipal contract set-aside programs, which spread to most large cities in the 1980s. With city hall increasingly controlled by minority coalitions and mayors, government officials were no more eager to police their own spoils system than were the notorious Irish city machines of the nineteenth century. In the 1990s, following the Supreme Court's requirement in *Croson* (1989) that jurisdictions seeking minority set-aside programs must identify specific events of discrimination and narrowly tailor their remedies, local governments responded by commissioning expensive "disparity studies" to prove that they were complicit in discrimination and hence obliged to establish minority set-aside remedies. American local governments in the 1990s thus introduced the novelty of spending tax dollars, often at costs exceeding $500,000 per disparity study, not to defend themselves against charges of racial discrimination but to prove their own guilt.[16]

A related category of practical complaint against affirmative action was waste of taxpayer dollars. Historically, government antidiscrimination measures had produced more efficient use of human resources, not less, by enlarging the labor pool and improving its competitive performance. But MBE programs short-circuited the government's traditional, low-bid procurement protocols. These had been the proud legacy of the Progressive reformers who attacked the corruption of the city machines. The minority preference mechanisms used in single-source contracts and in no-bid, bid-preference, and minority subcontracting arrangements, however, were more expensive than standard low-bid contracting and often less efficient as well. Some inefficiency was arguably a legitimate social cost of affirmative action programs, as many novice minority contractors made mistakes common to inexperienced entrepreneurs. Many others, however, over-charged prime contractors for their minority subcontract, knowing that nonminority prime contractors were barred from bidding without minority subcontractors. And some MBE contractors adjusted their operations to the favor-swapping routines of old-fashioned political graft, as had European immigrant entrepreneurs in the city machines of generations past. Newspapers occasionally publicized the more flagrant examples of racial and ethnic pork, such as Wedtech and the Rodriguez and Fanjul families. But the minority political alliances that created the set-aside programs generally screened participants from public scrutiny and its consequences.[17]

No less protective of affirmative action programs than Democrats in city hall were Democratic majorities in Congress, who controlled the House of Representatives for forty years before the Republican sweep of 1994. Democratic-controlled committees were generally uninterested in studies critical of affirmative action programs. The new Republican committee chairpersons of 1995, not surprisingly, held hearings and commissioned reports critical of the Democrats' favorite social programs, such as the SBA's 8(a) program.[18] But Congress under Republican control showed little enthusiasm for passing legislation to curb race-conscious affirmative action.[19] The federal government's largest affirmative action program in tax dollar volume, however, the SBA's 8(a) program, was so persistently flawed from the beginning that GAO reports to Congress, even during the years of Democratic control, criticized it for inefficiency, administrative sloppiness, dominance by a small number of large profitable firms, and MBE firm dependency on subsidized sole-source business.

On the whole, public exposés of corruption and inefficiency in affirmative action programs were ineffective against the protective lobbying of the civil rights coalition. Although the affirmative action issue in the late 1960s and early 1970s had helped split the Democrats' New Deal coalition, ushering in an era of Republican presidencies and conservative federal court appointments under Nixon, Ford, Reagan, and Bush, the advantages of client politics, ably exploited by the civil rights coalition in lobbying legislators and agency officials, helped neutralize the weight of public opinion against affirmative action. Even the conservative Republican leaders, such as House Speaker Newt Gingrich, omitted affirmative action reform from their 1995 Contract with America and minimized it in their subsequent legislative priorities. This behavior reflected a recognition by opponents of affirmative action that, despite majority support in public opinion, in the world of practical politics they would be attacked as racists by the civil rights coalition.

The practical advantages enjoyed by the civil rights coalition in the battle over affirmative action included effective control of the civil rights enforcement agencies in Washington and the equivalent bureaucracies in state and local governments. In the calculation of political muscle, this was a source of strength, not weakness, for affirmative action. But from the viewpoint of public legitimacy, it damaged the reputation for fairness of many government agencies and strengthened trends toward cynicism about government. It fueled resentment by whites that they were excluded from civil rights protections. Paradoxically, then, as affirmative action was strengthened in political power inside the beltways encircling American governing elites, it was diminished outside the beltway in perceived public legitimacy.[20]

Affirmative Action, Republicans, and Immigration

For the country as a whole, the strengths of affirmative action policy since the 1960s have not matched its weaknesses. One reason for this, little explored in the literature, is that mass immigration brought increasing pressures on both the logic and the structures of affirmative action. During the 1990s, controversy over immigration levels and over immigrants in affirmative action programs stimulated fresh debate over the definition of racial and ethnic minorities and the reasons and consequences for awarding government benefits on the basis of ancestry. High intermarriage rates among second-generation immigrants led to controversy over racial definitions to be used in the 2000 census, multiracial Americans objected to government requirements that individuals have a single racial identity, while the civil rights coalition urged the Clinton administration to prohibit multiracial categories in the 2000 census. During the Reagan presidency, however, rising immigration initially helped soften Republican opposition to affirmative action.

During the 1970s it was widely understood that race-conscious affirmative action was the government's response to the inner-city riots of 1965–68 and was designed almost exclusively for African-Americans. Federal jurists approved the new racial preference policies as remedies for past discrimination that included centuries of African slavery. Other minorities were vaguely understood by the public to be included, but their presence in affirmative action programs was incidental and modest. The largest such group, Hispanics, concentrated during the 1970s on expanding bilingual-bicultural education as a distinctively Latino model of affirmative action. Shaped in the 1970s by insurgent Chicano nationalism, bilingual education posed no threat to mainstream, black-oriented affirmative action, such as the expanding federal and state MBE programs. This began to change, however, during the 1980s. In particular, two policy controversies during the Reagan presidency were resolved in a way that reflected the growing demographic, economic, and political importance of mass immigration. They did so in a way that emphasized a quiet shift in the politics of both affirmative action and immigration among Reagan-Bush Republicans.

One controversy centered on whether Reagan would rewrite the affirmative action executive order inherited from the 1960s. Traditional Republican conservatives, led by the White House counselor and later attorney general, Edwin Meese III, and the assistant attorney general for civil rights, William Bradford Reynolds, urged Reagan to revise the order in a way that required color blindness in public policy. In 1984 and 1985, Meese, who chaired the cabinet's Domestic Policy Council, won support in his color-blindness campaign from the secretaries of Education, Energy, and the Interior. Opposing Meese and Reynolds, however, was a cabinet majority that included not only the labor secretary, defending his department's contract compliance agency, the OFCCP, but also the cabinet's ranking departments of State and Treasury, as well as the secretaries of Health and Human Services, Transportation, and Housing and Urban Development. Meese was backed by small business interests (the U.S. Chamber of Commerce and the Associated General Contractors) but opposed by big business (the National Association of Manufacturers). Faced with such strong opposition, Meese withdrew his proposal.

Why had the leaders of Reagan's conservative administration rallied to protect the affirmative action policies of the Carter administration? The evidence suggests several factors, including immigration.[21] One element was concern that rewriting the executive order would bring Democratic charges of racism that damaged Republicans at the polls. Another was worry by corporate leaders, who had negotiated government-approved affirmative action plans in the 1970s, that a color-blind policy would invite a flood of litigation and would benefit competitors who had not developed affirmative action plans and structures.[22] Moreover, corporate commitments to expand minority employment allowed businesses to hire Asian and Latino workers in large numbers, while often employing few blacks. Ironically, the affirmative action programs of private employers, in addition to providing government protection against "reverse discrimination" lawsuits by whites, also provided cover for firms to hire disproportionate numbers of immigrants relative to black workers. Among Republican leaders in the Reagan presidency, the efforts of cultural conservatives like Senator Simpson to restrict immigration were more than matched by the efforts of business/libertarian conservatives to expand it. In the final compromises that shaped the Immigration Reform and Control Act of 1986, business lobbyists worked with Hispanic political leaders to neutralize the bill's employer sanctions provisions.

By the mid-1980s, the politics of affirmative action and immigration were converging in unanticipated ways. This was demonstrated in the controversy over voting rights enforcement. The 1965 Voting Rights Act was due for renewal in 1982, and once again, traditional conservative Republicans in the Reagan administration supported color-blind procedures that equally protected the access of all citizens to the polls. In the 1982 amendments, the civil rights coalition in Congress, however, successfully replaced the 1965 statute's equal-treatment standard with an equal results formula designed to maximize not only the minority vote but also the election of minority candidates.[23] The Reagan administration was chastened by its 1982 defeat over the voting rights amendments, and this experience—Republican fear of being labeled racist—helped derail Meese's proposal to rewrite the executive order.

By the late 1980s, however, the Republican Justice Department had discovered surprising advantages in aggressively enforcing the voting rights law. Traditionally, such enforcement was championed by liberal Democrats, not conservative Reagan-Bush Republicans, because under the 1982 amendments, the Justice Department could require new electoral districts containing a majority of minority voters and hence likely to elect minority candidates. Although such "majority minority" districts overwhelmingly elected black or Latino candidates who were Democrats, Republican political strategists noticed that they drained minority voters from surrounding districts and thereby enhanced the election of Republicans. As a consequence, voting rights officials in the Reagan and Bush Justice Department began requiring majority-minority districts with a zeal that matched that of MALDEF and La Raza. Large-scale redistricting required by the 1990 census, chiefly reflecting immigration-driven population shifts, enabled the Bush Justice Department to create new majority-minority districts for legislative and congressional seats throughout the South and the Southwest. This strategy was crucial to winning the Republican sweep of Congress in November 1994. Although black and Hispanic Democrats won an unprecedented number of seats in Congress, Republican gains from the voting-rights redistricting were greater, capturing formerly Democratic districts drained of minority voters. The 2000 census, requiring even more widespread redistricting to accommodate immigration-driven population changes, offered George W. Bush's Justice Department a similar opportunity in 2001–2 to draw partisan advantage from the growing convergence of affirmative action and immigration policies.[24]

Strengths of Mass Immigration

The Republican shift toward high-immigration policies during the Reagan-Bush years mirrors the enthusiasm of the party's business constituency for an expanding (and hence cheapening and union-weakening) workforce to boost economic competitiveness and growth. Most economists agree that the return of mass immigration stimulated the American economy. Immigrants typically bring both lower wage costs and different skills to domestic production, thereby enhancing productive efficiency through labor specialization. Following the shock of high energy costs and "stagflation" in the 1970s, low-wage immigrant workers enabled American businesses to lower production costs and compete more successfully in global competition. Economists are divided on particular issues, such as the degree to which immigration produced job displacement and raised social service costs. But they generally agree that large-scale immigration has brought a net gain to the economy. The overall gain, however, has been small and the distribution of its benefits has been uneven, concluded a panel of experts selected in 1995 by the National Research Council, in response to a request by the Commission on Immigration Reform.[25]

How much net economic gain did immigration bring? Harvard economist George J. Borjas estimated that in a $8 trillion U.S. economy, the net gain in productive efficiency (the immigration surplus) amounts to only $8 billion a year.[26] This is a relatively trivial amount. But like the tip of an iceberg, the economic redistribution of income from labor to capital it signals is not trivial to the owners of companies that buy immigration services. These are concentrated in the six states containing almost three-quarters of the immigrants (California, New York, Texas, Florida, New Jersey, and Illinois), who by 2000 represented about 10 percent of the American workforce. The small net gain of $8-10 billion masks a substantial redistribution of income from the losers, the low-skilled native workers who compete with immigrants, to the winners, skilled native workers (white collar, technical, professional), owners of the firms employing immigrants, and the consumers who buy the goods and services produced by immigrants. For American consumers, low-wage immigrant workers provide cheaper restaurants, hotels, food products, clothing, cleaning and lawn care costs, and construction and transportation costs generally. Immigration thus redistributes wealth from labor to capital. Borjas estimates the total annual windfall going to the winners at $160 billion, or about 2 percent of GDP. This is a nontrivial amount. To its recipients, immigration has been a significant boon to the economy. Such an amount is well worth fighting for by the highly organized employers whose enthusiasm for high levels of immigration shine in the pages of the *Wall Street Journal* and *Fortune* magazine and whose generous contributions to political campaigns in both major parties ensures that immigration expansionist views are well attended in Congress.[27]

A second strength of immigration is the diversity it brings to American culture. This has always been a double-edged sword, both in American history, with its backlash movements against Catholics, Jews, Chinese, Japanese, Mexicans, and others, and in contemporary Europe, with heavy immigration pressures from Africa, Asia, the Near East, and the former Soviet empire. But the positive tradition symbolized by the Statue of Liberty and Ellis Island is deeply rooted in American culture. Polls demonstrating rising resistance to mass immigration after the 1960s also demonstrated a deep ambivalence that includes valuing cultural pluralism considerably beyond the charm of ethnic cuisine.[28] The Manhattan Project that produced the atomic bomb in 1945 and the annual roster of Nobel Prize winners testify famously to the nation's intellectual debt to immigrants. In 1995 the proportion of foreign born among U.S. Nobel laureates was 26 percent in chemistry, 31 percent in economics, 27 percent in literature, 32 percent in physics, and 31 percent in biomedical science.[29] The American media routinely celebrate this diversity, as do public schools and holidays, sports stars and celebrity rosters, political campaigns, university faculties, and corporate brochures.

The bottom line of multicultural tolerance, however, has been the public attitude toward interracial marriage, especially between whites and blacks. When the U.S. Supreme Court in the 1967 *Loving* case ruled unconstitutional Virginia's law banning interracial marriage, only 17 percent of whites in the United States (not just the South) approved of interracial relationships, and only 48 percent of blacks did so. Since then, the baby boomer generation, maturing in an age of rising immigration and globalization, has transformed American attitudes toward racial mixing. In 1991, only 27 percent of Americans over 50 years of age approved of marriage between blacks and whites, according to the Gallup poll. But 64 percent of Americans between the ages of 18 and 29 approved of interracial marriages. Moreover, approval of interracial marriages rose with increased education, income, urbanization, and interpersonal contacts. In the 1991 Gallup poll, 70 percent of college graduates approved of interracial marriage compared with 26 percent of Americans who did not graduate from high school.[30] Sixty-one percent of Americans with annual incomes over $50,000 approved of racially mixed marriages, compared to 37 percent of those with incomes under $20,000.[31] Looking back from the perspective of the twenty-first century, the attitudes of American society toward multicultural diversity circa 1950 would appear unrecognizeable, and the attitudes of the 1920s would be incomprehensible.

Third, one of the ironies of the immigration debate has been the failure of immigration expansionists to take advantage of a strong potential argument, one based on population and demographic trends. The arguments for immigration reform in the 1960s, which concentrated on eliminating the racism of national origins quotas in cold war competition with the Soviet bloc and China and fostering family reunification, were not controversial. Then in the 1970s and 1980s, when heavy immigration from Latin America and Asia coincided with domestic economic distress and helped generate a restrictionist reform drive, expansionists downplayed or ignored the soaring numbers of legal and illegal immigrants and attacked restrictionist proposals, such as FAIR's, as racist. Population-based arguments, to the degree that they were used at all, were offered chiefly by FAIR. They emphasized dangers from overburdening the nation's carrying capacity, and reflected the population control and environmentalist perspective of the progressive/liberal wing of the restrictionist movement.[32]

Despite FAIR's efforts, little heed was paid by Congress to demographic arguments during the Simpson-Mazzoli debates of the 1980s. Yet looking back from the twenty-first century, with the population of the world's industrial nations rapidly aging, and with their governments facing generational warfare as fewer workers are available to support growing numbers of retirees, the argument could be made by expansionists that the United

States benefited because rising immigration compensated for falling birthrates after 1965. In the 1970s, the United States achieved fertility levels consistent with zero population growth. Had the immigration reforms of 1965 produced the negligible increase in immigration that its sponsors expected, the United States today might as a consequence share with Europe, Japan, and South Korea the problem of subreplacement fertility. In the fifteen-nation European Union, retirees accounting for 15.4 percent of the population in 2000 were expected to rise to 22.4 percent by 2025. To support these retirees might require either steep tax increases on declining workforces in European nations already highly taxed, or sharp reductions in the generosity of the European welfare state, or the admission of 30-35 million immigrants, or a controversial combination of these measures.[33] Despite population growth through immigration, the United States faced the need to provide retirement income and medical care for the baby boom generation in an economy characterized by a declining ratio of workers to retirees. In 1960 in the United States there were 5.1 workers per Social Security beneficiary. By 1996 the ratio had fallen to 3.3 It was projected by Social Security Administration analysts to fall to 2 by 2030.[34]

The subreplacement fertility debate involves controversial claims based on recent demographic projections that have not yet produced mature literature.[35] Demographic projections are essential exploratory tools, yet they are inherently unreliable, failing as they must to take into account the wars, natural disasters, epidemics, economic disruptions, religious and ideological movements, and other unpredictable phenomena that have always affected mankind. They fail, as well, to factor in favorable changes, such as breakthrough scientific developments or dramatic increases in economic productivity. There is no inherent reason why economic growth, producing higher per capita productivity and standards of living, need be accompanied by population growth. On the other hand, the subreplacement fertility debate reminds us that environmentalists may face a rising price for maintaining a green and livable world, in the form of stiffening political choices that may force citizens of industrial democracies to accept a more painful balance between such unpalatable options as reduced social welfare benefits, higher taxes, extended retirement age, and population growth through immigration.

Weaknesses of Mass Immigration

The greatest weakness brought by mass immigration to the United States is the unworkable system that the American political process devised to control it. It is anchored in a glaring contradiction symbolized by the outcome of policies designed to police the borders on the one hand, and on the other, policies designed to protect American jobs from undocumented workers. As a consequence of the compromises accompanying the passage of IRCA in 1986, the United States built a system that emphasized rigorous control of the borders to prevent illegal entry, while at the same time the employer sanctions program operated as a palpable sham. Because the American borders and airport networks were so easily breached, illegal entry became massive, routine, and abundantly rewarded by employers who ran little risk in offering jobs to fraudulently documented immigrants. Additionally, IRCA's amnesty provision, sold as a humanitarian measure that would remove the country's "shadow population" of fugitive aliens, instead replenished and even expanded the shadow population, in the process fueling demand for future amnesties.

The result of this nonfunctional system, not surprisingly, was widespread contempt for American law. As legal immigration bogged down in long waiting lists overseas under the heavily used visa preference system, incentives to work within the lawful system were overwhelmed by the ease of short-circuiting it. Increased legal immigration thus stimulated greater illegal traffic. Increasingly, family members of immigrants on overseas waiting lists for U.S. visas moved illegally to the United States, in order to earn money, qualify for amnesty programs, and potentially marry an American citizen. The American political system periodically made token, figleaf gestures toward policing the borders, then looked the other way as the great American job magnet pulled millions of illegal immigrants into low-wage employment.

Census Bureau statisticians discovered in 2001 that the United States had twice the number of illegal immigrants than officials thought—possibly 10 million or more, compared with earlier estimates of 6 million. "It looks like 5 million illegal immigrants were here that we didn't know about—maybe more," said Everett M. Erlich, commerce undersecretary in the Clinton administration.[36] Census officials expected in 2000 to count 275 million Americans. Census workers, however, actually counted 281.4 million. When Census Bureau statisticians adjusted the data to account for the significantly higher number of workers reported by businesses than by worker surveys, the number rose to 285 million. Census Bureau tabulators suggested nearly doubling their estimate of illegal immigrants who arrived during the 1990s from 2.8 million to 5.5 million. By these revised estimates, the number of immigrants coming to the United States between 1965 and 2000 rose to 35 million, an estimated 15 million of them arriving illegally.[37]

A second weakness of mass immigration is the economic price it extracted from low-income native workers. Although immigration's net impact on the American economy was tiny but positive—from an annual gain of about $8 billion in an $8 trillion U.S. economy, an increase in the income of natives of about 0.10 percent—this immigration "surplus" masked a significant internal redistribution of income from labor to capital. Because immigrants lowered wages, especially in manufacturing and personal service employment, native wages were reduced by approximately 3 percent. For high school dropouts, immigration reduced real wages by 5 percent. This meant an income transfer from workers to users of immigration services: the employers of immigrants and the consumers who buy the goods and services produced by immigrants. The total annual windfall going to the middle and upper-class winners in the $8 trillion economy of the late 1990s was $160 billion, or 2 percent of GDP.[38]

The main losers in this redistribution were not the immigrants, who had bettered their economic station by migrating. Low-income native workers were the real losers, chiefly poor (often rural) whites and urban blacks. Immigration was by no means a leading cause of affluent America's shockingly wide income gap between the rich and the poor. Since World War II, the American political economy has proven adept at producing abundance but inept at distributing it equitably. In 1949, when immigration levels were economically inconsequential, the bottom-ranked fifth of Americans received 4.5 percent of family income and the top-ranked fifth received 42.7 percent. But mass immigration after 1965 helped to widen rather than narrow the wage gap between rich and poor. In 1969, the bottom fifth of American families received 4.1 percent of aggregate household income and the top fifth received 43 percent. By 1996, the income share of the bottom fifth of American workers had fallen to 3.7 percent, and the top fifth share had risen to 49 percent.[39] Mass immigration was only one factor working to widen the wage gap, other forces being economic globalization, the shift from manufacturing to a service-based economy, the decline of organized labor, and corporate "outsourcing" overseas of production and assembly for American business products. But mass immigration, by flooding the labor market, weakened the bargaining position of American workers.

Immigrants lowered American wages because, with the exception of a small cohort of highly educated professional and technical immigrants (whose graduate education exceeded that of their native-born counterparts), most of the post-1965 "fourth wave" immigrants, especially those from Latin America, were poorly educated. According to the 1990 census, 25 percent of the foreign born had less than a ninth-grade education, compared with 10 percent of the native born. Forty-two percent of the foreign born had no high school diploma, compared with 23 percent of the native born. In 1995, workers with at least a high school education earned 41 percent more than high school dropouts, a gap that was widening in the high-tech U.S. economy. Immigration, by increasing the relative number of high school dropout workers, accounted for 44 percent of this wage gap. Moreover, 79 percent of the immigrants spoke a primary language other than English, a liability in most employment competition. Immigration after 1965 thus produced a mismatch with the American economy, bringing millions of poorly educated, low-skill workers to an economy chiefly in need of greater professional, technical, and administrative expertise.[40]

A third weakness of mass immigration centers on the nation's largest ethnocultural category of immigrants, Hispanics, and particularly on the largest group within that category, Mexicans. Hispanics in 1997 constituted about 45 percent of the 30 million foreign-born immigrants in the United States. The 2000 U.S. census counted 31.3 million Hispanics, one-third of them in California, and almost two-thirds foreign-born. Almost three-fourths of immigrants in 2000 were Hispanic. The country's Hispanic population was projected to surpass the number of black residents in the United States by 2005, thereby making Hispanics the nation's largest minority group. Like the country's 12 million Asian-Americans, also two-thirds foreign-born, American Hispanics were primarily an immigrant population.

As is well known, the blanket term *Hispanic* or *Latino* misleads by masking wide cultural differences associated with country of origin. Americans of Latin American origin have constituted ethnocultural "groups" chiefly in terms of their national origins, that is, as Mexicans, Puerto Ricans, Cubans, Salvadoreans. Many immigrants from the Caribbean, on the other hand, are not culturally or linguistically Hispanic—English-speaking West Indians and French-speaking Haitians, for example. Despite these wide cultural differences, the blanket term *Hispanic* or *Latino* has captured a statistical portrait of immigrant attributes that has been disturbingly negative. Median family income for Hispanics in 1997 was $28,142, compared to $51,850 for Asians, $46,754 for non-Hispanic whites, and $28,602 for non-Hispanic blacks. (This category excludes approximately 950,000 Hispanic blacks, chiefly from Puerto Rico, Cuba, and the Dominican Republic.) Whereas 83 percent of non-Hispanic whites in 1997 were high school graduates, compared with 74.9 percent of blacks and 84.9 percent of Asians, only 54.7 percent of Hispanics were high school graduates. In 1998, the Latino school drop-out rate was an alarming 33 percent. One-fourth of non-Hispanic whites in 1997 had at least four years of college, compared with 42.2 percent of Asians, 13.3 percent of blacks, and 10.3 percent of Hispanics.

Two-thirds of Hispanics were blue-collar and service workers, compared with 47 percent of non-Hispanic whites.[41] In New York City, a 1998 study of welfare rolls showed that 5 percent of persons on public assistance were white, 33 percent were black, and 59 percent were Hispanic.[42] As Linda Chavez notes in *Out of the Barrio*, upward mobility and suburbanization have been rapid for Hispanic-Americans, but this has been obscured by the continuing influx of poorly educated, low-income immigrants whose socioeconomic characteristics depress the scores for all Latinos.[43]

The Unique Role of Mexico

The low Hispanic scores, however, were chiefly depressed by the weak performance on socioeconomic indicators of Mexicans, by far the largest national group of immigrants in the United States. Although large-scale immigration from Mexico is a very recent phenomenon—in 1970, the Mexican immigrant population was less than 700,000—in 1997, Mexicans were 28 percent of U.S. immigrants. This figure increased to 35 percent when illegal immigrants are included, because Mexicans accounted for almost half of the illegal immigrants in the U.S. The Mexican-born population in the United States approached 8 million in 2000, and increased annually by approximately 150,000 legal and 175,000 illegal new arrivals. By 2000, 1 in 3 immigrant children in the United States had at least one Mexican-born parent.

Immigrants from Mexico were characteristically low-skilled and poorly educated. Almost two-thirds of adult Mexican immigrants have not completed high school, compared to fewer than one in ten natives. Fewer than half (48.3 percent) of Mexican-Americans had completed four years of high school or more in 1998, compared with 63.8 percent of Puerto Ricans, 67.8 percent of Cubans, 74.9 percent of blacks, 83 percent of whites, and 84.9 percent of Asians. Only 7.5 percent of Mexican-Americans in 1998 had four years of college, compared with 12 percent for Puerto Ricans and 22 percent for Cubans. The median family income of Mexicans in America in 1998 ($27,088) was significantly lower than that of Cubans ($37,537) and Central and South Americans ($32,030), and it exceeded among Hispanics only that of Puerto Ricans ($23,729). The same pattern held for unemployment levels in 1998 and for persons below the poverty level.[44] Of the 9–10 million immigrants living illegally in the U.S. in 2000, approximately half were Mexican.

Most disturbing was evidence that the second generation of Mexican-Americans, children born in the United States, were falling further behind non-Mexican immigrant children, rather than closing the gap—the traditional pattern of second generation success for American immigrants. In a study based on 2000 census data, economist Steven Camarota found that the high school dropout rates of native-born Mexican-Americans (both second and third generation) were two-and-one-half times that of other natives. Lower education levels resulted in lower earnings, lower average tax payments, and heavier use of means-tested programs. Based on estimates developed by the National Academy of Sciences for immigrants by age and education at arrival, the lifetime fiscal impact (taxes paid minus services used) for the average adult Mexican immigrant in 2000 was a negative $55,200. Mexican immigrants who had lived in the United States for more than 20 years, almost all of them legal residents, still had double the welfare use rate of natives.[45]

The roots of the problem lie in Mexico's history and culture and its unique geographic relationship to the United States. Mexico's population explosion since midcentury saw the country's population double and then quadruple, with birthrates per woman of 7.2 in the 1960s driving the population to almost 100 million by the century's end, a classic Third World pattern of impoverishment when coupled with a weak economy. Mexico's post-1960s economy had strengths in tourism and, by the 1990s, in manufacturing. More than 3,000 *maquiladora* export plants, mostly near the U.S. border, processed and assembled intermediate parts for U.S. manufacturers, thus providing more than 1 million jobs and accounting for half of Mexico's revenue from manufacturing exports. But Mexico's economy was also characterized by a large and tradition-bound agricultural sector, inefficient state-run extractive industries (including petroleum and natural gas), regressive labor laws, low wages and growth rates, and high levels of foreign debt, inflation, unemployment, and interest rates. Politically, Mexico was governed for most of the century by an entrenched and profoundly corrupt machine, the Pardido Revolucionario Institucional (PRI). By 2000, 40 percent of Mexico's population was subsisting on less than two dollars a day. The U.S.-Mexico wage gap, 7 to 1 in favor of American wage levels, was among the largest between contiguous countries. A U.S. manufacturing worker in 2000 earned four times the wages of a Mexican factory worker and 30 times that of a Mexican agricultural worker.[46]

These factors, when combined with proximity to the United States, a porous border, large American guest worker programs, and unenforced U.S. employer sanctions laws, produced a distinctive immigration pattern for Mexicans in the U.S. Its chief characteristics, compared to the patterns of non-Mexican immigrants (excluding Puerto Ricans), have been large-scale sojourner migrations by poorly educated, low-skilled workers, and linguistic and cultural isolation in the U.S. The Mexican government in the 1990s passed dual citizenship legislation to encourage voting in Mexican elections by Mexican migrants to the United States irrespective of American citizenship, and to maximize the size of the Mexican-born workforce in the United States and the $8 billion annual flow to Mexico from that population. Life in insular, Spanish-speaking communities of Mexicans in the U.S. weakened the forces of acculturation that fostered assimilation into the American mainstream by other immigrants. The proliferation since the 1970s of bilingual/bicultural education programs in American schools has further segregated and isolated Mexican (and Hispanic) children from the American mainstream and weakened the acquisition of English literacy and competence in school subjects leading to higher education and advancement in America's high-tech economy. Unlike most immigrants, who have aggressively sought American citizenship (the percentage of immigrants not U.S. citizens in 1997, for example, was below 3.5 for immigrants from Cuba, the Dominican Republic, El Salvador, China, India, Korea, the Philippines, and Vietnam), immigrants from Mexico have a non-citizenship rate exceeding 35 percent. The Mexican government has encouraged a pattern of dual citizenship, seeking with considerable success to export surplus labor to the United States, import migrant earnings, and retain the national loyalty of Mexican-born immigrants to the United States and their children.[47]

For Mexico, and hence for the United States, the turn of the twenty-first century also brought prospects for improvement, however. Mexico's net annual population growth rate, a ruinous 3.5 percent in the 1960s, had fallen by 2000 to 1.44 percent. By 2000, 70 percent of Mexican women practiced family planning, compared with 30 percent in the 1970s. As a consequence, the birth-per-woman figure had fallen from 7.2 in the 1960s to 2.4 in 2000. It is projected to reach 2.1 by 2005, a figure associated with zero population growth. This decline promises in turn to reduce Mexico's budget-draining primary school population by 10 percent by 2010. Economically, the creation of the North American Free Trade Association in 1994 has helped triple Mexico's exports, and the United States helped stabilize the peso following its collapse in 1996. Politically, the election to the Mexican presidency of Vincente Fox Quesada in 2000 broke the seventy-one-year stranglehold on power of the PRI. Fox, a free-trading, market-oriented corporate executive with fluent English and pro-American leanings, as president-elect promptly proposed an open-border future for Mexico and the United States—a proposal greeted cooly in the fall of 2000 by both the Bush and Gore presidential campaigns.[48] Within a year, however, the Fox government had moved to curb the flow of Mexicans across the U.S. border—

a first for Mexican national policy. The Fox initiative in the summer of 2001 consisted chiefly of video and television messages emphasizing deaths in border crossings and exploitation by smugglers. At the same time in the United States, the INS reported a 30 percent reduction in apprehensions along the Mexican border—a first for the INS in two decades. The INS announcement, predating the Fox initiative, suggested that the economic downturn and American job shrinkage played a significant role in reducing illegal immigration, together with strengthened Border Patrol defenses in urban areas, which shifted crossings from Mexico into more dangerous desert regions.

Fox's election did not change the still enormous gaps continuing to separate the United States and Mexico, such as the reality of $60 for a day's work in the United States and $5 in Mexico. Mexico's long-term prospects, however, were buoyed by one demographic projection in particular: declining Mexican birthrates meant that the average age of Mexico's population was projected to rise from twenty-seven in 2000 to thirty-eight by 2030. The increase in Mexico's working-age population (ages seventeen to sixty-five) relative to retirees meant that, by 2030, only one in eight Mexicans would be of retirement age. The force of this demographic projection is comparative: by the middle of the twenty-first century, Mexico will enjoy a ratio of workers to retirees that will be the envy of most developed nations.[49]

The Political Success of Expansionist Immigration Politics

How should we assess the balance of strengths and weaknesses in American immigration policy? From the beginning, U.S. policy has oscillated between flood and drought models, and the country has paid a heavy price in the excesses associated with each extreme. The immigration of 1880–1914 brought the industrial manpower and cultural pluralism commemorated by the Statue of Liberty and Ellis Island. But it was accompanied by expanding slums, disease, poverty, political corruption, wage depression, labor strife, crime, and violence. The immigration restriction laws of the 1920s brought a sudden drought. It provided a needed respite to speed immigrant acculturation into mainstream American life. It was also a period during which immigration from Latin America, geographically immune from the national origin quotas, continued to increase. Unfortunately, the immigration restriction of the 1920s was accompanied by spurious racial theories, religious bigotry, rural parochialism, and xenophobia enflamed by war and Bolshevism. In retrospect, the widespread concern among the country's Protestant policy elites in the Progressive era that

Europe's Jews were a dim-witted race was especially wrong-headed. In light of the disproportionate talent brought to America by Jewish immigrants, U.S. policymakers should have scoured the European continent to attract Jewish immigration.

The reforms of 1965 were commendably free of these prejudices. The Hart-Celler Law of 1965 began the country's inadvertent return to the immigration flood model. But the flood was hastened by powerful exogenous "push" forces: the global revolution in communications and travel, the disruptions of cold war competition and instability, and the ingenuity of aspiring immigrants in the Third World in exploiting the idiosyncracies of America's post-1965 visa preference system. The structure of the post-1965 immigration regime was not mature, however, until the passage of IRCA in 1986, when its political dynamics were clarified. They were conditioned by the effective political alliance of the expansionist left-right coalition, which peculiarly united, on immigration issues, the open-borders preferences of the Congressional Hispanic Caucus on the left and the *Wall Street Journal* on the right.

To defeat the reforms proposed by FAIR and other restrictionist organizations, the Latino-led minority rights coalition, following the model of the Congressional Black Caucus, effectively racialized the immigration issue. To House Speaker Tip O'Neill—who proclaimed that "all politics is local" —visas and green cards, grants of asylum and amnesty, were regarded as public goods, like federal contracts and social service grants. Their generous distribution helped incumbents get reelected. Like affirmative action benefits, they won for incumbents support from well-organized clientele groups at little direct cost to taxpayers through budget appropriations. O'Neill showered his contempt upon the unorganized American majorities that polls showed favored reduced immigration: "There is no constituency here," O'Neill explained,[50] meaning no organized beneficiary group with proven lobbying clout, such as La Raza and MALDEF, working closely with a constituency-based caucus in Congress.

The result of these political dynamics, the IRCA system that set the parameters followed by the immigration legislation of the 1990s, combined an unworkable employer sanctions law with a large guest worker program to provide cheap labor for growers, an amnesty program that rewarded lawbreakers and provided incentives for renewed illegal immigration, and budget increases for the INS to strengthen the border against illegal entry and provide legislators cover against voter resentment over illegal immigration. This system produced increases in both legal and illegal immigration. Its assets included large numbers of hardworking, low-cost laborers and the economic benefits this brought to the employers and consumers of immigrant services, including a strengthened worker-to-retiree ratio. On the negative side, the post-1960s immigration was generally characterized by low levels of migrant education and employment skills; increased lawlessness in the form of illegal entry and continued residence, fraudulent work documents, migrant smuggling and its attendant corruption, asylum claims coached by immigration lawyers to disguise economic distress as political oppression; and depressed wages for all low-skilled workers.

By the end of the 1990s, the expansionist coalition had overwhelmed restrictionist opponents. A booming American economy had eased resentment against immigrants. In a September 2000 Gallup poll, 44 percent of respondents said that immigrants helped America and 40 percent said they hurt, as opposed to the 1993 poll that showed 26 percent agreeing that immigrants helped and 64 percent saying they hurt.[51] Also by the end of the 1990s, the NAACP had abandoned its traditional restrictionist stance and joined the Congressional Black Caucus in solidarity with the Hispanic Caucus, itself increased from five founding members in 1976 to seventeen in 2000. Finally, by 2000 the AFL-CIO, under the leadership of President John Sweeney, had reversed labor's historic opposition to large-scale immigration. Thus by the end of the twentieth century, two of the restrictionists' traditional bases of support, African-American organizations and union leaders, had defected to the expansionist coalition—with Sweeney, like Mexico's Vincente Fox and the Hispanic Caucus leadership, calling for open borders.

In the election year maneuverings of 2000, presidential nominees Gore and Bush cautiously sidestepped the immigration issue. But political leaders from all parties, including the Greens and the Libertarians, generally favored increased immigration. Leading Republican legislators and governors supported the electronic industry's need for high-skilled workers and the growers' demand for guest workers. (The Congressional Hispanic Caucus, it should be noted, continued to oppose guest worker programs for growers, a point of rare agreement it shared with FAIR.) Democratic legislators representing high-immigration areas supported Hispanic Caucus demands for a Latino and Immigration Fairness Act that included an amnesty for 500,000 undocumented workers and green cards for refugees from El Salvador, Guatemala, Honduras, and Haiti.[52] Congress passed an amnesty provision creating a four-month window in early 2001 for up to 500,000 illegal residents to claim permanent resident status (the provision was buried in clause 245(i) of the massive, eleventh-hour budget bill signed by President Clinton in December 2000).[53] Overall, the trends in immigration politics heading into the new century were generally grim for FAIR.

In light of the mismatch between America's technologically sophisticated, knowledge-based economy and the low-skilled, poorly educated characteristics of most immigrants, FAIR's qualitative complaints about the inappropriate weight given to family reunification criteria over national needs were consistently vindicated, though seldom acted upon by Congress.[54] Moreover, in light of the shoddy, IRCA-based system shaped by the congressional politics of the 1980s and 1990s, FAIR's arguments appear persuasive for a technologically modern, law-respecting system grounded primarily in national needs rather than the family kinship of immigrants. The main ingredients included a computerized national identification system for checking worker eligibility and thereby eliminating the job magnet that fueled illegal immigration. Such systems, common among other nations in controlling immigration, were central to the efficient functioning of the Social Security Administration and other government agencies and private corporations in the United States, including the insurance industry, where false claims were common.[55] FAIR lobbied unsuccessfully for an end to the brothers and sisters preference and for sharp reductions in immigration during periods of high unemployment. During the economic contraction of 1978–83, for example, when unemployment averaged 8.2 percent of the labor force, or 9 million workers, 3.5 million immigrants joined the American labor market. But Congress paid little heed. FAIR had little to offer elected officials that could compete with the coordinated lobbying of the immigration and civil rights coalitions. La Raza, MALDEF, LULAC, and the organizations representing Hispanic elected officials were, after all, legitimately pursuing their own self-interest, as were the *Wall Street Journal* and the National Association of Manufacturers, in seeking open-borders immigration to swell their constituency ranks, expand their career opportunities and patronage, and provide low-cost, union-resistant labor to American employers. The primal fault lay not with the lobbyists but with a shortsighted, horse-trading system of policymaking grounded in the dynamics of client politics and the imperatives of incumbent reelection.

Collision Course

This book describes the surprising trajectory of civil rights and immigration reforms in modern America toward unintended consequences. The parallel stories of affirmative action and mass immigration from Latin America and Asia have been closely studied by American scholars, although customarily in isolation from one another. But both stories feature the unanticipated success of organized interest groups, loosely cooperating within the liberal coalition, in shifting national policy toward controversial new goals and then consolidating these shifts in the halls of government.

According to most accounts of American policymaking, these two stories feature persistent controversies, but not a collision course. Instead, the major players in the liberal coalition—the alphabet lobbies (including the ACLU, NAACP, MALDEF), the black and Hispanic congressional caucuses, liberal church groups, the civil rights and immigration bar—demonstrate solidarity through effective coalition politics. This achievement merits high marks on any scorecard of political acumen. In shifting civil rights policy from the equal individual rights standard of traditional liberalism to the equal results standard of hard affirmative action, for example, the civil rights coalition had to overcome the powerful appeal of constitutional color blindness, the statutory language and legislative intent of the Civil Rights Act, and strong resistance to race-conscious measures in American public opinion generally. To overcome such obstacles, the civil rights coalition exploited several strategic advantages, including a legacy among whites of national guilt over African-American slavery and segregation, the unique historic impoverishment of the nation's largest and most visible minority, the prestige of the Warren Court, and the protection of liberal judicial majorities during the 1970s and 1980s under the leadership of Justice William Brennan.

The civil rights coalition enjoyed expert leadership in exploiting the advantages of client politics. Coalition strategies included courting and often capturing operational control of the new agencies of civil rights enforcement, maintaining solidarity between African-American and Latino organizations despite increasing tensions at the grassroots, and nourishing the attractions that affirmative action offered to Republicans eager to foster minority business enterprise. Despite the setbacks of the 1990s in court decisions and voter referendums, the civil rights coalition could look back on a record of program growth and consolidation in affirmative action that included the quiet cooperation of Richard Nixon, Ronald Reagan, and Newt Gingrich.

Paralleling this success story of maximizing coalition agreement and minimizing conflict, however, has been a hidden story of deeply rooted policy contradictions inherent in the shift to affirmative action, exacerbated by the shift in immigration policy to mass migration from Latin America and Asia. At the heart of the concept of race-conscious affirmative action lay the notion of official minorities designated by government as protected classes. This status carried a presumption of eligibility for program benefits. That is, *all* members of the officially designated minority groups were presumed to be disadvantaged and hence eligible for preferences in employment, admissions, and government contracts. Conversely, *all* Americans not designated as minorities were presumed not to be disadvantaged, absent evidence demonstrating the contrary. In the SBA's 8(a) program, for example, which required applicants to demonstrate that they were both culturally and economically disadvantaged, minority group members were deemed economically disadvantaged *because* they were minorities and hence culturally disadvantaged by definition. This logic simplified the job of agency officials sorting claims: Minority identification automatically certified cultural and economic disadvantage.

The presumption of eligibility formula, however, posed contradictions that would grow more problematical with time.[56] First, it denied government benefits to poor whites—still the majority of poor Americans throughout the twentieth century—exclusively on the basis of their racial ancestry. Second, it protected benefits for minorities irrespective of their economic success. Not surprisingly, this attracted media attention to the anomaly of wealthy black, Hispanic, and Asian entrepreneurs who legally exploited their race or ethnicity, like the Fanjuls in Miami and the Rodriguezes in Washington, D.C., to further enrich themselves at public expense. Thus affirmative action success, in the form of growing affluence on the part of some protected minorities, progressively threatened the political legitimacy of affirmative action itself by undermining its equation of minority status and economic disadvantage.

From the beginning, affirmative action ironically had a time bomb of program success buried within it. Program failure was easier to explain, especially in the MBE program, where most MBE "firms" had only one employee, the owner. In such programs, a high tolerance for failure was shown by Congress and by sponsoring state and local governments. Success, however, was also a problem. In the SBA's 8(a) program, for example, agency managers needed a core of large successful firms to reach their contract budget goals, which tended to grow larger each year in procurement budgets as Congress responded to civil rights coalition lobbying by increasing the size of MBE allotments. But congressional oversight committees were frustrated by the failure of successful MBE firms to "graduate" from the set-aside programs, and they were embarrassed by media coverage of MBE millionaires. If high levels of income and education characterized an increasing proportion of families in a protected-class minority, how could all members of that minority be presumptively disadvantaged? If affirmative action was a temporary, catch-up program to compensate for past discrimination, as its sponsors had generally claimed during the 1970s (though not thereafter), what criteria should trigger its termination?

Protected-class eligibility for affirmative action benefits was especially difficult to justify for Asian-Americans. Although Americano of Chincac and Japanese ancestry had been subjected to systematic discrimination in America for generations, including exclusions from citizenship and, for Japanese-Americans, the suffering consequent to forced removal and internship during World War II, Asian-Americans had collectively surpassed white Americans in family income and education as early as the 1960s. The Civil Rights Commission, concerned chiefly with discrimination against black Americans, complained in a 1966 report that Asians were overrepresented in professional and technical employment. By 1997, despite significant immigration of low-income migrants from southeast Asia, the median family income of Asian-Americans was $51,850, compared with $38,972 for non-Hispanic white families, $26,628 for Hispanics, and $25,020 for blacks. In California, the legislature in 1987 found Asians overrepresented in the state's universities and removed them from the list of protected classes under state affirmative action programs. For Asians, despite a long history of oppression in America, affirmative action preferences and presumptions of cultural and economic disadvantage had never made sense. Although the Supreme Court in *Adarand* (1995) held race-conscious remedies appropriate only for minorities suffering documented discrimination, the politics of affirmative action impelled government officials to include all official minorities.

Similarly problematical was official minority status for Hispanics. Federal officials in the 1960s and early 1970s showed confusion over the triggering source of protected class status for Hispanics, sometimes labeling them as Spanish-speaking, sometimes as Spanish-surnamed, sometimes distinguishing between Hispanics (meaning chiefly Mexicans) and Puerto Ricans. In 1977, the OMB in Directive No. 15 attempted to provide consistency across federal agencies by defining a Hispanic as "a person of Mexican, Puerto Rican, Cuban, Central or South America or other Spanish culture or origin, regardless of race."[57] Did this include persons from Spain—and if so, why? Did it include Portuguese or Brazilians, who were not Spanish-speaking? Or Filipinos who were? Did it include persons from Latin American countries without "Spanish culture," whatever that meant, countries such as Belize, Guiana, or Surinam?

OMB Directive No. 15 defined "White" as "a person having origins in any of the original peoples of Europe, North Africa, or the Middle East," but noted that "the classifications should not be interpreted as being scientific or anthropological in nature." Yet government officials were obliged to interpret and apply the OMB's classifications when assessing claims for affirmative action benefits. The SBA, challenged in the 1980s by various groups seeking eligibility for the 8(a) minority contract program, concluded, on grounds that were never explained, that the Asian and Pacific Islander category extended westward as far as Pakistan, but stopped at the Afghan border. Fortunately, the SBA was not obliged to provide a scientific basis for such findings. As a by-product of such arbitrary line drawing, affirmative action programs came to include persons of European ancestry (Spaniards and Portuguese), but excluded persons of North African and Middle Eastern ancestry, such as Iranians and Hasidic Jews.

These problems of logic and coherence in the rationale for affirmative action programs and their criteria for eligibility, inherent from the beginning, were intensified by the tide of immigration from Asia and Latin America. The eligibility of 80 percent of immigrants to America for affirmative action programs made a mockery of the historical rationale that minority preferences compensated for past discrimination in America. By the late 1990s, Asians dominated the SBA's contract set-aside program in California, the federal government's largest state outlay for affirmative action. By 2000, non-Hispanic whites were no longer a majority in California, the nation's most populous state, and by 2008, they would no longer be a majority in Texas. By 2005, Hispanics were expected to displace blacks as the country's largest minority. Most significant, however, was the growing problem of assigning a single racial and ethnic identity to all Americans, as the OMB directives required. Mass immigration accompanied by growing racial and ethnic intermarriage made this practice politically unsustainable.

Assigning individuals to single, nonduplicative categories is an old tradition in America. The Constitution required the enumeration of slaves and free persons to apportion the House of Representatives, a task that launched America's decennial census on a long and, for the most part, distinguished career of counting and classification. The national origins quotas of the 1920s required assigning to all Americans of European ancestry a single country of origin—a Herculean and, ultimately, a scientifically impossible task. Civil rights statutes in the 1960s added new single-category requirements to support enforcement efforts in areas such as voting rights and bilingual education. For generations, the Census Bureau asked Americans to assign themselves to nonduplicative categories, especially racial ones. In cases of uncertainty, children were assigned to the race of their mother, or their race was identified visually by the census enumerator. But dual or multiple racial assignments were not permitted. Tiger Woods could identify himself as African or Asian, but not both, and certainly not also as part Caucasian or Native American, which he did when he called himself a "Cablinasian" to reflect his own four-way identification.

For persons of mixed racial or ethnic parentage, the OMB directed government officials to select "the category which most closely reflects the individual's recognition in his community." This was a highly subjective judgment for government officials to make. Government policy after 1960 relied increasingly on self-identification. But government policy continued to prohibit individuals from claiming, or employers from reporting, more than one racial category for individuals. Although mixed-race parentage was widespread among African-Americans, U.S. government policy for generations had followed the notorious one-drop rule in racial classifications. Ironically, this policy was not changed by the "color-blind" thrust of the civil rights revolution of the 1960s. Both racial segregation before the 1960s and race-conscious affirmative action after the 1960s required government fidelity to the one-drop rule of (white) racial purity.

Large-scale immigration from Latin America and Asia, however, changed all this. Beginning in the 1980s and increasing in the 1990s, the native-born children of post-1965 immigrants began to marry and have children outside of their racial and ethnic group. The trend toward interracial parentage was strong among Asians, Hispanics, and American Indians, and weak among blacks. Between 1970 and 1990, the number of multiracial children under 18 quadrupled to 2 million. In 1990, more than half of all native-born, young (ages 25–34) Asians married non-Asians, and two-fifths of Hispanics in this group married non-Hispanics. By 1994, there were 1.3 million interracial married couples, compared with 310,000 in 1970, and an additional 500,000 interracial couples who were not married but living together. Even among blacks, with traditionally low rates of interracial marriage, mixed-race unions began to increase. Among better educated young black men (ages 20–29), 6 percent married nonblacks in 1980 and 11 percent married non-blacks in 1997. By 2000 more than 40 percent of third-generation Asian-Americans married people of different ethnic backgrounds. Among Hispanics, almost two thirds married non-Latinos.[58]

The parents and children of these racially and ethnically mixed unions increasingly objected to government requirements, including public school celebrations of ethnic diversity, that individuals select the racial identity of one of their parents and reject the other. They formed more than thirty national organizations, making extensive use of the internet to lobby for a multiracial category in state classifications (twelve states had done so by 1995) and in the 2000 census.[59] This effort won House hearings in 1993, followed by an OMB review that, unlike the agency deliberations of the past, included open sessions and public testimony. Most black and Hispanic interest groups opposed a multiracial category, fearing that it would diminish their constituency numbers and reduce their internal cohesion. In 1997 the OMB, in a compromise decision, rejected a multiracial category for the 2000 census but approved checking more than one box to indicate race.[60] In March 2000, an election year, the OMB issued a directive welcomed by civil rights groups urging the Clinton administration to block a multiracial category. "Mixed-race people who mark both White and a non-white race will be counted as the latter for purposes of civil rights monitoring and enforcement," the OMB ruled.[61] The U.S. government thus left the twentieth century as it had entered it, clinging to the antebellum one-drop rule, even as millions of the immigrants' native-born children and grandchildren, by marrying and having children outside their racial and ethnic group, were transforming the country into Tiger Woods's America.[62]

Despite the Clinton administration's insistence on minority-only counting in the 2000 census for purposes of civil rights monitoring and enforcement, however, the census report itself listed the new multiracial and multiethnic categories as Americans for the first time had selected them. They included fifty-seven possible combinations of six single-race categories (white, black, American Indian and Alaskan Native, Asian, Native Hawaiian and other Pacific Islander, and "Some Other Race"). Adding Hispanic ethnicity as a choice doubled the sixty-three boxes available for selecting one's racial identity. The new multicultural options promised to transform the way race was viewed in America, breaking the single-race-only, one-drop rule model even as the OMB attempted to retain it to mollify the civil rights lobbies. Henceforth, all government agencies would be required to report data in the new format. Private employers, required to adopt the new reporting method by 2003, were expected to abandon their "visual surveys," whereby employers determined the racial identity of employees without asking them, and switch to employee identification. Schools, colleges, and universities were given until 2004-5 to make the changes.[63] The American Anthropological Association, noting that scientists who sequenced the human genome announced in 2000 that the DNA of human beings was 99.9 percent alike, regardless of race, recommended eliminating the term "race" in the 2010 census.[64]

Economics, Policy Logic, and Demographics

Will affirmative action survive the growing assaults against it? One should not lightly predict the demise of a major government benefits program of any kind in America, especially one so deeply entrenched and skillfully defended. In the 1990s, narrow conservative majorities on the U.S. Supreme Court, in decisions such as *Adarand Constructors v. Pena* (1995), sharply curbed minority preference policies in government contracts and other affirmative action programs, but stopped short of ruling them unconstitutional per se and requiring color-blind policies. Prohibiting minority preferences in state and local government programs was achieved through voter referendums in several western states, notably California, Washington, and Arizona, where heavy immigration coincided with economic distress. But federal affirmative action programs and federal court requirements were unaffected by these state initiatives. And throughout the 1990s, the Supreme Court failed to clarify the permissible constitutional role of race-conscious admissions in colleges and professional schools, despite conflicting rulings in the appeals circuits.

By 2000, however, affirmative action faced a renewed and potentially more dangerous attack. It was the product of a program maturing in a society that received 26 million immigrants from Latin America and Asia whose ancestry immediately qualified them as eligible for affirmative action benefits. Although most of these immigrants may not have known of this eligibility or attempted to exercise it, they and their children benefited from it in the general labor market. American employers valued most immigrant workers as hardworking, noncomplaining, low-cost, and reliable. Commonly preferring immigrant workers to high-cost, less tractable native workers, employers emphasized a diversity rationale in "hiring by the numbers" under affirmative action plans. The EEOC, dismayed that employers acting under affirmative action plans were hiring millions of immigrants while leaving high unemployment among inner-city blacks, filed lawsuits in the 1980s to compel employers to follow a stricter racial proportionality in their workplace. The EEOC legal offensive largely failed, however, in courts increasingly populated by Reagan-appointed judges. Meanwhile the immigrants themselves, through their economic and educational achievements and their marriages and parenting, began to reshape the racial and ethnic mix in ways that undermined the affirmative action regime.

The new attack on affirmative action was three-pronged. Though none of the three lines of argument was new, all had gained force as immigration accelerated and immigration success challenged the traditional equation of minority status and social and economic disadvantage. By the 1990s, the three arguments were beginning to displace the old constitutional and moral claims about color blindness that had failed to stop race-conscious affirmative action in the 1970s. First, opponents argued that minority preferences were economically unfair, because beneficiaries include a growing constituency of affluent minorities while continuing to exclude poor nonminorities. Second, opponents charged that affirmative action was logically incoherent, because the government's expanding list of official minorities, especially within the extraordinarily broad and varied categories of Hispanic and Asian, included some groups and excluded others on arbitrary and contradictory grounds. Third, and perhaps most threatening to the affirmative action regime, opponents charged that the government's single-minority categories, and the one-drop rule on which they rested, offended racial and ethnic sensibilities themselves and denied the reality of a racially mixed American population.

By 2000, the dispute over including multiracial classifications in the census promised to subvert the single-race-only scheme that underpinned presumptive eligibility for official minorities. Even though the OMB, in a rear-guard action, required that all persons claiming both white and racial minority ancestry in the census be counted as a minority for civil rights monitoring purposes, the new multiracial categories in the census carried implicit policy consequences. Like the minority categories added in the 1950s to the fair employment surveys, the new multiracial categories took on a logic and momentum of their own. Under the new census format, for example, the familiar five classifications of the ethnoracial pentagon were reported in overlapping ranges rather than in discrete totals. Thus in the 1990 census the number of Hispanics in America was listed as 22.4 million, whereas the 2000 census counted between 31.8 million and 35.3 million Hispanics. The total number of Asians, listed as 7.3 million in 1990, jumped to a range of 10.5 to 12.8 million. As the two largest immigrant blocs grow in size, their edges blur.

African-Americans, though urged by several black rights organizations to check black race only on the census form, surprised observers when more than 5 percent checked at least a second box. Since previous noncensus studies had demonstrated that most African-Americans were of mixed racial ancestry, the black response to the racial options in the 2000 census was revealing both because the share of African-Americans selecting a multiracial identity was large, relative to expectations, and because it was small, relative to reality. To most African-Americans, the cultural solidarity enforced by the one-drop rule had long trumped the genetic reality of mixed-race ancestry. The changes measured and foretold by the overlapping racial categories in the 2000 census, however, made the one-drop rule and its corollary, the one-race-only rule, increasingly indefensible. Yet without these rules, which defined eligibility for affirmative action programs, how could affirmative action itself be maintained?

A widely-cited demographic projection based on 2000 census data concluded that "[t]he future U.S. population will not consist of a distinct set of races and ethnic groups. Indeed, it will not be possible to describe the future U.S. population in terms of mutually exclusive racial and ethnic groups with distinct cultures, languages, looks, and unique race/ethnic identification."[65] By 2150, intermarriage will have so thoroughly mixed the racial and ethnic ancestry of Americans that the old twentieth century distinctions between American Indians, Hispanics, Asians, and "non-Latino whites" will be meaningless. Black intermarriage rates, low in most of the twentieth century but tripling after 1980, remain the demographic wild card. In the 2000 census, 33.9 million checked the African-American or black box alone. An additional 2.5 million, however, checked black and another racial designation.

Such a multi-racial and multi-ethnic population threatened the heart of the affirmative action system. Since 1970 the EEOC, contract compliance officials enforcing Title VI, and federal courts applying disparate impact standards of statistical representation all had relied on single-category totals from the Census Bureau and employer reports to provide the benchmark data needed to demonstrate underrepresentation for specific minorities. This system was devised in the heat of the 1960s race riots and was designed to speed black hiring. To shield the new race-conscious affirmative action requirements from "quota" charges and reverse-discrimination lawsuits, as we have seen, the Nixon administration and its successors had blurred the hard edge of proportional representation targets for minorities by permitting employers to submit percentage ranges rather than specific numerical targets as hiring goals. This intentional measure of defensive slack in the affirmative action system, however, had the unintended consequence of allowing American employers to hire millions of Asian and Hispanic immigrants as protected-class minorities while often employing proportionally few blacks. In 2000 the Census Bureau's new multi-racial/ethnic categories further blurred the racial and ethnic boundaries upon which affirmative action enforcement relied.

"We've opened Pandora's box," warned Robert Hill, a member of the Census Bureau Committee on Race and Ethnicity.[66] "The higher black multiracial responses are, the more likely it is that they might erode affirmative action and civil rights enforcement," Hill said. "We're worried about it. That's why we objected to the multiracial categories in the first place." Howard University sociologist Roderick Harrison, founding director of the Databank at the Joint Center for Political and Economic Studies and chief of the U.S. Census Bureau's Racial Statistics Branch, warned that the new multiracial census categories opened affirmative action programs to potentially ruinous lawsuits.[67]

Increasingly, the unintended consequences of the immigration reforms of the 1960s were colliding with the unintended consequences of the civil rights reforms of the 1960s. The combined assaults of the federal courts, the state-level initiatives, the continuing opposition of public opinion majorities, and above all the multiracial future that intermarrying immigrant children and grandchildren were bringing to America, threatened to be fatal to the minority preference programs won by the civil rights coalition in the 1970s.

The immigration expansionist coalition, on the other hand, entered the twenty-first century with impressive political bargaining power against weakening opposition. The three forces undermining the foundations of affirmative action policy—economic disparities, policy contradictions, and demographic trends—have had a neutral impact or have strengthened high-immigration policies. The economic boom of the 1990s dampened resentment of immigrant job competition, while increasing employer pressures for a workforce enlarged by immigration. America's post-IRCA immigration policy, although grounded in a profound contradiction between a defend-the-borders imperative and an unworkable employer sanctions law, rested on a legislative consensus that supported the major expansionist proposals—liberal family reunification preferences, high levels of legal immigration, guest worker programs for growers and high-tech industries, and generous provisions for asylum. The federal courts, while alarming the civil rights and voting rights bar by narrowing the scope of affirmative action policies, have posed no equivalent threat to the immigration bar. The U.S. Supreme Court in its 2000–2001 term continued to affirm the constitutional rights of immigrants irrespective of their visa status, criminal record, or deportation orders.[68] Demographically, heavy immigration from Asia and Latin America pleased employer groups and sweetened large-scale immigration for the Republican Party. Politically, heavy immigration from Latin America strengthened Latino rights organizations, especially within the Democratic Party, and enabled them to neutralize traditional opposition to immigration expansion from African-American leaders and organized labor. By racializing the immigration issue, Hispanic rights organizations also neutralized opposition from cultural conservatives and populists who opposed the shift away from European immigration.

Despite these political and legal successes, however, the immigration policies of the post-1965 era left America vulnerable to the expanding global market in international misery. The bonanza of free-market economic globalization produced unprecedented abundance in the industrial democracies of the Northern Hemisphere that dangerously outpaced the performance of struggling nations in Africa, Latin America, and much of

Asia. Post-cold war studies of persons "internally displaced" by growing instability, civil war, and economic collapse showed an increase from 1.2 million in eleven countries in 1982 to 20 million in thirty-five to forty countries in 1995.[69] Collapsing political and economic orders in Central America and the Caribbean (for example, Guatemala, El Salvador, Cuba, and Haiti), South America (especially Colombia and Equador), Asia (particularly North Korea, Myramar, and Indonesia), and most of sub-Saharan Africa were driving vast new populations into flight.

In these imperiled, mostly southern sectors of the globe, 3 billion people struggled to survive on less than two dollars a day, 1.5 billion lacked clean drinking water, half of the children were not in school, one-third of the workers were unemployed or severely underemployed, and corruption was rampant. In much of Africa and Asia, AIDS was spreading at pandemic scale, bleeding desperate societies of 15–20 percent of their shrinking GDP. The revolution in transportation and communications magnified the appeal and proximity of target destinations in the affluent democracies. An estimated 40,000 illegal immigrants entered Europe in 1993, and 500,000 entered in 2000.[70]

The exploding new market in human misery nourished sophisticated worldwide smuggling networks run by international mafias.[71] "Coyotes" charging $500 to escort immigrants across the Rio Grande were upstaged by "snakeheads" charging $50,000 to smuggle Chinese into America. In 2000, an estimated fifty thousand Chinese sneaked into America; only one in ten ended up in INS custody.[72] The interception, beaching, or sinking of overcrowded smuggler ships was increasingly featured by American and European media. More symptomatic evidence, however, of the new economic muscle of human smuggling, fast-rivaling the dollar volume and corruptive power of drug smuggling, was the indictment by federal prosecutors in 2000 of the leaders of one of New York's busiest immigration law firms for receiving $1.2 million in fees from Chinese smuggling rings and for helping smugglers hold illegal immigrants hostage until the fee for passage was paid.[73]

Against such forces, the porous U.S. immigration system seemed almost defenseless. The world's most powerful economy was paired with probably the most easily penetrated system of immigration control among the magnet industrial democracies of the world. In a Brookings Institution study of the federal government's greatest achievements and failures since World War II, 450 historians and political scientists ranked controlling immigration second among the top five failures of the postwar era.[74] The United States has already paid a high price for that failure, especially in the coin of contempt for American lawful processes. Given the forces building behind a worldwide flight from the collapsing societies to the rich democracies, America may yet pay a higher price still, especially following a global economic downturn. Throughout history, the American economy has periodically fallen into steep declines, as have the economies of all nations. Also historically, the United States has reshaped its immigration policy infrequently, but sharply, following periods of intensifying debate over immigration. The shock of the terrorist attack on the World Trade Center and the Pentagon on September 11, 2001 sent the American economy into recession and abruptly changed the political environment of the immigration debate. Proposals for open borders with Mexico and Canada and another round of amnesty for illegal immigrants were replaced by demands for tight border security and computerized monitoring of the status and whereabouts of foreign visitors and immigrants.[75] Should the combination of economic and physical insecurity—a painful novelty for Americans—grow sufficiently severe under the strains of the new and uncharted war against global terrorism, American policy may once again make a broad swing of the pendulum, replacing a permissive regime of mass entry with a new restrictionist regime that may be severe. Only time can reveal how these new forces play out in the 21st century.

Notes

1. Introduction

1. For a critical account of the immigration and affirmative action issues in California's political culture in the 1980s and 1990s, see Peter Schrag, *Paradise Lost: California's Experience, America's Future* (Berkeley: University of California Press, 1999).

2. Richard Lee Colvin and Doug Smith, "Proposition 227 Foes Vow to Block It Despite Wide Margin," *Los Angeles Times*, 4 June 1998, 1.

3. These news reports are summarized in James S. Robb, *Affirmative Action for Immigrants: The Entitlement Nobody Wanted* (Petoskey, Mich.: Social Contract Press, 1995).

4. Silverman, quoted in Robb, *Affirmative Action for Immigrants*, 9.

5. Lawrence H. Fuchs, "What Do Immigrants Deserve?" *Washington Post*, 29 January 1995, C2.

6. Christopher Edley Jr. and George Stephanopoulos, "Affirmative Action Review: Report to the President," 19 July 1995.

7. Steven A. Holmes, "On Civil Rights, Clinton Steers Bumpy Course between Left and Right," *New York Times*, 20 October 1996, 14.

8. James P. Smith and Barry Edmonston, eds., *The New Americans: Economic, Demographic, and Fiscal Effects of Immigration* (Washington, D.C.: National Academy Press, 1997).

9. Kevin F. McCarthy and Georges Vernez, *Immigration in a Changing Economy: California's Experience* (Santa Monica, Calif.: RAND, 1997).

10. *Immigration Reform: Employer Sanctions and the Question of Discrimination* (Washington: General Accounting Office, 1990).

11. Michael D. Reagan, *Regulation: The Politics of Policy* (Boston: Little, Brown, 1987).

12. Allan J. Cigler and Burdett A. Loomis, eds., *Interest Group Politics*, 4th ed. (Washington: Congressional Quarterly Press, 1995); Jeffrey M. Berry, *The New Liberalism: The Rising Power of Citizen Groups* (Washington, D.C.: Brookings Institution Press, 1999).

13. Paul M. Sniderman and Edward C. Carmines, *Reaching Beyond Race*

(Cambridge: Harvard University Press, 1997); Kenneth K. Lee, *Huddled Masses, Muddled Laws: Why Contemporary Immigration Policy Fails to Reflect Public Opinion* (Westport, Conn.: Praeger, 1998).

14. Nicholas Laham, *The Reagan Presidency and the Politics of Race* (Westport, Conn.: Praeger, 1998).

15. Ellis Cose, *A Nation of Strangers: Prejudice, Politics, and the Populating of America* (New York: Morrow, 1992).

16. George R. La Noue, "To the `Disadvantaged' Go the Spoils?" *Public Interest*, winter 2000, 91–98.

17. Hugh Davis Graham, *The Civil Rights Era: Origins and Development of National Policy, 1960–1972* (New York: Oxford University Press, 1990); John David Skrentny, *The Ironies of Affirmative Action: Politics, Culture, and Justice in America* (Chicago: University of Chicago Press, 1996).

18. John David Skrentny, *The Minority Rights Revolution* (Cambridge: Harvard University Press, 2002).

19. Steven M. Gillon, *"That's Not What We Meant to Do": Reform and Its Unintended Consequences in Twentieth-Century America* (New York: Norton, 2000); Marc K. Landy and Martin A. Levin, eds., *The New Politics of Public Policy* (Baltimore: Johns Hopkins University Press, 1995).

20. Thomas Byrne Edsall with Mary D. Edsall, *Chain Reaction: The Impact of Race, Rights, and Taxes on American Politics* (New York: Norton, 1991).

21. David M. Reimers, *Unwelcome Strangers: American Identity and the Turn against Immigration* (New York: Columbia University Press, 1998).

2. Civil Rights Reform in the 1960s

1. Richard Kluger, *Simple Justice: The History of Brown v. Board of Education* (New York: Knopf, 1976).

2. C. Vann Woodward, *The Strange Career of Jim Crow*, 3d rev. ed. (New York: Oxford University Press, 1974).

3. Wilbur J. Cash, *The Mind of the South* (New York: Knopf, 1941).

4. Herbert H. Hyman and Paul B. Sheatsley, "Attitudes toward Desegregation," *Scientific American*, July 1964, 18, 35–39.

5. Howard N. Rabinowitz, *The First New South, 1865–1920* (Arlington Heights, Ill.: Harlan Davidson, 1992); William A. Link, *The Paradox of Southern Progressivism, 1880–1930* (Chapel Hill: University of North Carolina Press, 1992).

6. Grace Elizabeth Hale, *Making Whiteness: The Culture of Segregation in the South, 1890–1940* (New York: Pantheon, 1998).

7. Quoted in Mark Curriden and LeRoy Phillips Jr., *Contempt of Court: The Turn-of-the-Century Lynching That Launched a Hundred Years of Federalism* (New York: Faber and Faber, 1999), 329.

8. Link, *The Paradox of Southern Progressivism*, 141–42; E. M. Beck, *A Festival*

of Violence: An Analysis of Southern Lynchings, 1882–1930 (Urbana: University of Illinois Press, 1995); Curriden and Phillips, *Contempt of Court*, appendix 1, 353–56. Annual lynchings in the South averaged 167 in the 1890s, 93 between 1900, and 1909, 62 in the 1910s, 31 in the 1920s, and 13 in the 1930s.

9. *Buchanan v. Warley*, 245 U.S. 60 (1917); Roger L. Rice, "Residential Segregation by Law, 1910–1917," *Journal of Southern History* 34 (1968): 179–99.

10. Woodward, *Strange Career of Jim Crow*, 82–93.

11. Howard N. Rabinowitz, *Race Relations in the Urban South, 1865–1890* (New York: Oxford University Press, 1978); Rabinowitz, "More than the Woodward Thesis: Assessing the Strange Career of Jim Crow," in Rabinowitz, ed., *Race, Ethnicity, and Urbanization* (New York: Columbia University Press, 1984), 23–41.

12. The classic political formulation is V. O. Key Jr., with Alexander Heard, *Southern Politics in State and Nation* (New York: Knopf, 1949). For social science analysis before *Brown*, see Gunnar Myrdal, *An American Dilemma* (New York: Harper, 1944); Gordon W. Allport, *The Nature of Prejudice* (Cambridge, Mass.: Addison-Wesley, 1954); and Walter A. Jackson, *Gunnar Myrdal and America's Conscience: Social Engineering and Racial Liberalism* (Chapel Hill: University of North Carolina Press, 1990). David W. Southern, *Gunnar Myrdal and Black-White Relations: The Use and Abuse of an American Dilemma, 1944–1969* (Baton Rouge: Louisiana State University Press, 1987) criticizes the inadequacies of Myrdal's liberal legacy.

13. Key, *Southern Politics*.

14. Dewey W. Grantham, *The Life and Death of the Solid South* (Lexington: University of Kentucky Press, 1988), 78–149.

15. Steven F. Lawson, *Black Ballots: Voting Rights in the South, 1944–1969* (New York: Columbia University Press, 1976).

16. David J. Garrow, *The Montgomery Bus Boycott and the Women Who Started It: The Memoir of Jo Ann Gibson Robinson* (Knoxville: University of Tennessee Press, 1987); Adam Fairclough, *To Redeem the Soul of America: The Southern Christian Leadership Conference and Martin Luther King, Jr.* (Athens: University of Georgia Press, 1987).

17. Clayborne Carson, *In Struggle: SNCC and the Black Awakening of the 1960s* (Cambridge: Harvard University Press, 1981); William H. Chafe, *Civilities and Civil Rights: Greensboro, North Carolina, and the Black Struggle for Freedom* (Chapel Hill: University of North Carolina Press, 1980).

18. August Meier and Elliott Rudwick, *CORE: A Study in the Civil Rights Movement, 1942–1968* (New York: Oxford University Press, 1973); Catherine A. Barnes, *Journey from Jim Crow: The Death of Segregation in Southern Transit* (New York: Columbia University Press, 1983), 44–161; David J. Garrow, *Protest at Selma* (New Haven, Conn.: Yale University Press, 1978). On the protest demonstrations in Albany, Georgia, in 1962, see David J. Garrow, *Bearing the Cross: Martin Luther King, Jr. and the Southern Christian Leadership Conference* (New York: Random House, 1986), 173–230; and Fairclough, *To Redeem the Soul of America*, 85–110.

19. Garrow, *Bearing the Cross*; Taylor Branch, *Parting the Waters: America in the King Years, 1954–1963* (New York: Simon and Schuster, 1988).

20. Robert Weisbrot, *Freedom Bound: A History of America's Civil Rights Movement* (New York: Norton, 1990).

21. Numan V. Bartley and Hugh Davis Graham, *Southern Politics and the Second Reconstruction* (Baltimore: Johns Hopkins University Press, 1975); Steven S. Lawson, *Running for Freedom: Civil Rights and Black Politics in America Since 1941* (New York: McGraw-Hill, 1991).

22. Hugh Davis Graham, *The Civil Rights Era: Origins and Development of National Policy, 1960–1972* (New York: Oxford University Press, 1990), 125–77; Denton L. Watson, *Lion in the Lobby: Clarence Mitchell Jr.'s Struggle for Passage of the Civil Rights Laws* (New York: William Morris, 1990); Michael Pertschuk, *The Giant Killers* (New York: Norton, 1986), 148–80.

23. Hugh Davis Graham, "The Civil Rights Act and the American Regulatory State," *Legacies of the 1964 Civil Rights Act*, ed. Bernard Grofman (Charlottesville: University Press of Virginia, 2000), 43–64.

24. Charles and Barbara Whalen, *The Longest Debate: A Legislative History of the 1964 Civil Rights Act* (Cabin John, Md.: Seven Locks Press, 1985); James Patterson, *Grand Expectations* (New York: Oxford University Press, 1996), 524–92; Steven F. Lawson, *In Pursuit of Power: Southern Blacks and Electoral Programs, 1965–1982* (New York: Columbia University Press, 1985).

25. Hugh Davis Graham, "Race, History, and Policy: African-Americans and Civil Rights Since 1964," *Journal of Policy History* 6 (winter 1994): 12–39.

26. Hugh Davis Graham, *Civil Rights and the Presidency* (New York: Oxford University Press, 1992), 87–116; Stephen C. Halpern, *On the Limits of the Law: The Ironic Legacy of Title VI of the 1964 Civil Rights Act* (Baltimore: Johns Hopkins University Press, 1995), 331–39.

27. James Heckman and Brooks Paynor, "Determining the Impact of Federal Anti-Discrimination Policy on the Economic Status of Blacks: A Study of South Carolina," *American Economic Review* 79 (March 1989): 173; John J. Donohue III and James Heckman, "Continuous versus Episodic Change: The Impact of Civil Rights Policy on the Economic Status of Blacks," *Journal of Economic Literature* 29 (December 1991): 1603–43.

28. Jonathan Leonard, "The Impact of Affirmative Action Regulation and Equal Employment Law on Black Employment," *Journal of Economic Perspectives* 4 (fall 1990): 49; Dave M. O'Neill and June O'Neill, "Affirmative Action in the Labor Market," *Annals of the American Academy of Political and Social Science* 532 (September 1992): 88–103.

29. Garrow, *Protest at Selma*, 18, 20; Lawson, *In Pursuit of Power*.

30. *New York Times*, 23 May 1954.

31. 347 U.S. 483, brief for appellants on reargument, 15.

32. Quoted in John David Skrentny, *The Ironies of Affirmative Action* (Chicago: University of Chicago Press, 1996), 7.

33. Quoted in Graham, *Civil Rights Era*, 150–51.

34. Quoted in Skrentny, *Ironies of Affirmative Action*, 3.

35. Graham, *Civil Rights Era*, 33.

36. Ibid., 30–46.

37. Quoted in ibid., 42.

38. Ted Robert Gurr, ed., *Violence in America*, vol. 2 (Newbury Park, Calif.: Sage, 1989); James W. Button, *Black Violence: Political Impact of the 1960s Riots* (Princeton: Princeton University Press, 1978).

3. Immigration Reform in the 1960s

1. Roger Daniels and Otis L. Graham Jr., *Debating American Immigration, 1882–present* (New York: Rowman and Littlefield, 2001).

2. Madison Grant, *The Passing of the Great Race* (New York: Scribner, 1916).

3. Grant reasoned from the science of Darwin and Mendel that the mixing of two races "gives us a race reverting to the more ancient, generalized, and lower type." Thus "the cross between any of the three European races and a Jew is a Jew." Quoted in John Higham, *Strangers in the Land: Patterns of American Nativism, 1860–1925* (New Brunswick, N.J.: Rutgers University Press, 1955), 156.

4. Ibid., 131–93.

5. Robert G. Spinney, *City of Big Shoulders: A History of Chicago* (DeKalb: Northern Illinois University Press, 2000), 123–45.

6. John Bodnar, *The Transplanted: A History of Immigrants in Urban America* (Bloomington: Indiana University Press, 1985); Roger Daniels, *Coming to America: A History of Immigration and Ethnicity in American Life* (New York: Harper-Collins, 1990).

7. Allen F. Davis, *Spearheads for Reform: The Social Settlements and the Progressive Movement, 1890–1914* (New Brunswick, N.J.: Rutgers University Press, 1984); Otis L. Graham Jr., *The Great Campaigns: Reform and War in America, 1900–1928* (Malabar, Fla.: Krieger, 1987).

8. Daniel T. Rodgers, "In Search of Progressivism," *Reviews in American History* 10 (1982): 113–31.

9. Wilson, quoted in E. P. Hutchinson, *Legislative History of American Immigration Policy, 1798–1965* (Philadelphia: University of Pennsylvania Press, 1981), 167.

10. Ibid., 166–68. The chief target of the Asiatic barred zone, especially in the House, seemed to be the Indian subcontinent, since with the exception of certain professional classes, Chinese had been excluded since 1882 and Japanese by the Gentlemen's Agreement of 1907. The Senate's Asiatic barred zone in 1917 was adopted rather than an explicit ban on "Hindus" in the House bill.

11. Marion T. Bennett, *American Immigration Policies* (Washington, D.C.: Public Affairs Press, 1963), 41.

12. *Ozara v. United States*, 260 U.S. 178 (1922).

13. *Terrance v. Thompson*, 263 U.S. 197 (1923).

14. Woodrow Wilson, *History of the American People* (New York: Harper and Brothers, 1902), 5: 212.

15. U.S. Immigration Commission of 1911, *Report*. See Hutchinson, *Legislative History*, 143–55.

16. Johnson had long consulted with leading racialist proponents of immigration restriction, including Prescott F. Hall of the Immigration Restriction League, Madison Grant, and Harry L. Laughlin, a prominent eugenicist from Cold Spring Harbor, New York. In 1923 the Eugenics Research Association at Cold Spring Harbor elected Albert Johnson its president. Johnson's 1924 bill, by putting European immigration on 2 percent quotas computed from the 1890 census rather than 3 percent quotas from the 1910 census, would cut the Italian quota from 42,000 to about 4,000, the Polish from 31,000 to 6,000, the Greek from 3,000 to 100. Higham, *Strangers in the Land*, 312–24.

17. Senator David Reed, quoted in Stephen Thomas Wagner, "The Lingering Death of the National Origins Quota System: A Political History of United States Immigration Policy, 1952–1965" (Ph.D. diss., Harvard University, 1986), 12.

18. Opposition leaders in the House were Adolph Sabath from Chicago and Samuel Dickstein and Fiorello La Guardia from New York, all Democrats.

19. Higham's *Strangers in the Land* was joined in the 1950s by Oscar Handlin, *The Uprooted* (Boston: Little, Brown, 1951); Handlin, *Race and Nationality in American Life* (Boston: Little, Brown, 1957); and Robert A. Divine, *American Immigration Policy, 1924–1952* (New Haven: Yale University Press, 1957). Divine's work was more policy-oriented than Higham's intellectual and cultural history and more sympathetic to the restrictionists of the McCarran-Walter era. In the 1960s, immigration scholarship shifted against assimilationist traditions of "Americanization," questioning the desirability of acculturation and emphasizing cultural survival and ethnic persistence. See Marion T. Bennett, *American Immigration Policy* (Washington: Public Affairs Press, 1963); Roger Daniels, "Federal Policy Towards Immigration," in *Reader's Guide to American History*, ed. Peter J. Parish (Chicago: Fitzroy Dearborn, 1997), 337–38.

20. Fresh scholarship on the restrictionist era in American history, 1882 to World War II, includes Stephen Wagner's 1986 study, his unpublished Harvard dissertation; Desmond King, *Making Americans: Immigration, Race, and the Origins of a Diverse Democracy* (Cambridge: Harvard University Press, 2000); and Daniels and Graham, *Debating American Immigration*.

21. Glazer quoted in Otis L. Graham Jr., "The Unfinished Reform: Regulating Immigration in the National Interest," in *Debating American Immigration*, 142–43.

22. Letter, Gompers to J. H. Reiter of Haverford College, 28 April 1921, H. Keith Thompson collection, Hoover Institution on War and Peace, Stanford University.

23. Wagner, "National Origins Quota System," 101–57.

24. Ibid., 158–236.

25. Otis L. Graham Jr. and Elizabeth Koed, "Americanizing the Immigrant, Past and Future: History and Implication of a Social Movement," *Public Historian* 15 (fall 1993): 24–49.

26. Erik Barnouw, *Tube of Plenty: The Evolution of American Television* (New York: Oxford University Press, 1990), 105–10, 117–30, 172–84.

27. Betty K. Koed, "The Politics of Reform: Policymakers and the Immigration Act of 1965" (Ph.D. diss., University of California, Santa Barbara, 1999), 1–42.

28. Hutchinson, *Legislative History*, 461–91.

29. David M. Reimers, *Still the Golden Door* (New York: Columbia University Press, 1985), 11–36; Koed, "Immigration Act of 1965," 43–66.

30. Wagner, "National Origins Quota System," 237–309.

31. Koed, "Immigration Act of 1965," 67–112.

32. Hugh Davis Graham, *The Civil Rights Era* (New York: Oxford University Press, 1990), 153–76.

33. Wagner, "National Origins Quota System," 384–458; Koed, "Immigration Act of 1965," 155–68.

34. Graham, "Unfinished Reform," 135–44.

35. See generally Hutchinson, *Legislative History*, 308–13, 492–520.

36. Koed, "Immigration Act of 1965," 97–101.

37. Wagner, "National Origins Quota System," 401–2.

38. Koed, "Immigration Act of 1965," 192–219.

39. Hutchinson, *Legislative History*, 492–520.

40. Wagner, "National Origins Quota System," 421–24.

41. Celler quoted in *Congressional Quarterly Almanac 1965* (Washington, D.C.: Congressional Quarterly, 1966), 183.

42. Koed, "Immigration Act of 1965," 192–218.

43. Ibid., 169–91.

44. Reimers, *Still the Golden Door*, 37–60.

45. In 1945, the Bracero program contracted for 49,500 Mexican guest workers and 63,500 Mexicans were apprehended for illegal entry into the United States. In 1954, the corresponding figures for Mexico were 309,000 guest workers and 1,076,000 apprehensions. *Congress and the Nation* (Washington, D.C.: Congressional Quarterly, 1965), 762.

46. Kennedy quoted in Koed, "Immigration Act of 1965," 171–72.

47. Roger Daniels, "Two Cheers for Immigration," in Daniels and Graham, *Debating American Immigration*, 43.

48. In the House, Republicans supported the immigration reform bill (H.R. 2580) by a vote of 109–25; northern Democrats voted 179–8 for the bill and a majority of southern Democrats opposed it 30–62. In the Senate, Republicans supported the bill (S. 500) 24–3; northern Democrats supported it 43–2, and southern Democrats opposed it 9–13.

4. Origins and Development of Race-Conscious Affirmative Action

1. John David Skrentny, *The Ironies of Affirmative Action* (Chicago: University of Chicago Press, 1996), 3.

2. The race-conscious remedies of hard affirmative action thus originate in

1969. The slippery-slope tensions between the soft nondiscrimination-plus-outreach affirmative action required by the Kennedy and Johnson administrations and the hard minority-preference policies developed in the 1970s reach back to Kennedy's executive order of 1961. In various indirect ways, the antecedents of proportional representation as a remedy for racial discrimination reach back into the mists of history. For antecedents of affirmative action, see Paul D. Moreno, *From Direct Action to Affirmative Action: Fair Employment Law and Policy in America, 1933–1972* (Baton Rouge: Louisiana State University Press, 1997); Thomas Sugrue, "The Tangled Roots of Affirmative Action," *American Behavioral Scientist* 41 (April 1998): 886–97.

3. Joan Hoff, *Nixon Reconsidered* (New York: Basic Books, 1994); Hugh Davis Graham, "Richard Nixon and Civil Rights: Explaining an Enigma," *Presidential Studies Quarterly* 26 (winter 1996): 93–106.

4. *Contractors Association of Eastern Pennsylvania v. Secretary of Labor*, 442 F.2d 159 (3d Cir. 1971), cert. denied, 404 U.S. 424 (1971); Hugh Davis Graham, *The Civil Rights Era* (New York: Oxford University Press, 1990), 322–45.

5. James T. Patterson, *Grand Expectations* (New York: Oxford University Press, 1996), 723–25; Hugh Davis Graham, *Civil Rights and the Presidency* (New York: Oxford University Press, 1992), 150–69.

6. Herbert S. Parmet, *Richard Nixon and His America* (Boston: Little, Brown, 1990).

7. Ehrlichman, quoted in Graham, *Civil Rights Era*, 160.

8. Laurence H. Silberman, "The Road to Racial Quotas," *Wall Street Journal*, 11 August 1977; Graham, *Civil Rights Era*, 329–31.

9. James E. Jones Jr., "The Bugaboo of Employment Quotas," *Wisconsin Law Review* 40 (1970): 341–55; Robert D. Schuwerk, "The Philadelphia Plan: A Study in the Dynamics of Executive Power," *University of Chicago Law Review* 39 (1972): 732–39.

10. George Meany, "Labor and the Philadelphia Plan," *Wall Street Journal*, 13 January 1970.

11. Graham, *Civil Rights Era*, 336.

12. Skrentny, *Ironies of Affirmative Action*, 195–96.

13. Silberman, quoted in Graham, *Civil Rights Era*, 438.

14. Paul Burstein, *Discrimination, Jobs, and Politics: The Struggle for Equal Employment Opportunity in the United States since the New Deal* (Chicago: University of Chicago Press, 1985).

15. James Q. Wilson, *Bureaucracy: What Government Agencies Do and Why They Do It* (New York: Basic Books, 1989), 72–89.

16. Hugh Davis Graham, "The Origins of Affirmative Action: Civil Rights and the Regulatory State," *Annals* 523 (September 1992): 50–62.

17. James Q. Wilson, ed., *The Politics of Regulation* (New York: Basic Books, 1980).

18. Stephen C. Halpern, *On the Limits of the Law: The Ironic Legacy of Title VI of the 1964 Civil Rights Act* (Baltimore: Johns Hopkins University Press, 1995),

81–189; Jeremy Rabkin, "Office for Civil Rights," in *Politics of Regulation*, ed. James Wilson, 304–33.

19. Lyndon B. Johnson, Howard University commencement address, 4 June 1965, *Public Papers of the Presidents: Johnson 1965*, 1:635–36. See Gareth Davies, *From Opportunity to Entitlement: The Transformation and Decline of Great Society Liberalism* (Lawrence: University Press of Kansas, 1996), 65–74.

20. Joe R. Feagin and Clairece Booher Feagin, *Discrimination American Style: Institutional Racism and Sexism* (Englewood Cliffs, N.J.: Prentice-Hall, 1978).

21. Edward J. Erler, "Sowing the Wind: Judicial Oligarchy and the Legacy of *Brown v. Board of Education*," *Harvard Journal of Law and Public Policy* 8 (1985): 399–426.

22. The contractors were citing language from Title VII of the Civil Rights Act prohibiting them as employers from discriminating on account of race. For the equivalent language in Title VI, sec. 601, see note 25.

23. Skrentny, *Ironies of Affirmative Action*, 161–66.

24. 442 F.2d 159 (3d Cir. 1971).

25. See Halpern, *Limits of the Law*, 331–40.

26. *United States v. Jefferson County Board of Education*, 372 F.2d at 869. See J. Harvie Wilkinson III, *From Brown to Bakke: The Supreme Court and School Integration, 1954–1978* (New York: Oxford University Press, 1980).

27. Coleman Bretz Stein Jr., *Sink or Swim: The Politics of Bilingual Education* (New York: Praeger, 1986); Lawrence H. Fuchs, *The American Kaleidoscope* (Hanover, N.H.: Wesleyan University Press, 1990), 458–73.

28. Hugh Davis Graham, *The Uncertain Triumph: Federal Education Policy in the Kennedy and Johnson Years* (Chapel Hill: University of North Carolina Press, 1984), 155–58, 217–21.

29. Hugh Davis Graham, "Civil Rights and the Carter Presidency," in *The Carter Presidency*, ed. Gary M. Fink and Hugh Davis Graham (Lawrence: University Press of Kansas, 1998), 213–16.

30. The National Archives has been unable to locate the files of the OCR in the 1960s and 1970s, but OCR documents relating to the regulations of 1970 and the Lau Remedies may be found in the Shirley Hufstedler Papers in the Carter Library; all quotations from OCR documents are drawn from boxes 12–15 of the Hufstedler Papers.

31. Gareth Davies, "The Early Politics of Bilingual Education, 1967–1974," *Journal of American History*, forthcoming.

32. Ibid.; Armando B. Rendon, "Chicano Manifesto," in *"Takin' It to the Streets": A Sixties Reader*, ed. Alexander Bloom and Wini Breines (New York: Oxford University Press, 1995), 177–78.

33. John David Skrentny, *The Minority Rights Revolution* (Cambridge: Harvard University Press, 2002).

34. Graham, "Carter Civil Rights," 214.

35. Joseph A. Califano Jr., *Governing America* (New York: Simon and Schuster, 1981), 312–13.

36. Malcolm N. Danoff, *Evaluation of the Impact of ESEA Title VII Spanish/English Bilingual Education Program* (Palo Alto, Calif.: American Institutes of Research, 1978), quoted in Califano, *Governing America*, 313; Noel Epstein, *Language, Ethnicity, and the Schools: Policy Alternatives for Bilingual-Bicultural Education* (Washington, D.C.: Institute for Educational Leadership, 1977).

37. Willis D. Hawley and Beryl A. Radin, *The Politics of Federal Reorganization: Creating the U.S. Department of Education* (New York: Pergamon Press, 1988).

38. Graham, "Carter Civil Rights," 206–10.

39. George R. LaNoue, "Split Visions: Minority Business Set-asides," *Annals* 523 (September 1992): 104–16.

40. *Fullilove v. Klutznick*, 448 U.S. 448 (1980), 527–32.

41. Graham, "Carter Civil Rights," 209.

42. Marc K. Landy and Martin A. Levin, eds., *The New Politics of Public Policy* (Baltimore: Johns Hopkins University Press, 1995).

43. Reagan, quoted in Hugh Davis Graham, "The Politics of Clientele Capture: Civil Rights Policy in the Reagan Administration," in *Redefining Equality*, ed. Neal Devins and Davison Douglas (New York: Oxford University Press, 1997), 103.

5. The Return of Mass Immigration

1. Steven M. Gillon, *"That's Not What We Meant to Do": Reform and Its Unintended Consequences in Twentieth-Century America* (New York: Norton, 2000).

2. In 1968 Stanford biologist Paul Ehrlich published a best-selling polemic, *The Population Bomb* (New York: Ballantine, 1968), and University of California, Santa Barbara ecologist Garrett Hardin published his classic essay on the population dilemma, "The Tragedy of the Commons," in the prestigious journal *Science*, 13 December 1968.

3. E. P. Hutchinson, *Legislative History of American Immigration Policy, 1798–1965* (Philadelphia: University of Pennsylvania Press, 1981), 519.

4. David E. Simcox, *U.S. Immigration in the 1980s* (Boulder, Colo.: Westview Press, 1988), 19.

5. David M. Reimers, *Still the Golden Door: The Third World Comes to America* (New York: Columbia University Press, 1992), 95.

6. Ibid., 92–117. Reliance on foreign medical school graduates to staff residencies, especially in less desirable inner-city hospitals, became a permanent part of American medical practice. During the 1980s and 1990s, American medical schools graduated about 16,000 aspiring physicians a year, a number almost 30 percent short of the 22,500 entry-level residencies filled by new physicians. Graduates of foreign medical schools took up most of the slack, filling 25 percent of the new residencies. Katherine S. Mangan, "Should Medical Schools Admit More Applicants?" *Chronicle of Higher Education*, 4 August 2000.

7. Peter J. Duignan and L. H. Gann, *The Spanish Speakers in the United States: A History* (Lanham, Md.: University Press of America, 1998).

8. Matt S. Meier and Feliciano Ribera, *Mexican Americans/American Mexicans* (New York: Hill and Wang, 1993), 113–16.

9. Mark Reisler, *By the Sweat of Their Brows: Mexican Labor in the United States, 1900–1940* (Westport, Conn.: Greenwood Press, 1976); Meier and Ribera, *Mexican Americans/American Mexicans.* Given geographic proximity and ease of border crossing, few Mexicans in the United States in the first half of the twentieth century sought naturalization. Of the 320,000 Mexican-born living in the United States in 1930 who were over twenty-one years of age, only 5.5 percent had gone through naturalization.

10. David Simcox, "Mexico's Dilemma: Finding a Million Jobs a Year," in *U.S. Immigration in the 1980s,* ed. David Simcox (Boulder, Colo.: Westview Press, 1988), 203–4.

11. Nicholas Laham, *Ronald Reagan and the Politics of Immigration Reform* (Westport, Conn.: Praeger, 2000).

12. Reimers, *Still the Golden Door,* 157–206.

13. Kenneth K. Lee, *Huddled Masses, Muddled Laws: Why Contemporary Immigration Policy Failed to Reflect Public Opinion* (Westport, Conn.: Praeger, 1998), 21–32.

14. In the controversy over bilingual education, influential studies by critics include Noel Epstein, *Language, Ethnicity, and the Schools: Policy Alternatives for Bilingual-Bicultural Education* (Washington, D.C.: Institute for Educational Leadership, 1977); and Keith A. Baker and Adriana de Kanter, "Effectiveness of Bilingual Education: A Review of the Literature" (Washington, D.C.: U.S. Department of Education, Office of Planning, Budget, and Evaluation, September 1981). For arguments supporting bilingual education, see James Crawford, *Bilingual Education: History, Politics, Theory, and Practice* (Trenton, N.J.: Crane, 1989).

15. Thomas Muller and Thomas Espenshade, *The Fourth Wave: California's Newest Immigrants* (Washington, D.C.: Urban Institute, 1985), 125–44. See also Kevin F. McCarthy and R. Burciago Valdez, *Current and Future Effects of Mexican Immigration in California* (Santa Monica, Calif.: RAND Corporation, 1985).

16. *Congressional Quarterly Almanac 1972* (Washington, D.C.: Congressional Quarterly Press, 1972), 537.

17. Mary Elizabeth Brown, *Shapers of the Great Debate on Immigration* (Westport, Conn.: Greenwood Press, 1999), 261–74; Ann Cooper, "Immigration Reformer Stirs Melting Pot," *National Journal,* 17 May 1986, 1210; David M. Reimers, *Unwelcome Strangers: American Identity and the Turn against Immigration* (New York: Columbia University Press, 1998), 43–63. FAIR's membership ranged around 70,000. Tanton in 1983 organized U.S. English, with 180,000 members, to support English as the nation's official language. FAIR, however, took no position on bilingual/bicultural issues.

18. FAIR's views are available on the web at www.fairus.org, and at www.thesocialcontract.org, the web site of the *Social Contract,* a quarterly immigration reform journal.

19. One early FAIR initiative was a lawsuit that it lost. In *Federation of American Immigration Reform v. Klutznick*, 486 F. Supp. 564 (D.D.C. 1980), federal courts rejected FAIR's claim that aliens living in the country illegally should not be counted for purposes of electoral apportionment.

20. Roy Beck and Leon Kolankiewicz, "The Environmental Movement's Retreat from Advocating U.S. Population Stabilization (1970–1998): A First Draft History," in *Environmental Politics and Policy, 1960s–1990s*, ed. Otis L. Graham Jr. (University Park: Pennsylvania State University Press, 2000), 123–56; Reimers, *Unwelcome Strangers*, 43–64.

21. Social science studies frequently cited in FAIR literature during the 1980s debate include George J. Borjas and Marta Tienda, "The Economic Consequences of Immigration," *Science*, 6 February 1987; Leon Bouvier, *The Impact of Immigration on U.S. Population Size* (Washington: Population Reference Bureau, 1981); Vernon M. Briggs Jr., *Immigration Policy and the American Labor Force* (Baltimore: Johns Hopkins University Press, 1984); Otis L. Graham Jr., "Uses and Misuses of History in the Debate over Immigration Reform," *Public Historian* 8 (spring 1986): 41–64; Lawrence E. Harrison, *Underdevelopment Is a State of Mind: The Latin American Case* (Lanham, Md.: University Press of America, 1985); Philip Martin, *Illegal Immigration and the Colonization of the American Labor Market* (Washington, D.C.: Center for Immigration Studies, 1986); David S. North, *Enforcing the Immigration Law* (Washington, D.C.: New Transcentury Foundation, 1980); Muller and Espenshade, *The Fourth Wave*; Michael S. Teitelbaum, *Latin Migration North: The Problem for U.S. Foreign Policy* (New York: Council on Foreign Relations, 1985).

22. For Gallup poll questions and data on immigration, see *The Gallup Poll: Public Opinion*, published annually by Scholarly Resources in Wilmington, Delaware.

23. Ellis Cose, *A Nation of Strangers: Prejudice, Politics, and the Populating of America* (New York: William Morrow, 1992), 165–66.

24. Lynne Duke, "Poll of Latinos Counters Perceptions on Language, Immigration," *Washington Post*, 16 December 1992. See also Rudolpho de la Garza, *Mexican, Puerto Rican, and Cuban Perspectives on America* (Boulder, Colo.: Westview Press, 1992).

25. *U.S. Immigration Policy and the National Interest: Final Report and Recommendations of the Select Commission on Immigration and Refugee Policy with Supplemental Views by Commissioners* (Washington, D.C.: Government Printing Office, 1981).

26. Peter H. Schuck, "The Politics of Rapid Social Change: Immigration Policy in the 1980s," *Studies in American Political Development* 6 (spring 1992): 37–92.

27. Nancy Humel Montwieler, *The Immigration Reform Law of 1986: Analysis, Text, Legislative History* (Washington, D.C.: Bureau of National Affairs, 1987).

28. Immigration Reform and Control Act of 1982, Joint Hearing before the Subcommittee on Immigration, Refugees, and International Law of the House

Committee on the Judiciary and the Subcommittee on Immigration and Refugee Policy of the Senate Committee on the Judiciary, 97th Cong., 2d sess., 1 and 20 April 1982; Roger L. Conner, oral history interview with Otis L. Graham Jr., 27 January 1989, FAIR archive, Washington, D.C.

29. Craig Allan Kaplowitz, "Mexican Americans, Ethnicity, and Federal Policy: The League of United Latin American Citizens and the Politics of Cultural Disadvantage" (Ph.D. diss., Vanderbilt University, 1999).

30. Ford Foundation annual reports, 1968–99. Between 1968 and 1999 Ford contributed $56,958,572 to MALDEF, La Raza, LULAC, the National Immigration Forum, and the immigration project of the National Lawyers Guild. See Joseph Fallon, "Buying Open Borders," *Social Contract* 10 (summer 2000): 256–60; and Fallon, "Funding Hate: Foundations and the Radical Hispanic Lobby," *Social Contract* 11 (fall 2000): 56–72. Latino organizations attacked FAIR as racist, citing early FAIR grants from the Pioneer Fund (a claim denied by both parties), an organization formed in the 1930s and attacked by the left for promoting racial purity. Peter Marks, "Special-Interest Groups Widening Political Attack Ads," *New York Times*, 14 May 2000.

31. The relevant web sites are, for the National Immigration Forum, www. immigrationforum.org; for La Raza, www.nclr.org; for MALDEF, www. maldef.org; for LULAC, www.lulac.org.

32. Peter Skerry, *Mexican Americans: The Ambivalent Minority* (Cambridge: Harvard University Press, 1993), 323–30.

33. Peter Skerry, "The Racialization of Immigration Policy," in *Taking Stock*, ed. Morton Keller and R. Shep Melnick (New York: Cambridge University Press, 1999), 81–122.

34. Quoted in Cose, *Nation of Strangers*, 167.

35. Nadine Cohodas, "Immigration Reform Measure Now Hanging by a Thread," *Congressional Quarterly Weekly Report*, 28 July 1984, 1839–40.

36. Nadine Cohodas, "Immigration Bill Stalls over Farm Issue," *Congressional Quarterly Weekly Report*, 21 June 1986, 1411–12; Cohodas, "Congress Clears Overhaul of Immigration Law," *Congressional Quarterly Weekly Report*, 18 October 1986, 2595–98.

37. Roberto Suro, *Watching America's Door: The Immigration Backlash and the New Policy Debate* (New York: Twentieth Century Fund Press, 1996), 38.

38. Elisabeth Rosenthal, "Chinese Town's Main Export: Its Young Men," *New York Times*, 26 June 2000; Ko-lin Chin, *Smuggled Chinese* (Philadelphia: Temple University Press, 1999).

39. Nancy Cleeland, "Granjenal's Life Ebbs with Exodus," *Los Angeles Times*, 3 August 1997; Ginger Thompson, "Exodus of Migrant Families Is Bleeding Mexico's Heartland," *New York Times*, 17 June 2001.

40. Robert Warren, "Annual Estimates of the Unauthorized Immigration Population Residing in the U.S. and Components of Change, 1987–1997," Office of Policy and Planning, U.S. Immigration and Naturalization Service, September 2000. The INS report was obtained through subpoena and released

by Texas Republican Lamar Smith, chairman of the House Subcommittee on Immigration. According to the INS study, nearly 500,000 migrants entered America illegally each year during the mid-1990s. This number was offset by about 145,000 who returned home of their own accord, 40,000 deportations, 20,000 deaths, and 150,000 receiving green cards as part of the normal legalization process.

41. Quoted in Schuck, "Politics of Rapid Social Change," 64.

42. Most of the social science research on majority-minority redistricting has involved African-American rather than Hispanic-majority districts. Most empirical research supports the conclusion that representation for minority voter interests is best served by dispersed rather than concentrated electoral districting, but that majority-minority districts most effectively elect minority candidates. See Carol Swain, *Black Faces, Black Interests* (Cambridge: Harvard University Press, 1993); Kenny J. Whitby, *The Color of Representation: Congressional Behavior and Black Interests* (Ann Arbor: University of Michigan Press, 1997); Charles Cameron, David Epstein, and Sharyn O'Halloran, "Do Majority-Minority Districts Maximize Substantive Black Representation in Congress?" *American Political Science Review* 90 (December 1996): 794–812.

43. IRCA required employers screening job applicants to complete Form I-9, the Employment Eligibility Verification, and maintain the records for three years.

44. Statement of Sharon M. Hughes, executive vice president, National Council of Agricultural Employers, "Verification of Eligibility for Employment and Benefits," *Hearings*, Subcommittee on Immigration and Claims, House Judiciary Committee, 104th Cong., 1st sess., 30 March 1995.

45. General Accounting Office, *Immigration Reform: Employer Sanctions and the Question of Discrimination*, Washington, D.C., March 1990, 67. To support its conclusion that the employer sanctions provision had "apparently" reduced illegal immigration, the GAO observed that most violations (36,354) charged by the INS in enforcing the law were for employer failure to complete filling out Form I-9. INS enforcement action against employers for knowingly hiring or continuing to employ unauthorized aliens produced fines of $6.1 million settled against 2,534 employers, from a pool of 4.6 million employers.

46. Schuck, "Politics of Rapid Social Change," 67–80; Cose, *Nation of Strangers*, 204–8.

47. "Sizable Boost in Immigration OK'd," *Congressional Quarterly Almanac 1990* (Washington, D.C.: Congressional Quarterly Press, 1990), 474–85.

48. Kevin F. McCarthy and George Vernez, *Immigration in a Changing Economy: California's Experience* (Santa Monica: RAND, 1997); Reimers, *Unwelcome Strangers*, 31–41.

49. Peter Schrag, *Paradise Lost: California's Experience, America's Future* (New York: New Press, 1998), 229–34.

50. In a unanimous 1971 decision, *Graham v. Richardson*, 403 U.S. 365, the Supreme Court declared alienage, like race, a "suspect" category, a classifica-

tion justifiable only by a compelling government interest. "Classifications based on alienage, like those based on nationality or race," the Court ruled in *Graham*, "are inherently suspect and subject to close judicial scrutiny. Aliens as a class are a prime example of a "discrete and insular" minority . . . for whom such heightened judicial solicitude is appropriate."

51. Lee, *Huddled Masses, Muddled Laws*, 89–126.

52. Commission on Immigration Reform, *U.S. Immigration Policy: Restoring Credibility* (Washington, D.C.: Government Printing Office, 1994).

53. *Congressional Quarterly Almanac 1996* (Washington, D.C.: Congressional Quarterly, 1997), 719.

54. Reimers, *Unwelcome Strangers*, 131–49.

55. Steven A. Holmes, "Incomes Up and Poverty Is Down, Data Show," *New York Times*, 27 September 2000.

56. "AFL-CIO Shifts Stance, Seeks to Aid Immigrants," *Washington Post*, 3 June 2000; Steven Greenhouse, "Campaign to Attract New Union Membership Helps to Restore Labor's Political Muscle," *New York Times*, 30 May 2000.

57. Steven Greenhouse, "Coalition Urges Easing of Immigration Laws," *New York Times*, 16 May 2000.

6. The Strange Convergence of Affirmative Action and Immigration Policy

1. James S. Robb, *Affirmative Action for Immigrants: The Entitlement Nobody Wanted* (Petoskey, Mich.: Social Contract Press, 1995).

2. David M. Reimers, *Unwelcome Strangers: American Identity and the Turn Against Immigration* (New York: Columbia University Press, 1998), 25–41.

3. Lawrence H. Fuchs, "What Do Immigrants Deserve?" *Washington Post*, 29, January 1995.

4. Fuchs, "The Changing Meaning of Civil Rights, 1954–1994," in *Civil Rights and Social Wrongs*, ed. John Higham (University Park: Pennsylvania State University Press, 1997), 82.

5. Reimers, *Unwelcome Strangers*, 3.

6. Nathan Glazer, "The Case for Racial Preferences," *Public Interest*, spring 1999, 48.

7. Glenn C. Loury, "How to Mend Affirmative Action," *Public Interest*, spring 1997, 33–43.

8. Orlando Patterson, *The Ordeal of Integration* (Washington, D.C.: Civitas/Counterpoint, 1997), 192, 193.

9. A prominent exception was women, technically not a minority group. After the ratification of the women's suffrage amendment, the twentieth-century feminist movement was deeply split between the sex-blind model of equal rights for men and women, as symbolized by the Equal Rights Amendment (ERA), and the social feminist model, which emphasized inherent differences

between the sexes and promoted special protective legislation for working women. Equal rights feminists, ineffective through the 1950s, regained national leadership behind the ERA during the 1960s and 1970s. Following the presidential election of Ronald Reagan and the defeat of the ERA, feminist leaders shifted back toward the difference model and pressed for affirmative action preferences for women, such as Women Business Enterprise (WBE) set-aside contracts in government procurement. See Rosalind Rosenberg, *Divided Lives* (New York: Hill and Wang, 1992).

10. Hugh Davis Graham, "Race, History, and Policy: African-Americans and Civil Rights since 1964," *Journal of Policy History* 6 (winter 1994): 12–39.

11. The President's Committee on Civil Rights, *To Secure These Rights* (Washington, D.C.: Government Printing Office, 1947), x.

12. For a detailed description and close analysis of the development of official minorities, see John David Skrentny, *The Minority Rights Revolution* (Cambridge: Harvard University Press, 2002).

13. The discussion of Mann's construction of survey forms for the president's contract compliance committee is based on an unpublished manuscript by Harold Orlans, "The Origin of Protected Groups." Orlans's paper, prepared as part of a Commission on Civil Rights study of affirmative action in higher education in 1986 that was not completed, was generously provided by John Skrentny.

14. The 1969 Philadelphia Plan defined Spanish Surnamed Americans as "all persons of Mexican American, Puerto Rican, Cuban or Spanish origin or ancestry."

15. See, for example, the General Accounting Office, *Small Business: Problems Continue with SBA's Minority Business Development Program*, GAO/RCED-93–145, 17 September 1993.

16. The SBA's 1973 regulation named five groups as presumptively culturally disadvantaged: "blacks, American Indians, Spanish-Americans, Asian-Americans, and Puerto Ricans." The curious distinction between Spanish-Americans and Puerto Ricans testifies to the imprecision and general sloppiness of the closed bureaucratic processes that produced official minority designations to govern affirmative action policy during its formative years.

17. In the 1990s, businesses with annual revenues of $100 million were in the 8(a) program. The personal income limitations on participating 8(a) firm owners was $250,000, a figure that excluded the worth of the owner's residence or business. In construction, for example, firm size limitations made 98 percent of the country's construction businesses economically eligible for the 8(a) program. See hearings before the Committee on Small Business, U.S. House of Representatives, 104th Cong., 2d sess., 18 September 1996.

18. In fiscal year 1994, for example, of the 5,628 firms participating in the 8(a) program, only 0.5 percent of the owners were not in the presumptively eligible groups (nine women, nine disabled, and eight white men).

19. On clientele capture in civil rights regulation, see Hugh Davis Graham,

"Since 1964: The Paradox of American Civil Rights Regulation," in *Taking Stock*, ed. Morton Keller and R. Shep Melnick (Cambridge: Cambridge University Press, 1999), 187–218; and James Q. Wilson, *Bureaucracy* (New York: Basic Books, 1989), 75–89.

20. Skrentny, *Minority Rights Revolution*, chap. 4.

21. On the problem of the race-sex analogy in affirmative action, see Graham, *Civil Rights Era*, 205–33, 393–449; and Skrentny, *Minority Rights Revolution*, chap. 4.

22. Quoted in Alfred W. Blumrosen, *Black Employment and the Law* (New Brunswick, N.J.: Rutgers University Press, 1971), 117.

23. U.S. Commission on Civil Rights, *The Federal Civil Rights Enforcement Effort, 1970* (Washington, D.C.: Government Printing Office, 1970).

24. Thomas Sowell, *The Economics and Politics of Race* (New York: Morrow, 1983).

25. Herbert Hammerman, "Affirmative-Action Stalemate: A Second Perspective," *Public Interest*, fall 1988, 130–34.

26. The bill's House sponsor, Baltimore Democrat Parren Mitchell, was chairman of the Congressional Black Caucus and sponsor of the 10 percent minority contract set-aside provision in the 1977 public works law. Mitchell, who had omitted American Indians from his original bill as well as Asians (Indians were later added in conference committee), explained that the omissions were "inadvertent." See Hugh Davis Graham, "Civil Rights Policy in the Carter Presidency," in *The Carter Presidency*, ed. Gary M. Fink and Hugh Davis Graham (Lawrence: University Press of Kansas, 1998), 202–23.

27. Office of Management and Budget, Directive No. 15: Race and *Ethnic Standards for Federal Statistics and Administrative Reporting*, 12 May 1977.

28. See George R. LaNoue and John C. Sullivan, "Presumptions for Preferences: The Small Business Administration's Decisions on Groups Entitled to Affirmative Action," *Journal of Policy History* 6 (1994): 439–67. The author is indebted to LaNoue and Sullivan for details of the SBA's 8(a) petitioning process.

29. U.S. citizenship was required in the 8(a) program.

30. Norton quoted in LaNoue and Sullivan, "Presumptions," 448.

31. Memo, Harry Schwartz and Bob Malson to Stu Eizenstat, "Application of Hasidic Jews for Designation as a Socially Disadvantaged Group Entitled to Minority Procurement Set-Aside and Minority Subcontractor Benefits," 21 February 1980, box 17, Domestic Policy Staff-Eizenstat file, Jimmy Carter Library.

32. SBA quoted in LaNoue and Sullivan, "Presumptions," 453. The SBA also rejected a 1987 petition from disabled veterans, ruling that disabled veterans were handicapped, not minorities. In 1988, Congress responded to intense lobbying by feminist organizations by authorizing a WBE program under the 8(a) program.

33. *University of California Regents v. Bakke*, 438 U.S. 193 (1978); *United Steelworkers of America v. Weber*, 443 U.S. 193 (1979); *Fullilove v. Klutznick*, 448 U.S. 448 (1980).

34. Congress in 1988 passed an overhaul measure to revamp the scandal-plagued SBA 8(a) program, but black and Hispanic members of the House Small Business Committee weakened the statute. During fiscal year 1995, the SBA graduated three firms from the 8(a) program, the first graduations in the program's history.

35. See, for example, General Accounting Office, *Small Business: Problems in Restructuring SBA's Minority Business Development Program*, GAO/RCED-92–68, 31, January 1992; *Small Business: Problems Continue with SBA's Minority Business Development Program*, GAO/RCED-93–145, 17 September 1993; *Small Business: SBA Cannot Assess the Success of Its Minority Business Development Program*, (GAO/T-RCED-94–278, 27 July 1994).

36. Phyllis Berman and Alexandra Alger, "The Set-Aside Charade," *Forbes*, 13 March 1995; William P. Cheshire, "A Fast Track for Minority Millionaires," *Tampa Tribune*, 9 April 1995.

37. "Attorney General Meese Comes and Goes . . . amidst Clouds of Controversy," *Congress and the Nation*, Vol. 7, 1985–88 (Washington, D.C.: Congressional Quarterly, 1990), 756–57.

38. *Wedtech: A Review of Federal Procurement Decisions*, Senate Subcommittee on Oversight of Government Management, Committee on Governmental Affairs, 100th Cong., 1st sess. (Washington, D.C.: Government Printing Office, 1988).

39. Conflict of interest charges against Meese, many of them, including Wedtech, involving arrangements with his friend and law school classmate, E. Robert Wallach, included negotiations over a proposed oil pipeline in Iraq and evading capital gains taxes on "Baby Bell" securities holdings.

40. Marilyn W. Thompson, *Feeding the Beast: How Wedtech Became the Most Corrupt Little Company in America* (New York: Scribner, 1990); James Traub, *Too Good to Be True: The Outlandish Story of Wedtech* (New York: Doubleday, 1990).

41. Wedtech's contract price for building the auxiliary engines was $99.9 million, whereas the army's pricing analyst had calculated a fair-market price of $19 million.

42. *City of Richmond v. J. A. Croson Co.*, 488 U.S. 469 (1989); George R. LaNoue, "Split Visions: Minority Business Set-Asides," *Annals*, 523 (September 1992): 104–16.

43. W. Avon Drake and Robert D. Holsworth, *Affirmative Action and the Stalled Quest for Black Progress* (Urbana: University of Illinois Press, 1996).

44. Howard Schneider and James Ragland, "4 Dominated D.C. Minority Contracting," *Washington Post*, 1 June 1992.

45. Jane Mayer and Jose de Cordoba, "Sweet Life: First Family of Sugar Is Tough on Workers, Generous to Politicians—Aided by U.S. Price Supports, the Fanjuls Get Wealthy and Dine with Presidents," *Wall Street Journal*, 29 July 1991; Jack Egan, "A New Battle for the Sultans of Sugar," *U.S. News and World Report*, 17 July 1995.

46. Phyllis Berman and Alexandra Alger, "The Set-Aside Charade," *Forbes*,

13 March 1995; William P. Cheshire, "A Fast Track for Minority Millionaires," *Tampa Tribune*, 9 April 1995.

47. For recent case studies of competition between immigrants and native black Americans in employment, see Michael Lichter and David Waldinger, "Producing Conflict: Immigration and Management of Diversity in Multiethnic Metropolis," *Color Lines: Affirmative Action, Immigration, and Civil Rights Options for America*, ed. John David Skrentny (Chicago: University of Chicago Press, 2001), 147–67; and Jennifer Lee, "Racial and Ethnic Meaning behind *Black*: Retailers' Hiring Practices in Inner-City Neighborhoods," *Color Lines*, 168–88.

48. Frank Dobbin and John R. Sutton, "The Strength of a Weak State: The Rights Revolution and the Rise of Human Resources Management Divisions," *American Journal of Sociology* 104 (September 1998): 441–76.

49. Lauren B. Edelman, Stephen Petterson, Elizabeth Chambliss, and Howard S. Erlanger, "Legal Ambiguity and the Politics of Compliance: Affirmative Action Officer's Dilemma," *Law & Policy* 13 (January 1991): 73–97.

50. Erin Kelly and Frank Dobbin, "How Affirmative Action Became Diversity Management: Empower Response to Antidiscrimination Law, 1961–1996," *Color Lines*, 87–117; Dobbin and Sutton, "The Strength of a Weak State," 456.

51. William Julius Wilson, *When Work Disappears: The World of the New Urban Poor* (New York: Random House, 1996), 246.

52. Ibid., 111–46. According to Wilson's data, 85 percent of the Mexican Americans in his sample and 73 percent of the Puerto Ricans were not born in the mainland United States. Nearly all of the blacks and non-Hispanic whites were native-born. Oddly, he included no Asians in his sample.

53. Jacquelyne Johnson Jackson, "Seeking Common Ground for Blacks and Immigrants," in *U.S. Immigration in the 1980s*, ed. David Simcox (Boulder, Colo.: Westview Press, 1988), 92–103.

54. Philip Martin, "Network Recruitment and Labor Displacement," *U.S. Immigration in the 1980s*, ed. David Simcox, 67–91; Roger Waldinger, *Still the Promised City? African-Americans and New Immigrants in Postindustrial New York* (Cambridge: Harvard University Press, 1996).

55. Jennifer Lee, "Cultural Brokers: Race-Based Hiring in Inner-City Neighborhoods," *American Behavioral Scientist* 41 (April 1998): 936.

56. *EEOC v. Chicago Miniature Lamp Works*, 2622 F.Supp. 1281 (N.D.Ill. 1985) at 1295.

57. *EEOC v. Chicago Miniature Lamp Works*, 947 F.2d 292 (7th Cir. 1991) at 305.

58. *EEOC v. Consolidated Service Systems*, 989 F.2d 233 (7th Cir. 1993) at 238. In 1994, the EEOC in its Chicago offensive finally won a case, *EEOC v. O&G Spring and Wire Forms Specialty*, 38F. 3rd 872 (7th Cir. 1994). But the success was of little practical use to the EEOC because the target firm, O&G, had hired no African-Americans. Founded by a Polish immigrant who used word-of-mouth recruiting to hire mostly Polish immigrants and Latinos, O&G presented the court with the rare vulnerability of an "inexorable zero."

59. Jack Miles, "Blacks vs. Browns," *Atlantic Monthly*, October 1992, 41–68; Lou Cannon, *Official Negligence* (New York: Times Books, 1997), 334–46.

60. Peter Skerry, "Borders and Quotas: Immigration and the Affirmative Action State," *Public Interest*, winter 1989, 94–97; Skerry, *Mexican Americans: The Ambivalent Minority* (New York: Basic Books, 1993), 297–99.

61. General Accounting Office, *Hispanic Employment at the USPS*, GAO/GGD-93-58R, 3 September 1993.

62. George J. Borjas, *Heaven's Door: Immigration Policy and the American Economy* (Princeton: Princeton University Press, 1999); Daniel S. Hamermesh and Frank D. Bean, eds., *Help or Hindrance? The Economic Implications of Immigration for African Americans* (New York: Russell Sage, 1998); Kevin F. McCarthy and Georges Vernez, *Immigration in a Changing Economy: The California Experience* (Santa Monica, Calif.: RAND, 1997).

63. Roger Waldinger, "Producing Conflict," in *Color Lines*, ed. John Skrentny, 147–67; Waldinger, "Black-Immigrant Competition Reassessed: New Evidence from Los Angeles," *Sociological Perspectives* 40 (1997): 365–85.

64. John Aubrey Douglass, "Anatomy of Conflict: The Making and Undoing of Affirmative Action at the University of California," *American Behavioral Scientist* 41 (April 1998): 938–59; Peter H. Schuck, "Reflections on the Effects of Immigrants on African Americans—and Vice Versa," in *Help or Hindrance?* eds. Daniel S. Hamermesh and Frank D. Bean, 361–75.

65. National Science Foundation, *Foreign Participation in U.S. Academic Science and Engineering: 1991*, NSF-93-302, 1993; David S. North, *Soothing the Establishment: The Impact of Foreign-Born Scientists and Engineers on America* (Lanham, Md.: University Press of America, 1995); Maryann Jacobi Gray, Elizabeth Rolph, and Elan Melamid, *Immigration and Higher Education* (Santa Monica: RAND, 1996).

66. Susan T. Hill, Delores Thurgood, and Martha Bohman, *Selected Data on Science and Engineering Doctorate Awards* (Washington, D.C. National Science Foundation, 1993); Scott Stossel, "Uncontrolled Experiment: America's Dependency on Foreign Scientists," *New Republic*, 29 March 1999, 17–22.

67. Robb, *Affirmative Action for Immigrants*, 49–79.

68. John Aubrey Douglass, "Anatomy of Conflict: The Making and Unmaking of Affirmative Action at the University of California," in *Color Lines*, ed. John Skrentny, 118–45.

69. Steve Johnson, "Stanford Offers Born-in-U.S. Minority Bonus," *San Jose Mercury News*, 24 October 1993; Robb, *Affirmative Action for Immigrants*, 58.

70. Julia Angwin and Laura Castaneda, "The Digital Divide: High-Tech Boom a Bust for Blacks, Latinos," *San Francisco Chronicle*, 4 May 1998; Tamar Jacoby, "Color Bind: The African American Absence in High Tech," *New Republic*, 29 March 1999, 23–27.

71. Ariana E. Cha, "Asians Share of Federal Contracts Soars," *San Jose Mercury News*, 31 December 1997; Report to the U.S. Congress on Minority Small Business and Capital Ownership Development for Fiscal Year 1995 (Washington: Small Business Administration, n.d.). The SBA, avoiding politically awk-

ward dollar-breakdown totals by ethnic group, reported instead the number and percentage of participating companies by ethnic groups. In fiscal year 1995, for example, this was 47 percent for black firms, 25 percent for Hispanics, 21 percent for Asians, and 6 percent for Native Americans.

7. Winners and Losers

1. Although southern whites after the 1960s continued a partisan shift begun in the 1950s from the Democratic Party to the Republican Party, a process that was accelerated by the presidential campaigns of Arizona senator Barry Goldwater in 1964 and Alabama governor George C. Wallace in 1968, they generally expressed beliefs about race relations similar to those of conservative Republicans nationwide. These beliefs varied by economic class, with poor whites resenting the alliance of national elites and minority clients, but generally they included accepting nondiscrimination as required by the Civil Rights Act and the Voting Rights Act, while rejecting school busing for racial balance, race-conscious affirmative action, and racial gerrymandering in electoral districts. Numan V. Bartley, *The New South, 1945–1980* (Baton Rouge: Louisiana State University Press, 1995), 278–80, 398–409.

2. Daniel Seligman, "Affirmative Action Is Here to Stay," *Fortune*, 19 April 1982, 143–62; Anne B. Fisher, "Businessmen Like to Hire by the Numbers," *Fortune*, 16 September 1985, 26–30; Steven A. Holmes, "Affirmative Action Plans Are Part of Business Life," *New York Times*, 22 November 1991; William G. Bowen and Derek Bok, *The Shape of the River: Long-Term Consequences of Considering Race in College and University Admissions* (Princeton, N.J.: Princeton University Press, 1998).

3. Stephan Thernstrom and Abigail Thernstrom, *America in Black and White* (New York: Simon and Schuster, 1997), 183–202. The Thernstroms, critics of race-conscious remedies, do not distinguish between soft and hard affirmative action, but emphasize the extent and momentum of black middle-class growth before the 1970s when race-conscious affirmative action expanded.

4. Paul Burstein, *Discrimination, Jobs, and Politics* (Chicago: University of Chicago Press, 1998). Asians, like women, have benefited chiefly from soft affirmative action, where the emphasis has been on nondiscrimination enhanced by outreach programs. This approach has characterized EEO enforcement in the U.S. armed services, the computer software industry, higher education faculty, and the professions, especially law, medicine, and engineering. On affirmative action in the military, see Richard J. Payne, *Getting Beyond Race* (Boulder, Colo.: Westview Press, 1998), 81–106.

5. Lyndon Baines Johnson, Howard University commencement address, 4 June 1965, *Public Papers of the Presidents: Johnson, 1965*, 1: 635–36.

6. Joe R. Feagin and Clairece Booher Feagin, *Discrimination American Style: Institutional Racism and Sexism* (Malabar, Fla.: R. E. Krieger, 1986).

7. Hugh Davis Graham, "The Civil Rights Act and the American Regulatory State," in *Legacies of the 1964 Civil Rights Act*, ed. Bernard Grofman (Charlottesville: University of Virginia Press, 2000), 43–64.

8. Seymour Martin Lipset, "Affirmative Action and the American Creed," *Wilson Quarterly*, winter 1992, 52–62; Paul M. Sniderman and Thomas Piazza, *The Scar of Race* (Cambridge, Mass.: Belknap Press, 1993); Paul M. Sniderman and Edward C. Carmines, *Reaching Beyond Race* (Cambridge: Harvard University Press, 1997).

9. Ben Gose, "Most Students Oppose Racial Preferences in Admissions, Survey Finds," *Chronicle of Higher Education*, 5 May 2000, A52; Arthur Levine, *When Hope and Fear Collide* (San Francisco: Jossey-Bass, 1998); Levine, "The Campus Divided, and Divided Again," *New York Times*, 11 June 2000.

10. "California's Expanding Minority Population," *California Opinion Index* (San Francisco: Field Institute, July 1988), 5.

11. "Asians Say They Fare Better than Other Minorities," *Los Angeles Times*, 20 August 1993, A1.

12. Peter Skerry, *Mexican Americans: The Ambivalent Minority* (Cambridge: Harvard University Press, 1993), 275–312.

13. Caution is required in interpreting polling and voting evidence concerning affirmative action, because responses vary with the wording of the questions. Majorities support wording that emphasizes equal individual rights, as in California's successful Proposition 209 in 1996. In a referendum the following year in Houston, however, voters supported affirmative action because proponents had worded the question to emphasize special outreach measures, which most voters favor.

14. William Julius Wilson, *The Truly Disadvantaged* (Chicago: University of Chicago Press, 1987), 109–24; Elijah Anderson, *Streetwise: Race, Class, and Change in an Urban Community* (Chicago: University of Chicago Press, 1990).

15. An exception has been the closer scrutiny surrounding official recognition of tribal status by the Bureau of Indian Affairs, owing partly to expanding gambling casino operations.

16. George R. La Noue, "Selective Perception: The Role of History in the Disparity Study Industry," *Public Historian* 17 (spring 1995): 13–20; La Noue, "Social Science and Minority Set-Asides," *Public Interest*, winter 1993, 49–62.

17. A perceptive case study of the Richmond, Virginia, set-aside program that was found unconstitutional by the U.S. Supreme Court in *City of Richmond v. J. A. Croson* (408 U.S. 469) in 1989 is W. Avon Drake and Robert D. Holsworth, *Affirmative Action and the Stalled Quest for Black Progress* (Urbana: University of Illinois Press, 1996).

18. In 1998, Republican congressional leaders supported amendments to the $150 billion highway bill that would substitute race-neutral and gender-neutral criteria for the bill's 10 percent affirmative action goal for disadvantaged (minority and women) businesses. In the House, the amendment proposed by Marge Roukema (R-N.J.) was defeated by a vote of 194–225, with

Republicans voting 191–29 and Democrats 3–195. In the Senate, the amendment proposed by Mitch McConnell (R-Ky.) was defeated 58–37.

19. See, for example, *Group Preferences and the Law*, hearings before the House Subcommittee on the Constitution of the Committee on the Judiciary, 104th Cong., 1st sess., serial no. 74, 3 April, 1 June, and 25 October 1995.

20. Hugh Davis Graham, "Since 1964: The Paradox of American Civil Rights Regulation," in *Taking Stock: American Government in the Twentieth Century*, ed. Morton Keller and R. Shep Melnick (Cambridge: Cambridge University Press, 1999), 187–218.

21. Nicholas Laham, *The Reagan Presidency and the Politics of Race* (Westport, Conn.: Praeger, 1998), 17–132; Hugh Davis Graham, "The Politics of Clientele Capture: Civil Rights Policy and the Reagan Administration," in *Redefining Equality*, ed. Neal Devins and Davison M. Douglas (New York: Oxford University Press, 1998), 103–19.

22. Seligman, "Affirmative Action Is Here to Stay"; Fisher, "Businessmen Like to Hire by the Numbers"; Holmes, "Affirmative Action Plans Are Part of Business Life"; Robert R. Detlefser, *Civil Rights Under Reagan* (San Francisco: ICS Press, 1991), 133–56.

23. *Congress and the Nation, 1981–1984* (Washington: Congressional Quarterly, 198), 680–81; Abigail Thernstrom, *Whose Votes Count? Affirmative Action and Minority Voting Rights* (Cambridge: Harvard University Press, 1987).

24. Studies of electoral behavior in the 1990s support the view that majority-minority districts limit minority influence to a few safe districts while marginalizing the minority vote elsewhere, thereby weakening minority bargaining power and increasing Republican electoral success. Carol Swain, *Black Faces, Black Interests: The Representation of African Americans in Congress* (Cambridge: Harvard University Press, 1993); Kevin Hill, "Does the Creation of Majority Black Districts Aid Republicans?" *Journal of Politics* 57 (May 1995): 384–401; Charles Cameron, David Epstein, and Sharyn O'Holloran, "Do Majority-Minority Districts Maximize Substantive Black Representation in Congress?" *American Political Science Review* 90 (December 1996): 794–812. In the 1991–94 round of electoral redistricting following the 1990 census, the number of black state legislators increased by 130 and Hispanic legislators by 29, but the number of states in which Democrats controlled both houses of the state legislature fell from 30 to 18, a 40 percent drop.

25. James P. Smith and Barry Edmonston, eds., *The New Americans: Economic, Demographic, and Fiscal Effects of Immigration* (Washington, D.C.: National Academy Press, 1997).

26. George J. Borjas, *Heaven's Door: Immigration Policy and the American Economy* (Princeton, N.J.: Princeton University Press, 1999), chap. 5.

27. Rachel M. Friedberg and Jennifer Hunt, "The Impact of Immigration on Host Country Wages, Employment, and Growth," *Journal of Economic Perspectives* 9 (spring 1995): 23–44; George J. Borjas, Richard B. Freeman, and Lawrence F. Katz, "Searching for the Effect of Immigration on the Labor Market," *American*

Economic Review 86 (1996): 246–51; Vernon M. Briggs Jr., *Mass Immigration and the National Interest* (Armonk, N.Y.: M. E. Sharpe, 1996), chap. 8; Steven A. Camarota, *The Wages of Immigration: The Effect on the Low-Skilled Labor Market* (Washington, D.C.: Center for Immigration Studies, January 1998).

28. Kenneth K. Lee, *Huddled Masses, Muddled Laws: Why Contemporary Immigration Policy Fails to Reflect Public Opinion* (Westport, Conn.: Praeger, 1998).

29. Smith and Edmonston, *The New Americans*, 383–86.

30. George Gallup Jr. and Frank Newport, "For the First Time, More Americans Approve of Interracial Marriage than Disapprove," *Gallup Poll Monthly*, August 1991, 60–62.

31. Payne, *Getting Beyond Race*, 153–54.

32. David M. Reimers, *Unwelcome Strangers* (New York: Columbia University Press, 1998), chap. 3; Leon F. Bouvier and Lindsay Grant, *How Many Americans? Population, Immigration, and the Environment* (New York: Random House, 1995). Economist Julian L. Simon championed the economic benefits of immigration in *The Economic Consequences of Immigration* (Washington, D.C.: Cato Institute, 1989). Ben J. Wattenberg, *Are World Population Trends a Problem?* (Washington, D.C.: American Enterprise Institute, 1985), describes the economic virtues of world population growth and makes the case for open international borders to maximize labor mobility and productivity.

33. *Replacement Migration: Is It a Solution to Declining and Aging Populations?* (New York: United Nations Population Division, 2000); Roger Cohen, "Europe's Love-Hate Affair with Foreigners," *New York Times*, 17 December 2000.

34. Social Security Advisory Board, "Social Security: Why Action Should be Taken," Baltimore, July 1998, 7.

35. *Replacement Migration*; Jack Miles, "Saving the Germans from Extinction," *Social Contract* (fall 1995): 23–27; Geoffrey McNicoll, "Reflections on `Replacement Migration,'" *People and Place* 8 (2000): 1–47; Leon F. Bouvier, "Replacement Migration," *Social Contract* 10 (fall 2000): 80–84.

36. Aaron Zitner, "Immigrant Tally Doubles in Census: U.S. Has Twice as Many Undocumented Workers as Estimated," *Los Angeles Times*, 10 March 2001.

37. Paul Magnusson, "The Border Is More Porous than You Think," *Business Week*, 9 April 2001, 94–95; Roberto Suro, "Recasting the `Melting Pot,' " *American Demographer* 21 (March 1999): 30–37.

38. Borjas, *Heaven's Door*, chap. 4.

39. Frank Levy, *The New Dollars and Dreams: American Incomes and Economic Change* (New York: Russell Sage, 1998), esp. chap. 6 and appendix tables A1 and A2.

40. Briggs, *Mass Immigration and the National Interest*; George J. Borjas, *Friends or Strangers: The Impact of Immigrants on the U.S. Economy* (New York: Basic Books, 1990); George J. Borjas, Richard B. Freeman, and Lawrence F. Katz, "How Much

Do Immigration and Trade Affect Labor Market Outcomes?" *Brookings Papers on Economic Activity*, no. 1 (Washington, D.C.: Brookings Institution, 1997).

41. *Statistical Abstract of the United States: 1999* (Washington: Census Bureau, 1999), tables 51–56, 262, 743, 768–69.

42. Rachel L. Swarms, "Hispanic Mothers Lagging as Others Escape Welfare," *New York Times*, 15 September 1998. In New York, the majority of Hispanic people on welfare in 1998 were Puerto Ricans, followed by Dominicans, the city's fastest-growing group of immigrants.

43. Linda Chavez, *Out of the Barrio: Toward a New Politics of Hispanic Assimilation* (New York: Basic Books, 1991).

44. *Statistical Abstract of the U.S.: 1999*, table 55. Unemployment rates in America's booming economy in 1998 were Hispanic (total) 4.9 percent; Mexican and Puerto Rican 5.0; Cuban 3.7, Central and South American 4.4. Equivalent figures for persons below the poverty line were Hispanic (total) 27.1, Mexicans 27.9, Puerto Ricans 34.2, Cubans 19.6, Central and South Americans 21.5. The poverty rate for blacks was 23.6 percent and for whites, 8.4.

45. Steven A. Camarota, *Immigration from Mexico: Assessing the Impact on the United States* (Washington, D.C.: Center for Immigration Studies, 2001). See also R. S. Oropesa and N. Landale, "Immigration Legacies: The Socioeconomic Circumstances of Children by Ethnicity and Generation in the U.S.," working paper 95–OIR, Department of Sociology and Population Research Institute, Pennsylvania State University, 1995; Joel Perlmann and Roger Waldinger, "Second Generation Decline? Children of Immigrants, Past and Present—A Reconsideration," *International Migration Review* 31 (winter 1997): 893–922.

46. Michael C. Meyer et al., *The Course of Mexican History* (New York: Oxford University Press, 1999); Michael J. Mazarr, *Mexico 2005: The Challenges of a New Millennium* (Washington: CSIS Press, 1999); Dale Story, *Industry, the State, and Public Policy in Mexico* (Austin: University of Texas Press, 1986).

47. Skerry, *Mexican Americans*, chap. 10; Frank D. Bean and Marta Tienda, *The Hispanic Population of the United States* (New York: Russell Sage, 1987); Kevin F. McCarthy and R. Brugiaga Valdez, *Current and Future Effects of Mexican Immigration in California* (Santa Monica, Calif.: Rand, 1986); Thomas Muller and Thomas J. Espenshade, *The Fourth Wave: California's Newest Immigrants* (Washington: Urban Institute, 1986), chaps. 3, 5 and 6; David S. Gutierrez, *Walls and Mirrors: Mexican Americans, Mexican Immigrants, and the Politics of Ethnicity* (Berkeley: University of California Press, 1995).

48. Ginger Thompson, "Fox Urges Opening of U.S.-Mexican Border," *New York Times*, 16 August 2000.

49. James F. Smith, "Changes in Population Create Opportunities for Mexico's Fox," *Los Angeles Times*, 23 September 2000; George J. Borjas, "Mexico's One-Way Remedy," *New York Times*, 18 July 2000.

50. "O'Neill Blocks Immigration Bill in House," *Congressional Quarterly Almanac 1984* (Washington, D.C.: Congressional Quarterly, 1985), 287.

51. Eric Schmidt, "Americans (a) Love (b) Hate Immigrants," *New York Times*, 14 February 2001.

52. Nick Anderson, "Immigrant Issues Top Agenda," *Los Angeles Times*, 22 September 2000.

53. Jane Gross, "Immigration Law Change Causes Snarl," *New York Times*, 20 February 2001.

54. FAIR was not always consistent. In criticizing the expanding H1-B visa program in the 1990s, which provided temporary skilled workers, primarily highly educated Asians, to fuel the economy's high-tech sector, FAIR voiced legitimate complaints about indenture-like working arrangements and displacement of native American workers, but was slow to acknowledge that the H1-B workers, unlike the migrant stoop-labor guest workers, brought valuable human capital skills that met national economic needs.

55. Mark Miller, "Employer Sanctions in Europe," Washington, D.C., Center for Immigration Studies, spring 1987; David Simcox, "Secure Identification: A National Need—A Must for Immigration Control," Washington, D.C., Center for Immigration Studies, fall 1989.

56. George R. La Noue and John C. Sullivan, "Gross Presumptions: Determining Group Eligibility for Federal Procurement Preferences," 41 *Santa Clara Law Review* 103 (2000).

57. Because "Hispanic" was an ethnic rather than a racial category, Hispanics could be any race. In the 2000 census survey, 48 percent of Hispanics listed themselves as white, 42 percent as "some other race," 2 percent as black, and 6 percent as belonging to two or more races.

58. Reynolds Farley, *The New American Reality* (New York: Russell Sage, 1996); Joel Perlmann, *Reflecting the Changing Face of America: Multiracials, Racial Classification, and American Intermarriage* (Annandale-on-Hudson, N.Y.: Jerome Levy Economics Institute of Bard College, 1997).

59. The organizations included the Association of Multi-Ethnic Americans, Project RACE (Reclassify All Children Equally), and the Biracial Family Network. Lobbying was coordinated through a website, "Interracial Voice" (www.webcom.com/intvoice). See Payne, *Getting beyond Race* 161-73.

60. Office of Management and Budget, "Revisions to the Standards for the Classification of Federal Data on Race and Ethnicity," *Federal Register* 62 (30 October 1997), 58782-90.

61. Office of Management and Budget, "Guidance on Aggregation and Allocation of Data on Race for Use in Civil Rights Monitoring and Enforcement," OMB Bulletin No. 00-02, 9 March 2000; Steven A. Holmes, "New Policy on Census Says Those Listed as White and Minority Will Be Counted as Minority," *New York Times*, 11 March 2000.

62. Olivia Winislow, "Does It All Add Up?" *Newsday*, 11 February 2001; Lexington, "Tiger, Tiger, Burning Bright," *Economist*, 12 June 2001.

63. Haya El Nasser, "Census to Define Multiracial in Myriad Ways," *USA Today*, 28 February 2001.

64. Deborah Kong, "A Question of Race," *Los Angeles Times*, 29 June 2001.

65. Barry Edmonston, Sharon M. Lee, and Jeffrey S. Passel, "Recent Trends in Intermarriage and Immigration and their Effects on the Future Racial Composition of the U.S. Population," paper presented at the conference on "Multiraciality: How Will the New Census Data be Used?" Jerome Levy Economics Institute of Bard College, September 22–23, 2000, 23.

66. Hill quoted in Robert Rosenblatt, "Census Illustrates Diversity from Sea to Shining Sea," *New York Times*, 13 March 2001.

67. Roderick Harrison, "Inadequacies of Multi-Response Data in the Federal Statistical System," paper presented at the conference on Multiraciality, Bard College, September 22–23, 2000.

68. Linda Greenhouse, "Justices Place Limits on Detention in cases of Deportable Immigrants," *New York Times*, 29 June 2001.

69. Roberta Cohen and Francis M. Deng, *Masses in Flight* (Washington, D.C.: Brookings Institution Press, 1998).

70. Roger Cohen, "Illegal Immigration Increases Sharply in European Union," *New York Times*, 25 December 2000; Christopher S. Wren, "World Needs to Add 500 Million Jobs in 10 Years," *New York Times*, 25 January 2001.

71. Sebastian Rotella, "As Crises Converge on Equador, an Exodus," *Los Angeles Times*, 13 July 2000; Norimitsu Onishi, "Out of Africa or Bust, with a Desert to Cross," *New York Times*, 4 January 2001.

72. Paul J. Smith, ed., *Human Smuggling: Chinese Migrant Trafficking and the Challenge to America's Immigration Tradition* (Washington, D.C.: Center for Strategic and International Studies, 1997); Kyle David and Rey Koslowski, *Global Human Smuggling* (Baltimore: Johns Hopkins University Press, 2001); Vanessa Ho, "U.S. Confronts Growing People-Smuggling Trade," *Seattle Post-Intelligencer*, 25 April 2001.

73. Susan Sachs, "Law Firm Is Charged with Aiding Smugglers of Chinese Immigrants," *New York Times*, 21 February 2000.

74. Paul C. Light, *Government's Greatest Endeavors of the Second Half of the Twentieth Century* (Washington, D.C.: Brookings Institution, 2000), website www.brookings.edu/GS/CRS/50ge. The top five postwar achievements of the federal government were rebuilding Europe after World War II; expanding the right to vote; providing equal access to public accommodations for all Americans; reducing disease through vaccinations and research; and reducing workplace discrimination. The top five failures were devolving responsibilities to the states; controlling immigration; simplifying taxes; expanding urban mass transit; and renewing poor communities.

75. Susan Sachs, "Changes Called Likely in Policy on Immigration," *New York Times*, 24 September 2001; Gene McNary, "We Must Control Our Borders," *St. Louis Post-Dispatch*, 26 September 2001.

Index